The Reenactment in Contemporary Screen Culture

The Reenactment in Contemporary Screen Culture

Performance, Mediation, Repetition

Megan Carrigy

BLOOMSBURY ACADEMIC
NEW YORK • LONDON • OXFORD • NEW DELHI • SYDNEY

BLOOMSBURY ACADEMIC
Bloomsbury Publishing Inc
1385 Broadway, New York, NY 10018, USA
50 Bedford Square, London, WC1B 3DP, UK
29 Earlsfort Terrace, Dublin 2, Ireland

BLOOMSBURY, BLOOMSBURY ACADEMIC and the Diana logo are trademarks of
Bloomsbury Publishing Plc

First published in the United States of America 2021
This paperback edition published 2022

Copyright © Megan Carrigy, 2021

For legal purposes the Acknowledgements on p. x constitute an extension
of this copyright page.

Cover design: Jade Barnett
Cover image © Tom Van Eynde

All rights reserved. No part of this publication may be reproduced or transmitted in any form or by any means, electronic or mechanical, including photocopying, recording, or any information storage or retrieval system, without prior permission in writing from the publishers.

Bloomsbury Publishing Inc does not have any control over, or responsibility for, any third-party websites referred to or in this book. All internet addresses given in this book were correct at the time of going to press. The author and publisher regret any inconvenience caused if addresses have changed or sites have ceased to exist, but can accept no responsibility for any such changes.

Library of Congress Cataloging-in-Publication Data
Names: Carrigy, Megan, author.
Title: The reenactment in contemporary screen culture :
performance, meditation, repetition / Megan Carrigy.
Description: London ; New York : Bloomsbury Academic, 2021. |
Includes bibliographical references and index.
Identifiers: LCCN 2021004262 (print) | LCCN 2021004263 (ebook) |
ISBN 9781501359385 (hardback) | ISBN 9781501359378 (eBook) |
ISBN 9781501359361 (ePDF)
Subjects: LCSH: Historical reenactments in mass media.
Classification: LCC P96.H548 C37 2021 (print) |
LCC P96.H548 (ebook) | DDC 302.2309–dc23
LC record available at https://lccn.loc.gov/2021004262
LC ebook record available at https://lccn.loc.gov/2021004263

ISBN: HB: 978-1-5013-5938-5
PB: 978-1-5013-8017-4
ePDF: 978-1-5013-5936-1
eBook: 978-1-5013-5937-8

Typeset by Newgen KnowledgeWorks Pvt. Ltd., Chennai, India

To find out more about our authors and books visit www.bloomsbury.com
and sign up for our newsletters.

For Leo Carrigy Browning who wasn't born when this project first took shape but has been at the centre of my life ever since.

Contents

List of figures	viii
Acknowledgements	x
Introduction	1
1 'To do; to perform': In-person reenactment, remediation and documentary performance	29
2 Between document and diegesis: Reenactment and researched detail in the biopic	57
3 Dramatizing forensic crime reconstruction: Investigation, trace and deixis in police procedural television	87
4 Restaging the cinema: Reproducibility and the shot-for-shot remake	117
5 Trial by media: Fugitive testimony, demonstrative evidence and computer animation in the courtroom	145
Conclusion	165
References	171
Index	189

Figures

1.1	The camera peers in through the window as Khieu Ches performs his routines in an empty cell. *S-21: The Khmer Rouge Killing Machine*.	40
1.2	Two reenactments of the opening of the bank vault are juxtaposed as Al Pacino performs side by side with John Wojtowicz. *The Third Memory* at the Renaissance Society at the University of Chicago, 2–30 April 2000.	46
1.3	Cameras are embedded in the action, influencing decisions about the staging of the performance. *The Battle of Orgreave*.	54
2.1 a, b	Theron's performance in *Monster* can be compared to Wuornos's own performance as herself in *Aileen: Life and Death of a Serial Killer*.	69
2.2	The success of Swank's performance hinges on her ability to pass as male, a feat that marked Teena himself as a successful performer. The close-up in the opening scene of the film references a widely publicized photo of Teena. *Boys Don't Cry*.	73
2.3 a, b	Key moments from two debates between Briggs and Milk about Proposition 6 shown in *The Times of Harvey Milk* are brought together in *Milk*, the mise en scène mimicking the gymnasium used for the debate in Orange County.	83
3.1	In 'The Soldier on the Grave' (1:21), Brennan, Hodgins, Zack and Angela lean over a body, Hodgins's tweezers pointing to a computer image of a magnified bullet wound, their discovery prompting Brennan and Angela to attempt a reconstruction of what happened. *Bones* (2005–17).	109
3.2	In 'Pilot' (1:1), Angela creates a reenactment of the struggle between a victim and perpetrator based on the defensive wounds on the bones of the victim's hand. Brennan and	

	Angela show the reenactment to the rest of the investigative team who surround the holograph. *Bones* (2005–17).	111
3.3 a, b, c, d	In 'Pilot' (1:1), a snap-zoom reenacts the path and impact of a bullet *CSI*-shots and invokes an endoscopic camera metaphorically. Explanations by the investigators make the bullet-hole perform multiple accounts of its inscription. *CSI: Crime Scene Investigation* (2000–15).	112
4.1 a, b	In *Psycho* the filmmakers attempted to replicate the narrative, framing, blocking and editing of the original *Psycho*.	126
4.2	Farocki is ghosted into *What Farocki Taught*, the double exposure facilitating his co-presence with the reenactment of his performance from *Inextinguishable Fire*.	133
4.3 a, b	The traveling helicopter shot at the opening of *Psycho* achieved what Hitchcock had envisaged for *Psycho*.	138

Acknowledgements

This book has its origins in a research project I began at the University of New South Wales. My thanks go first and foremost to Jodi Brooks for her rigorous guidance during this time. I would also like to thank Lisa Trahair for her support at several stages during its development. Thanks also to Christian Iseli whose invitation to present at the ZDOK conference, 'Do It Again: Reenactment in Documentary Film', at Zurich University of the Arts in 2016 provided me with the best possible conditions to reflect on the evolution of my thinking about this project.

Working with Bloomsbury, thanks go first to Katie Gallof, senior commissioning editor at Bloomsbury Academic, for taking on this project and shepherding it through the review and publication process so successfully and good-naturedly. Thanks also to assistant editor, Erin Duffy, who helped me with many details of the manuscript preparation process, and to the production editor, who managed the editing, proofing and printing processes. I also appreciate the anonymous reviews I received that helped to shape the book into its current form.

Thanks to the Renaissance Society at the University of Chicago, Marian Goodman Gallery and the artist Pierre Huyghe for permission to reproduce the image on the cover of this book of the exhibition *The Third Memory* at the Renaissance Society at the University of Chicago, 2–30 April 2000. Photographer: Tom Van Eynde.

An earlier version of Chapter 2 was published as 'Hilary Swank and Charlize Theron: Empathy, Veracity, and the Biopic' in *Star Bodies and the Erotics of Suffering*, edited by Rebecca Metereau and Colleen Glenn and published by Wayne State University Press in 2015. An earlier version of Chapter 3 was published as 'Re-staging the Cinema: *Psycho*, Film Spectatorship and the Redundant New Remake' in *Screening the Past*, issue 34, as part of a special issue titled 'Untimely Cinema: Cinema Out of Time' edited by Jodi Brooks and Therese Davis. I am grateful to the editors for permission to reprint this material here.

My colleagues at New York University have been a source of inspiration and comfort over many years and I have grown immensely in their company. I especially want to thank Mal Semple and Janet Alperstein for their mentorship and support.

On the home front, I thank Holly Smolly, who sat under my feet and kept me company during many hours I spent at my desk, and Sal Browning, as always, for her love and support. Thanks also to my parents, Ann and Neil Carrigy.

Introduction

The long-held belief that the reenactment was a form of historical representation unworthy of critical attention has been challenged during the first decades of the twenty-first century in the disciplines of history, performance studies and art history. At the same time, and no doubt tied to this critical reassessment, reenactments are increasingly pervasive in national and religious celebrations, on stages, inside and outside galleries and museums and on cinema, television and computer screens. The disciplinary field of film and media studies, however, has largely continued to neglect the persistent, widespread use of reenactment in film, television and other media. One of the strengths of the critical work on the reenactment that has emerged in history, performance studies and art history is its emphasis on the reenactment as a highly mobile, multimodal and dispersed representational form. This scholarship has shown that ideas of reenactment cross media and cultural forms and the reenactment's capacity for adaptation has been vital to its persistence over centuries.

Diverse history-themed genres: Historians on reenactment

Reenactments were long regarded by historians as a dubious and banal form of historical representation and an illegitimate form of historical thinking. For some they were essentially a marginal, amateur and unscholarly form of cultural expression, a naïve hobby for weekend enthusiasts, 'merely the present in funny dress', as Dening (1994: 4) put it, rather than a legitimate historical practice. Others tended to associate the reenactment as an expression of popular culture, criticizing the historicist and clichéd 'consumption-oriented spectacles' (Hansen 1991: 30) and 'Disneyfied history' (Lowenthal 1985: xv) produced by commercial operators in contexts where 'gore, adventure and personal transformation sell' (Agnew 2004: 328). Hewison (1987: 83) expresses an opinion shared by many historians that reenactments turn the past into commodities designed to be diverting, pleasing and placating: 'An actress mourning by a coffin may do her best to evoke the hardships of working class life in 1900, but her performance is an entertainment that helps to make the past seem picturesque and pleasing.' The use of reenactment in the heritage industry has been charged with being 'bad' historical representation, accused not only of not being 'real' history but, worse than that, being a threat to 'real' history. 'Vivid spectacles and straightforward narratives' are considered irresponsible, rose-coloured and vague: 'bogus' history 'entertainingly and authoritatively presented' (Hewison 1987: 137–8, 144).

Since historians have begun to reassess the reenactment, there has been a concerted effort to define the place of the reenactment both within the history industry and the academy. There has also been a revived interest in Collingwood's reenactment doctrine, which aligns the idea of reenactment with the practice of historiography by arguing that, in order to write about it, a historian needs to be able to mentally 'reenact the past in his own mind' ([1956] 1994: 246). Scholarly focus on reenactment is connected to broader efforts to come to terms with the commodification, consumption and construction of historical knowledge and discourses in popular culture (de Groot 2016). McCalman and Pickering (2010: 3) propose that reenactment, in its many variants, has now 'become the most widely consumed form of popular history'. Although there has been little agreement about the way in which the reenactment should be defined, the broad diversity of historical representations that historians have recognized as reenactments has made it a rich and burgeoning area of study. Agnew (2004: 327) conceives of reenactment as a form of historical thinking that spans 'diverse history-themed genres – from theatrical and "living history" performances to museum exhibits, television, film, travelogues, and historiography'. Agnew, among other historians, draws attention to the reenactment's capacity to break down traditional categories and distinctions and to transgress, interrogate and destabilize existing historical interpretations.

Lamb (2008) has proposed a taxonomy for the diverse kinds of reenactment that historians study, by grouping together those employed in different media (living history museums, public performances, television series, films, historical novels, etc.), based on their dramatic and investigative strategies. 'House', for example, one of Lamb's four categories (the others are 'pageant', 'theatre' and 'realist'), is characterized by investments in personal relationships and the 'private particulars' of everyday experiences. It includes living history villages (such as Colonial Williamsburg, the outdoor living history museum in the United States) and reality television series such as *1900 House* (2001), *Frontier House* (2003) and *The Colony* (2005), which place participants in recreated historical situations. Cook (2004: 487–8), on the other hand, groups these kinds of reality television programmes into the category of 'investigative reenactments', a category comprising examples that set out 'to learn something about the past through the activity of reenactment itself and to communicate those findings to a wider audience'. King (2012: 11–12), too, who positions her work in the fields of women's studies and the post-humanities but has also been published alongside these historians, likewise emphasizes the diversity and range of media and institutional contexts in which the reenactment is operating, including fan fiction, gaming, museums and television. She also points to the interweaving of different approaches to reenactment within reality television programmes, performances by hobby reenactors and museum displays. Her approach draws on Latour's (1991) conceptualization of a 'parliament of things' to think about how interactions between people, skills, devices, processes and infrastructures associated with these television productions shape and constrain the work of reenactment.

While most historians acknowledge that in such taxonomies, and in wider conceptualizations, the reenactment has been fully incorporated into popular media forms, historians have tended to concern themselves with the role of performance in the reenactment. The concept of mediation has received far less attention than dramatization and investigation. Gapps (2003: 106–7), for example, conceives of reenactment in terms of 'bodily, sensory engagement', emphasizing participation and immersion. Reenactments create opportunities for 'connection to the past through performance, props, and stages of authenticating histories'. Agnew (2004: 330) also describes reenactment as 'a body-based discourse in which the past is reanimated through physical and psychological experience'. This reflects the broader conceptualization of reenactment as 'a form of affective history' (Agnew 2007: 301) with emphasis being placed on the sensory, experiential and identificatory potential of the form. McCalman and Pickering (2010: 6), who emphasize the reenactment's relationship to the history of realism across literature, painting, theatre, film and television, describe the practice of reenactment as 'slip[ing] between the two "reals"; a desire to learn from the literal recreation of the past, and, at the same time to experience history somatically and emotionally – to know what it felt like'. There are a few exceptions: de Groot (2016) explores developments in online gaming, Elder (2009) draws on an existing body of work on television genres and Schwarz (2007) and Healy (2009) pay close attention to formal techniques of narration, cinematography, editing and soundtrack. But overall there has been a general tendency among historians to extend conceptualizations associated with dramatization, staging and live performance to analysis of reenactment in film and television.

Etymology and technical reproducibility

When it comes to understanding the place of reenactment in screen-based media, emphasis on performance and dramatization has its limitations. These stand out more starkly in the etymology of the word 'reenactment' provided by the *Shorter Oxford English Dictionary* (*SOED*), which demonstrates that the significance of repetition and technical mediation for the reenactment has increased over time. According to the *SOED*, the noun 'reenactment' only came into usage in the early nineteenth century. One of the *SOED*'s earliest definitions of the verb 'to enact' places performance and dramatization at its core, describing it as to 'represent (a scene, play, etc.) on or as on a stage; play (a part); take part in (a drama or scene in real life)'. It is this definition that remains central to conceptualizations of the reenactment among historians across the diverse manifestations they have identified. According to the *SOED*, this definition, which emerged in the fifteenth century, remained relatively constant and therefore adequate for describing the full range of representational activities, until the mid-nineteenth century. At this point, however, the term 'to reenact' emerges and begins to be conceptualized as 'to act or perform again; reproduce'.

This new conceptualization emerges at a time when new mass-reproduction technologies are beginning to impact dramatically on a range of, especially Western, societies around the globe. Benjamin (1968) and Weber (1996), among others, identify the mid-nineteenth century as the beginning of the 'age of technical reproducibility', a period in which, 'with the increasing mechanization of reproductive techniques, the traditional distinction between production and reproduction begins to break down' (Weber 1996: 82, 87). From the mid-nineteenth century onwards, repetition became tied up in forms of technical reproducibility. That this definition of 'to reenact' should have emerged at this point suggests that, while the practice of reenactment predates technically reproducible media, the reenactment, live or mediated, has become informed by the logic of technical media. While the reenactment continues to exist in both live and mediated forms, it has been transformed through its incorporation within forms of technical media – something that necessarily has implications for its theorization. Most historians have drawn primarily on the pre-nineteenth-century lineage of the reenactment, however, without fully thinking through the consequences of its technical mediation.

Schwarz (2004: 102) argues that there is a reluctance among historians to 'think about the consequence of media forms *as mediated*', a reluctance that stems from the fear that 'mediated time threatens to destabilize the very foundations of historical interrogation ... that mediated times transform historical times'. He argues that

> cinema, radio and television not only created new narrative times and organized new sensations of time (real and imagined, so long as those distinctions work); they also depended for their existence on unprecedented time frames and created new indices of social, or historical, time. (99)

Yet historical time, Schwarz (2004: 93, 100) argues, has generally been understood to be 'external, social and in some sense objective'. To challenge this, he proposes that historians address the question, 'How can we grasp the transactions between mediated times and historical time?' by building on the insights about time and mediation that have been developed specifically by film, television and radio scholars.

The etymology I have outlined suggests that the reenactment offers a productive form through which to pursue this kind of dialogue. The reenactment, traditionally regarded as the domain of history (and its practice that of performance), rather than of media, is also a representational form predicated on and drawing attention to itself as a repetition. My conceptualization of the reenactment shifts the emphasis from a broader interest in staging, dramatization and performance among historians to the contention that for a reenactment to be recognized *as* a reenactment, it needs to foreground that it is staging and performing an event that has already taken place. The reenactment is always caught between two agendas. First, it sets out to be a repetition of a previous event. Second, it sets out to foreground itself as a reenactment and it does so by emphasizing its theatrical, performative nature. Consequently, the most sustained representational code of the reenactment, in all its diverse forms, is its presentational mode of address which has been central to the way in which a reenactment has signalled itself historically, in both its pre-and post-cinematic history.

Even though presentational mode may manifest differently across genres, media and representational forms, it has more typically been understood as naïve rather than entailing self-reflexivity. However, as I will discuss, scholarly work in documentary studies has begun to conceptualize the reenactment precisely in terms of its self-reflexivity. Other notable exceptions in film and media studies scholarship include Griffiths (2003: 28, 3), who, in an essay on the relationship between nineteenth-century panoramas and early cinematic reenactments, argues that reenactments 'frequently signal their authored status in overt and self-conscious ways', making them 'highly reflexive speech acts'; and Pierson (2009: 2), who, in relation to what she terms 'avant-garde reenactments', argues that 'the element of performance introduces a reflexive dimension into this mode of historical representation that it has not always been credited with'.

Productive repetition: Art and performance studies

Primarily it has been in the fields of art history and performance studies that the reenactment has been conceptualized as a strategic form of repetition apt for exploring relationships between technical reproducibility, mediation, performance and concept of the event. Bangma (2006: 14, italics in the original), for example, proposes using reenactment as a 'framing concept that would open up questions about the more *fundamentally* mediated nature of experience and memory'. In this context, the tension in the reenactment between the attempt at repetition and the need to draw attention to itself as a performance has been most explicitly understood as the reenactment's greatest strength. In dance, too, scholars and practitioners are exploring the possibilities of reenactment as a self-reflexive mode for restaging dance works that can challenge the 'regimes of historicity' associated with traditional practices of reconstruction (Franko 2018: 11). There has been an unmistakable move in these fields to define the reenactment against the impression of 'a trapped medium, fundamentally conservative' (Blackson 2007: 33) and to draw attention to the work of reenactment beyond the 'uncritical repetitions' and 'entertaining diversion' (Hoyne 2009: 7, 37) produced by many living history and heritage projects.

The reassessment of the reenactment in these fields has been made possible by, and is a response to, a growing body of artistic work that utilizes reenactment inside and outside gallery spaces, museums and theatres. Exhibitions include *Ahistoric Occasion: Artists Making History* at Mass MOCA (2006); *Playback_ Simulated Realities* at Edith Russ House (2006); *History Will Repeat Itself* at KW Institute for Contemporary Art, Berlin (2007); *Not Quite How I Remember It* at Power Plant gallery in Toronto (2008); the event *Reenact* organized by Casco and Mediamatic in Amsterdam (2004); and the sidebar programme of the 2015 Art of the Real Film Festival at the Lincoln Center in New York, titled *Repeat as Necessary: The Art of Reenactment*, which showcased film and video artists restaging the work of earlier artists and filmmakers. Key works from the canon of performance art are also being reenacted on stages, inside and outside gallery spaces, as part of a phenomenon stretching across Europe and North America. Curated exhibitions of such work include *A Little Bit of History Repeated* at Kunst-Werke in 2001, *A Short History of Performance* at the Whitechapel Art Gallery between 2002 and 2006 and *Seven Easy Pieces* by Marina Abramovic at the Solomon R. Guggenheim Museum in 2005.

Works responding to the canon of performance art are themselves necessarily performances of performances. Often, as Lutticken (2005: 5) points out, they are performances based on the *documentation* of an original performance, marking that original performance as a fundamentally mediated event. In Lutticken's view the documentation produced by a reenactment can also become performative, highlighting the fundamentally mediated nature of both the reenactments and the performances on which they are based. Schneider's (2011: 10) approach to the reenactment also explores conceptualizations of performance, disappearance, liveness and documentation that have been central to the field of performance studies. Like historians Agnew and Gapps, she emphasizes the role of affect and the body in reenactment. She examines the work of performance artists alongside those of American Civil War reenactors in her analysis of what she describes as reenactment's 'knotty and porous relationship to time'. Reenactment, she proposes, challenges our habituation to time as linear instead showing us that time can be 'malleable, tactile, given to recurrence, given to cross-affiliate assemblage, given to buckling, given to return' (174). The work of reenactment, she proposes, serves to emphasize that the past is not 'over', that it is always incomplete.

The famous storming of the Winter Palace sequence in *October* (Sergei Eisenstein, 1927), a film commissioned for the tenth anniversary of the Russian revolution, is a particularly notable cinematic example of the past being enacted through commemoration. Indeed, Nowell-Smith goes as far as to argue that Eisenstein's storming sequence has shaped our understanding of revolution to such an extent that it has 'become history':

> The most powerful single image of the Russian Revolution is probably that of the storming of the Winter Palace in October 1917. But the image that has become history is not a documentary one: it is the one provided by Eisenstein in *October*, a fictional reconstruction. (1990: 162)

Many excerpts from it, and even still images, 'have become textbook images, "quoted" as documents in other films and displayed in exhibitions devoted to the history of the Revolution' (Alexandrov cited in Taylor 2002: 76). And 'countless documentaries', says Bordwell (1993: 96), have treated shots from it 'as newsreel footage'. One such borrowing occurs in the opening of HBO's *Stalin* (1993), where 'unidentified footage from Eisenstein's *October* is freely mixed with genuine archive material' (Rosenthal 1999: 11 n. 2). The sequence has frequently been misread – and, indeed, circulated – as documentary footage, lending it a new referential and historical status in its subsequent history.

Several film scholars and historians (von Geldern, Taylor, Bordwell, Bibikova, Buck-Morss) have also shown that the famous storming of the Winter Palace sequence in *October* was heavily influenced by *The Storming of the Winter Palace*, a popular, state-sponsored mass spectacle staged in the Winter Palace Square in Petrograd (now St Petersburg) on 7 November 1920 as a central event in the city's celebrations for the third anniversary of the October Revolution. The theatrical reconstruction was played out in the very location where the actual storming had occurred three years earlier, the Palace Square and its surrounds becoming simultaneously 'a stage and a real historical place' (von Geldern 1993: 201). It created what von Geldern (1993: 200) describes as 'a dynamic centre for the Revolution, the moment of creation essential to any foundation myth'. Produced and directed by Nikolai Evreinov and Nikolai Petrov and Alexander Kugel, designed by Yuri Annenkov and co-organized by Dmitri Temkim, the mass spectacle was a landmark event of 1920 in and of itself, and was instrumental in popularizing the idea that the 1917 storming of the Winter Palace was a climatic historical moment of the October Revolution.

By all accounts, this theatrical reenactment of the storming was more 'eventful' than the historical event, which, in von Geldern's words, was 'something of a letdown' (1993: 1–2). The Palace Square was peaceful on the actual day of the Revolution, with the storming of the Winter Palace occurring the day after power had been seized. And minimal blood was shed, the commanders having waited until most troops defending it had surrendered, before entering the Palace. Evreinov and his team, on the other hand, staged a storming that was much larger in scale and, as Bibikova (1990: 122) describes, 'far more dramatic (and more damaging to the building) than the original event'. By making a large-scale theatrical celebration of the actual events of 25 October 1917, the actors and creatives enacted a revolutionary energy that was not present in the historical storming: they shaped the Revolution 'as they celebrated it' (von Geldern 1993: 45). Indeed, Buck-Morss (2000) argues that in the act of commemoration, *The Storming of the Winter Palace* enacted a revolutionary energy in and for the present, rather than relegating it to the past, raising questions about the representability of the temporality and rhythm of revolution.

October was no more an exercise in historical accuracy than *The Storming of the Winter Palace* had been. Rather, it reenacted the revolutionary energy first enacted by *The Storming of the Winter Palace* and not present in the historical event. The thousands of extras in both the mass spectacle and the film sequence outnumbered the actual attackers who seized the Palace in 1917. Bordwell (1993: 80–2) argues that Eisenstein synthesized the 'revolutionary myth' of a massive crowd of revolutionaries that Evreinov had been responsible for creating, and that put the myth 'permanently on film', thereby turning 'the small detachment that invaded the Winter Palace' into 'for all time – a crowd of thousands'. Collectively, these two reenactments remediated the historical event into a properly 'revolutionary' event. *October* and *The Storming of the Winter Palace* not only reenacted the historical storming, they effectively enacted it.

The example of *October* and *The Storming of the Winter Palace* resonates with the suggestion by Lutticken (2005: 5–6, 19) that we think about reenactment as 'productive repetition' and as a self-reflexive 'performative strategy'. Indeed, Lutticken (2005: 55) refers to *October* and *The Storming of the Winter Palace* explicitly as part of his broader exploration of the idea that the reenactment has the potential to challenge those forms of historicism it seems set up to perpetuate. Blackson (2007: 29–30, 36) also points to the example of *The Storming of the Winter Palace*. Defining the reenactment specifically in terms of its 'distinct emancipatory agency', he argues that 'all reenactments are repetitions, but few repetitions become reenactments'. In a similar sentiment, Rushton (2006: 11, italics in the original), proposes that we emphasize 'not what reenactment *is* but what reenactment *does*'. Clearly, there is potential for dialogue across art history, performance studies and film and media studies in thinking about the reenactment as a representational form. Art historians, curators and performance studies scholars, like historians, have successfully engaged with the idea that the reenactment is not limited to a medium or cultural form.

Unfortunately, however, it is its broad dispersal across media and genres that has been at the heart of the problem posed by the reenactment for the disciplinary field of film and media studies. The reenactment's very ubiquity and diversity has meant that there is little agreement as to what is recognized *as* a reenactment in film and television. There remains no clear agreement as to what a reenactment is. Its history in these fields has been rather chaotic and therefore largely unrecorded. Attempts to come to terms with the use of reenactment in film and television have, like the practice itself, been scattered and the scholarly work on film and television reenactment has been piecemeal, fragmented and hard to find. It is hardly surprising, then, that both the problems and the insights that the reenactment can offer to film and media studies debates have for so long been unaddressed.

Genre trouble: Early American cinema

So chequered has its history been that the first decade of the American cinema constitutes one of the few areas in which the use made of the reenactment in film has become a serious element in critical debate. The earliest surviving reenactments in the American cinema are a pair of films entitled *Ambulance Call*, a 'staged actuality', in which a horse-drawn ambulance leaves its garage and turns towards the camera before exiting the frame, and *Ambulance at the Accident*, which were registered by the Edison Company in 1897. It is commonly agreed, however, that the practice of producing films modelled on topical events, staged in the style of actuality footage, first attracted attention in the United States in 1898. It was then that film producers realized that to satisfy the popular demand for topical material about the Spanish-American War, they did not have to be on the battlefield with a camera (Levy 1982: 246). These staged actualities became the first popular reenactments in American cinema. The practice was taken up promptly and widely and contributed to the conceptualization of the institution of cinema in American society as a visual newspaper, and as the industry capitalized on this, it gained in confidence and size (Musser 1994: 225). The attempt to meet the demand for topicality in the American cinema during its first decade extended well beyond the end of the Spanish-American War, with reenactments of events including boxing matches, prison escapes, executions, murders, robberies, fires, natural disasters and police apprehension of criminals.

Levy (1982: 249) has shown that the reenactments of the American cinema's first decade exemplified an era in which distinctions between categories such as newsreel, documentary, drama and reproduction were quite fluid and so identifying the kinds of films that were considered records or documents of a real event is less straightforward than one might have imagined. As Nowell-Smith insists in his discussion of the staged newsreels of the 1898 Spanish-American War:

> It would be wrong to regard this material has, in a serious sense, forged, since the deception planned did not really amount to a falsification of the historical record, and in any case the ethic of authenticity of the filmed record was not yet in place. (1990: 162)

Reenactments could be accommodated in a wide range of categories of films, as *Motion Pictures from the Library of Congress Paper Print Collection, 1894–1912* makes clear. As Levy (1982: 248) points out, some 're-constituted newsreels' are grouped with standard newsreels, while others, including *Execution by Hanging*, appear in both categories. Biograph's *Tenderloin Tragedy* (1907), in which an elderly man spends a night out on the town, collapses and dies, is the last film to be listed in the reproduction category and was also listed as 'drama'. Edison's *Ambulance Call* (1897) is the earliest title in the 'reproduction' list. Not only does it appear again as a 'drama' but also as a 'documentary', suggesting that it presented something of a taxonomic dilemma. In most instances, the wide variety of reenactment films – whether they depicted executions, natural disasters, police apprehension of criminals or whatever – stressed their topicality rather than their actuality and advertised themselves as reenactments.

This apparent flexibility in categorizing films using reenactment is not only evident in the diverse names given them at the time of their release but also in the way in which historians have since referred to them. At the time of their release, apart from 'reenactments', of course, early film reenactments were variously advertised as 'faithful duplications', 'reproductions', 'facsimile reproductions' and 'dramatic representations of current events' (Doane 2002: 155). The strategies of the reenactments themselves also range from table-top miniaturizations and bathtub models to carefully staged events using lots of actors, props and extras (Levy 1982: 249). The various terms employed by subsequent historians are intended either to reflect the reenactment's specific function or else to focus on subcategories of the reenactment. While 'reconstituted newsreels' and 'fake newsreels' are the terms Levy (1982: 243, 245, 247) usually uses, for the wider variety of reenactments, including, for example, execution films, he also uses the terms 'reenactments and reproductions', 'fake actuality film footage', 'staged actualities' and 'topical re-constructions'. By contrast, when describing the American coverage of the 1898 Spanish-American War, Nowell-Smith (1990: 161) puts the term 'newsreels' in inverted commas, noting that they contain 'large components of invention' and identifying instances where events were simulated and staged for the camera. The preferred term of both Doane (2002: 155) and Hansen (1991: 30–1) is 'dramatic reenactment', which they consider a subgenre of the early actuality.

These film historians and theorists, including Musser (1994), Hansen (1991), Doane (2002), Nowell-Smith (1990) and Levy (1982), have also shown that the reenactment both shaped and was shaped by the shift to narrative cinema. However, the tendency has been to conceive of the early film reenactment as a transitional form that lost currency with the rise of narrative cinema, focusing on the absorption and marginalization of its techniques after 1907. Musser (1991: 393) argues that between 1907 and 1909, 'reliance on the spectator's prior familiarity with a story was becoming rapidly outmoded' as filmmakers became increasingly skilled at communicating narrative. And, as less and less reliance was placed on the dramatic reenactment of topical events, the genre fell into a decline. Levy (1982: 249, 254) pinpoints 1907 as 'the year in which fake actuality disappeared', maintaining that, while it did not vanish entirely, it was no longer visible on the same scale and with the same self-consciousness that marked the earlier cinema. The narrative cinema had begun its rise, but no less significant for Levy is the fact that by this date camera equipment had become lightweight enough to enable its operator easier access to newsworthy events. Doane (2002: 155, 161) agrees, but with her conceptualization of the early reenactments as a subgenre of early actualities, she links their disappearance to the decline in the currency of the actuality, which the ascendancy of fictional narrative had also caused to be marginalized.

Levy, Doane and others have demonstrated that the early film reenactment played a crucial role in the development of film language, thus identifying it as a significant feature of the transition from actuality film production to narrative fiction. Levy (1982) and Doane (2002) have drawn attention to the absorption of the staging and editing techniques of the early film reenactment into the emerging conventions of narrative fiction. It is clear from Doane and Levy's discussions that techniques developed for reenactment films changed status and meaning as they developed and were incorporated into the conventions of narrative fiction. With the consolidation of these techniques into the conventions of narrative fiction, the reenactment's openly presentational mode of address; straightforward, undisguised emphasis on staging; foregrounding of performance and spectacle; and explicit association with a pre-existing event fell out of favour because the conventions of narrative cinema typically work to mask staging techniques in order to produce a self-contained fictional world. The shifting status of theatricality during the first decade of the cinema was directly connected to the emergence and solidification of a historically specific conceptualization of referentiality for the cinema. Only when looked back on later, when new cinematic conventions had taken over, were early cinema reenactments accused of deception and this has contributed to the marginalization of the reenactment as a form of historical representation that is unworthy of critical attention.

However, if we align the reenactment with what Gunning and Gaudreault call 'cinema of attractions', a term that drew attention to the exhibitionism that characterized the cinema's first decade and the persistence of an exhibitionist mode of address in cinema after 1907, it can help us to conceptualize the reenactment as both specific to the particularities of the early cinema and transhistorical. Gunning (1990: 59) argues that, with the rise of the narrative film, the cinema of attractions does not disappear, but rather 'goes underground, both into certain avant-garde practices and as a component of narrative films, more evident in some genres (e.g. the musical) than others'. Gunning (1990: 61) successfully challenged the commonly held view that while the films of cinemas early years were distinguished by direct address, those of the later period, when narrative fiction dominated, were characterized by spectatorial absorption: the distinction was far too neat. His now well-rehearsed argument – that there are still many diverse instances in which 'theatrical display dominates over narrative absorption' – has helped us to rethink the status of theatricality in the first decade of the cinema and in the subsequent developments of narrative and non-narrative cinema.

The broad acceptance of Gunning's argument that the cinema of attractions persisted as a component of narrative and non-narrative films has contributed significantly to the study of the cinema ever since. Scholars have investigated in detail the way in which the cinema of attractions operates within many kinds of cinema, well beyond the scope of avant-garde cinema and the musical genre, which were Gunning's initial examples. The reenactment embodies qualities that Elsaesser (2007: 211) argues have come to be associated with the cinema of attractions: 'reflexivity and self-reference, display and performativity'. The reenactment, like the cinema of attractions, is characterized by what Gunning (1990: 57) describes as a willingness 'to rupture a self-enclosed fictional world for a chance to solicit the attention of the spectator'. But film debates that have used Gunning's argument to help them rethink theatricality in the cinema have tended not to consider the reenactment. Making connections between the reenactment and the cinema of attractions enables me to show that the ways that the reenactment continues to impact on and trouble the referential dimensions of the cinema have largely gone unrecognized because its forms of theatricality fell out of favour. What is more, because Gunning detects evidence of his cinema of attractions across genres and across narrative and non-narrative filmmaking, he legitimizes a way of approaching the theatricality of the reenactment other than through the histories of documentary or fiction.

D. W. Griffith's epic 1915 feature film, *The Birth of a Nation*, a controversial film of tremendous significance in the history of the cinematic representation of history, demonstrates how, in the emerging conventions of narrative cinema, reenactment sequences were already calling attention to themselves in order to perform their authenticating function. Gunning (1990: 60), for whom Griffith's films are exemplars of the early development of the American narrative cinema, argues that the major shifts in film practice that took place between 1907 and 1913 represent 'the true *narrativization* of the cinema, culminating in the appearance of feature films which radically revised the variety format'. By the end of 1913 feature films had begun to dominate the American film industry:

> The transformation of filmic discourse that D.W. Griffith typifies bound cinematic signifiers to the narration of stories and the creation of a self-enclosed diegetic universe. The look at the camera becomes taboo and the devices of cinema are transformed from playful 'tricks' – cinematic attractions (Méliès gesturing at us to watch the lady vanish) – to elements of dramatic expression, entries into the psychology of character and the world of fiction.

Griffith played a central role in what Gunning (1991: 290) calls the 'cinema of narrative integration', in which all filmic elements are organized primarily for the purpose of storytelling. Yet Musser (2007: 409) also suggests, in the wake of Gunning's cinema of attractions argument, that while 'a presentational style is broadly characteristic of the pre-Griffith cinema', it 'also continues in the post-1908 era'. Griffith's *Birth of a Nation*, in his view, a key film in the developing classical model, marks an early and significant manifestation of the persistent tension between narrative integration and the presentational style of the attraction.

Specific moments in Abraham Lincoln's presidency that are reenacted in the first half of *Birth of a Nation* constitute key instances upon which discussion of the tension Musser identifies should focus. These reenactments find room in a broadly fictional diegesis, albeit one based in historical events, not only to link the narrative to a believable past but also to draw attention to themselves in the manner of an attraction. Operating very differently from scenes in which a fictional character drives the action, even on the battlefront, these reenactments in *Birth of a Nation* stand out *as* reenactments. They do so because they are signalled by intertitles that cite the source materials for the specific actions they contain. Not all dramatizations of historical events in *Birth of a Nation* are reenactments because they do not all seek to replicate an actual event as closely as possible. Rather those sequences that depict specific, well-documented events in Lincoln's presidency explicitly announce themselves as reenactments.

The first moment Griffith depicts from Lincoln's presidency is announced in an intertitle that reads 'The First Call for 75, 000 Volunteers. President Lincoln signing the proclamation. An HISTORICAL FACSIMILE of the

President's Executive Office on that occasion, after Nicolay and Hay in *Lincoln, a History*'. The intertitle cites the source for the account of the signing of the proclamation on 15 April 1861 as a ten-volume biography authored by two of Lincoln's secretaries, John Milton Hay and John George Nicolay, published in 1890. In the scene Lincoln (Joseph Henaberry) listens as the document is read aloud to a small group of people in his room, puts on his glasses, leans over his desk and begins to sign, overseen by a group of onlookers, who then take the document away. Lincoln remains at his desk, thoughtfully wiping his brow with a handkerchief. This brief simply played reenactment serves to contextualize the fictional scene that follows, in which the Stoneman brothers, taking up the president's call for volunteers, leave to join their regiment. As the film progresses, what goes on in Lincoln's office is constantly tied to the fictional narrative events and keeps them connected to a believable, historical past. For example, Mrs Cameron later appeals to Lincoln to pardon her elder son, Ben, who, it is rumoured, is to be hanged as a guerrilla. Lincoln is framed sitting at his desk at the same angle as he appeared in the reenactment of the signing of the call for volunteers earlier in the film. He puts on his glasses and leans over the same desk on which he signed the proclamation to write the pardon. The signing of the pardon is authenticated by the earlier reenactment of the signing of the call for volunteers.

The film's reenactment of Lincoln's assassination is announced by an intertitle that reads 'An HISTORICAL FACSIMILE of Ford's theatre as on that night, exact in size and detail, with the recorded incidents, after Nicolay and Hay in *Lincoln, a History*'. This is the same ten-volume biography by Hay and Nicolay, cited earlier as the source for Lincoln's proclamation signing. The assassination reenactment is also framed by additional intertitles that anchor it within a specific historical time and place – a gala performance at Ford's Theatre on 14 April 1865 – and with the specific historical timestamp of the assassination: 'Time 10:13. Act III, Scene 2'. Again, the details of the assassination itself are specific and replicate precisely what the assassin, John Wilkes Booth, did. Booth enters Lincoln's box downstage left, shoots him in the head and jumps over the balustrade of the box onto the forestage. At this point another intertitle appears – '*Sic semper tyrannis!*' – the line that some claim to have heard Booth shout as he crossed the stage and escaped via the stage right wings. Griffith contrives to include Phil and Elsie Stoneman in the audience, thus weaving the president's murder into the lives of the film's fictional characters.

The dispersal of the reenactment

As these early examples from *Birth of a Nation* highlight, the reenactment resurfaces frequently in forms that have been insufficiently acknowledged. While in its earliest forms in film, the reenactment operated as a genre – indeed, it was one of cinema's earliest genres – it has since become dispersed as a residual representational practice within a variety of film and television genres. It has continued not as a genre but in sequences in a range of other genres. Its dispersal across a fiction and non-fiction film forms calls into question not only the idea of a clean shift from the early cinema to narrative cinema but also the excessively neat distinction between documentary and fiction. That the reenactment began to be conceptualized as out of sync with the norms established in this first major paradigm shift for the cinema reveals much about the framework through which we have come to understand the cinema today. Fiction and non-fiction genres have now typically become distinguished generically in terms of different kinds of referential relationships they claim to negotiate between filmic and pro-filmic reality. The reenactment continues to embody the ontological ambivalence that characterized the early cinema, troubling the representational codes established on either side of cinema's primary generic distinction between fiction and non-fiction. It maintains vestiges of the weak ontological frontier that Levy, Doane, Hansen and Nowell-Smith identify between similar categories in the early cinema.

Notably, film and television reenactment has played a key role in the development of hybrid narrative forms. Docudrama is the term most widely used to describe a wide variety of documentary and fictional hybrids. The term has been used to encompass television docudrama tied to investigative journalism (Rosenthal 1999); docudrama tending more towards entertainment biographies and scandals (Paget 1998); and historical dramas such as *Schindler's List* (1993), *JFK* (1991) and *In the Name of the Father* (1993) (Lipkin

2002). Remarkably, the significance of reenactment in forging these hybrid generic forms, despite their extraordinary popularity, has largely escaped the close attention of film and media scholars. Lipkin (2002: ix–xi), for example, believes that docudrama itself has suffered fragmented and piecemeal critical attention because it slips through the cracks between fiction and documentary studies. Or, as Rosenthal (1999: 371) puts it, because it 'floats uneasily between documentary and fiction' and cannot be fully accounted for in either category. And Paget (1998: 1) relates the problem of docudrama to the fact that it makes a 'both/and' claim to drama and documentary that ruffles the underlying 'either/or' distinction that has been made between these modes, traditionally perceived in opposition. Paget (2002: 32) describes the actor in docudrama as 'negotiating backwards and forwards across the space between non-fiction and fiction'. Lipkin's (2002: xiv) definition of the docudrama genre is one that is based on true stories, told through a 'melodramatic staging of documentary materials' involving a 'combination of fiction and non-fiction, narrative and actuality' that 'ride the fence between narrative and documentary, blending the strategies of both'. He sees docudrama primarily as a means of 'get[ting] inside' a true story. Rosenthal (1999: 371) adds to these basic definitions by emphasizing the docudrama's social function of inciting public debate about current affairs.

Fundamental to all these attempts to define the docudrama is its basis in lived historical events, and essential to its way of presenting itself is its use of reenactment. Yet even those who have turned their attention to careful theorization of docudrama, including Lipkin, Paget and Rosenthal, have fallen short of explicitly acknowledging the centrality of reenactment in docudrama production, although they often refer to the role of 're-creation'. Lipkin (2011: 1–2), for example, conceptualizes docudramas as involving what he terms the 'performance of memory and memories', arguing that their promotion foregrounds the idea that 'docudrama performs what it re-creates'. It is as though the term 'docudrama' itself has subsumed the practice of reenactment and obscured the specific role it plays in this hybrid genre. Hoffer and Nelson (1999: 73), for example, also argue that television and film 'seldom have access to the "right moment" in events later deemed "newsworthy"', and it is this that gives docudrama such currency in contemporary moving-image practice. Implicit in this is the suggestion that the reenactment remains current and prevalent in cinema and television because it cannot be guaranteed that the camera will always be either able or available to capture significant events as they are unfolding.

The various ways in which reenactment functions across the docudrama spectrum can enable us to identify important distinctions between the genre's diverse practices. The use of reenactments in investigative documentaries, for example, is often seen to undermine the truth claims of the investigation, whereas its use in a film such as *In the Name of the Father*, a biographical courtroom drama about the false conviction of Gerry Conlon and his father and others for the 1974 Guildford pub bombings, lends an authenticity to many of its fictional dramatic techniques. Allowing for marked the variations in the reenactment's modes of operation, which will be explored in detail in this book, it is possible broadly to propose that reenactment is often typically seen to lend documentary drama and fiction authenticity, reflecting the different referential associations that staging, performance and theatricality have within non-fiction and fiction genres. Of course, these associations continue to evolve. The digital era has brought about further transformations to the reenactment, primarily because the digital image's challenges to understandings of photographic reference have impacted on ideas of historical representation.

As I proposed in my discussion of the etymology, the ways that the reenactment makes its referential claims have become tied up in its technical reproducibility. One of the disciplinary fields that has most rigorously addressed the changing referential status of the technically reproducible image is film theory. As a field interested in intermediality and transmedia forms, film theory offers frameworks for helping think through the workings of this successfully transdisciplinary form. Just like the reenactment, film and cinema are not static, unchanging concepts but have become thoroughly remediated in their encounter with digital production and distribution technologies. As Rodowick (2007: 23) argues, current technological transformations in moving-image production serve to highlight that 'cinema studies can stake no permanent claims on its disciplinary territories; its borders are in fact continually shifting'. The coexistence of different media technologies in contemporary film production and the dispersal of film across a broad range of media distribution platforms mean that it has become increasingly difficult to cordon off cinema and study it in isolation. As film theory continues to grapple with a period of intense technological change for the cinema, the transdisciplinary movement of the reenactment across media platforms provides a valuable accomplice for thinking through debates about the remediation of the film image.

Reenactment and reference: The indexical sign

In recent years, several established thinkers in Anglophone film theory, including Rodowick (2007), Mulvey (2006), Doane (2002) and Rosen (2001), have produced accounts of the changing contemporary media climate through investigations of the relationships between the concepts of technical reproducibility, time and reference. Film theory has tended to overlook the referential complexity of the reenactment, however, because debates about the referential status of the technically reproducible image have developed, by and large in relation to Charles Sanders Peirce's conceptualization of the indexical sign, one of a triad of signs developed by Peirce to explain different referential relationships between a signifier and its referent. In Peirce's taxonomy, there are three classes of signs – the icon, the index and the symbol – which are not mutually exclusive, and all three of which are at work in the film image. However, it is the index, characterized by a causal bond between itself and its referent, which has been the most prominent class of sign in film theory debates about reference. Peirce's (1932, II:159) conceptualization of the indexical qualities of the photographic image has been a cornerstone in debates about film's referential claims. He writes,

> Photographs, especially instantaneous photographs, are very instructive, because we know that in certain respects, they are exactly like the objects they represent. But this resemblance is due to the photographs having been produced under such circumstances that they were physically forced to correspond point by point to nature. In that aspect, then, they belong to the second class of signs, those by physical connection.

Film debates have located the referential dimensions of the film image in the forms of inscription that underlie the analogue photograph. The idea that the light reflected in the pro-filmic field has been burnt into the photochemical image, leaving an 'indexical trace' (Rosen 2001: 20) that remains as testimony to that physical, material contact, has traditionally established the referential claims of both the photographic and the film image. This conceptualization of the photochemical image as indexical trace builds not only on Peirce's account of the photograph but also Bazin's (1960) death mask in 'The Ontology of the Photographic Image' – and Barthes's ([1981] 2000) account of the relationship between the photograph, indexicality and the punctum in *Camera Lucida*.

The reenactment and the indexical image are generally regarded as standing in opposition to each other, and working with different understandings of reference. The referential relationship that the reenactment sets up between itself and a pre-existing event has typically been understood as one of resemblance, relegating the reenactment to the iconic sign, characterized by a relatively straightforward verisimilitude. The reenactment has typically been associated with researching, rehearsing, staging and performing a pre-existing event. By contrast, the image as indexical trace is associated with the inscription of a moment in time and with the unstaged, unrehearsed, pro-filmic event. These oppositions, between reenactment and trace, theatricality and the indexical image, have impacted on the reception of the reenactment throughout much of the history of its deployment in film and television. Now, as digital technologies coexist with, and increasingly replace, analogue processes across a range of media platforms, a major shift in the status of the pro-filmic field is underway in film and television production. Digital production processes are becoming more and more adept at producing images without staging or capturing a scene in front of a camera. As such, the pro-filmic field is becoming less and less necessary for image production. The imminent disappearance of photochemical celluloid prompted a crisis in those film debates previously entrenched in conceptualizing the referential dimensions of the film image in terms of the photographic basis of the analogue production process. Scholars are coming more and more to acknowledge the limitations of this approach. Doane (2007: 136), for example, argues that film debates have been so caught up in the 'drive to ground the photochemical image as trace' that there has been a misplaced emphasis on the trace, which she describes as 'only one genre of index, and not necessarily the most crucial or decisive'. There is an increasing recognition that what Gunning (2007: 30–1) calls the 'diminished concept of the index' as trace has, as he puts it, 'reached the limits of its usefulness in the theory of photography, film and new media'. With the passing of the centrality of the pro-filmic field to image production, the impending loss of the idea of the image as indexical trace has drawn attention to how narrow the conceptualization of indexicality has been in film theory.

Peirce's approach to the conceptualization of the indexical sign can be divided into two primary subcategories. There is the indexical trace, defined by a physical, material contact with a referent at a time in the past that remains as a form of testimony to a past interaction. But there are also deictic indices that direct and focus attention, setting up a co-present existential relationship between themselves and that to which they point, either literally or figuratively. Examples of deictic indices include shifters in language, demonstrative, relative and personal pronouns and the pointing finger. In Peirce's conceptualization, the pointing finger, which he identifies as 'the type of the class', works in a similar way to the 'hailing' function of deixis in language including shifters such as 'here', 'there' and the demonstrative pronoun 'this', which he argues are 'nearly pure indices, because they denote things without describing them' (Peirce 1992: 226). Both Gunning and Doane propose that if we think about the index as more than just a trace or impression, and pursue the performative and demonstrative dimensions of indexicality, we can acknowledge that the photographic process is not the only aspect of the film image that can be considered indexical. The critical rethinking of the forms and the parameters of indexicality in film has generated important work on rethinking the concept of medium specificity, the relationship between photography and film, cinematic realism, digital capture and remediation, as well as new approaches to the close up and to theorizing computer algorithms (Doane 2007).

I propose that the reenactment also be aligned with the indexical sign's more marginalized subcategory of the deictic index. The performative and demonstrative dimensions of the indexical sign, characterized by acts of showing and directing attention, have always been present in the reenactment. As I have outlined, the reenactment's primary investment in theatricality lies in the fact that, to be recognized as a reenactment, it must draw attention to the fact that it performs a pre-existing event. Its openly presentational mode of address and emphasis on staging, performance and spectacle have been its defining characteristics, essential to its ability to signal itself. Deixis has been central to the reenactment and a constant across the screen reenactment's many forms.

Chapter summary

Throughout this book I examine the relationship between self-reflexive theatricality in the reenactment and the ways in which its relationship to reference and authenticity are performed. The negotiation between theatricality and repetition in the reenactment has been continually reworked in relation to changes in the functions, status and referential relationships of the film and television genres in which the reenactment has appeared as well as wider transformations in the production and distribution of screen-based media.

As I have outlined, in film, the reenactment operated briefly as genre during the first decade of the cinema before it became associated with forms of historical representation found across different genres (including documentary, docudrama and historical fiction genres such as the biopic) as well as across different institutions (including cinema, television, galleries, museums, courtrooms and even medical research). The range of case studies in this book reflects the dispersal of the reenactment in contemporary screen culture. The book spans several subfields of film and media studies including film theory, documentary studies, genre studies and television studies. Pursuit of the reenactment across genres, media and institutional contexts is appropriate for dealing with the contemporary meaning and significance of the reenactment as a representational form and a strategy. Of course, it is not possible to address all aspects of the contemporary screen landscape in which the reenactment is operating and evolving within the scope of this study. There is still more work to be done on the use of reenactment in reality television, fan culture, gaming, virtual reality and augmented reality and ethnography, for example, among other areas.

My focus here is on thinking about how the reenactment, as a form predicated on repetition, has become tied to forms of technical repetition that are changing status, taking on different functions, meanings and referential relationships. Across the chapters, I consider different types and ways of conceiving events including media events, mediatized events, unstageable events, bodily events as well as representations of everyday habits and routines. I consider the idea that events are ongoing and can be made and remade as well as how our understanding of events is being influenced by the emerging ontologies of the digital. It is not only the idea of the event but also performance in the reenactment that has been impacted by the emergence of digital image production and the increasing circulation of technically reproducible images across media platforms. All the major examples discussed in this book have been produced after 1995, the year designated by a range of commemorative activities – scholarly, creative, industrial – as marking the centenary of cinema. Reflections on ongoing changes in the status of cinema as a cultural institution, prompted by these centenary celebrations, were expressly inflected with the coinciding decline and potential obsolescence of chemical and mechanical technologies that had long sustained the cinema. Much of the scholarship in film theory that I draw on in this book responds to these transitions and their implications.

I begin with a focus on documentary in Chapter 1, drawing on the efforts of scholars such as Kahana (2009), Margulies (2019), Nicols (2008) and Winston (1999) to develop critical frameworks to explore how and why the reenactment has undergone multiple marginalizations and resurgences in status and currency in documentary film, television and video. One of the most widely discussed strategies in the scholarship on documentary reenactment involves subjects reenacting events associated with their own lives. This strategy, which Margulies (2019) calls 'in-person reenactment', is prominent, for example, in Nichols's (2008) taxonomy of reenactment and in the special issue of *Framework* edited by Kahana (2009) titled 'Reenactment in Contemporary Documentary Film, Video and Performance'. I hone in on three case studies that take up this strategy. *S-21: The Khmer Rouge Killing Machine* (Rithy Panh, 2003) brings former inmates and prison staff together at the prison they occupied during Pol Pot's Democratic Kampuchea regime, now known as the Tuol Sleng Genocide Museum. *The Third Memory* (Pierre Huyghe, 2000) gives John Wojtowicz the opportunity to direct and perform a reenactment of his attempt to rob a Chase Manhattan Bank in 1972. *The Battle of Orgreave* (Mike Figgis, 2001) provides 'behind-the-scenes' insights into the preparation of an artwork that involves former coal miners, police officers and member of Britain's historical reenactment societies collaborating to produce a living history performance of events associated with the 1984–5 Miner's Strike in Britain. All three case studies connect the reenactment of individual actions with larger-scale events. Working with the idea that events are not discretely completed but carry on being remediated, subjects cooperate with filmmakers and other collaborators to stage and perform experiences associated with their younger selves, bringing with them the palpable sense that time has passed and the hindsight of the intervening years. I explore how the self-reflexive, performative strategies associated with in-person reenactment can produce media representations with the capacity to challenge and reconfigure an event's existing manifestations.

While there is considerable and growing discussion about the deployment of reenactment in documentary, the same cannot be said of its manifestations in film and television drama. In Chapter 2, I concentrate on the use of reenactment in the biopic, a subgenre of the historical film focused on the life of a documented historical person, and one of the fiction genres to which reenactment has been central. I work with three contemporary biopics – *Milk* (Gus Van Sant, 2008), *Monster* (Patty Jenkins, 2003) and *Boys Don't Cry* (Kimberly Peirce, 1999) – to consider some of the ways in which the increasing circulatory capacities of technical media have shaped the referential claims of the reenactment. I propose that a reenactment's accuracy can be certified through the dramatization of researched details associated with an event's mediation. I investigate how researched details drawn from documentation are integrated into the mise en scène, cinematography and soundtracks of these biopics and woven into their narrative worlds. I focus especially on the intensifying rivalry between the bodies of the actors in these biopics and the traces of the historical bodies they represent.

I continue to explore the deployment of reenactment in film and television drama in Chapter 3 with an examination of two popular police-procedural television dramas that are inspired by the principles of forensic investigation: *CSI: Crime Scene Investigation* (2000–15) and *Bones* (2005–17). Although the events being reenacted belong to the diegetic worlds of these series and do not typically have any basis in an external, pro-filmic reality – they are reenactments of fictional events within a fictional narrative – I use these case studies to expand my thinking about the incorporation and impact of reenactment in fictional narrative forms. The computer-generated reenactments devised for these shows – the infamous *CSI*-shots and the three-dimensional simulations produced by the 'Angelator' in *Bones* – serve an investigative function in the narrative, often playing a significant role in the verification of indexical traces, while leading audiences through the investigations. Indexical traces are brought to life and made to perform, the *CSI*-shot and the Angelator hailing the reenactment of their inscription. In this respect, they serve demonstrative as well as investigative functions. Their theatricality is, I propose, deictic: characterized by acts of showing, directing and focusing attention. Both series frequently devote considerable time and attention to the investigation of events that are so small in scale that can only be seen and understood with specific technologies. They explore emerging digital ontologies using computer-generated special effects to mimic styles and techniques associated with medical and forensic imaging. I contend that *CSI* and *Bones* make unstageable events spectacular by dramatizing possibilities for reenactment unleashed by innovations in computer-generated imaging technologies.

In Chapter 4, I conceptualize the shot-for-shot remake as a type of reenactment, comparing Gus Van Sant's 1998 remake of *Psycho* (Alfred Hitchcock, 1960) with Jill Godmilow's *What Farocki Taught* (1998), a remake of the short experimental essay film *Inextinguishable Fire* (Harun Farocki, 1969). Van Sant's film is situated within the Hollywood studio system while Godmilow's is connected to practices associated with reenactment in the art world but as shot-for-shot remakes they share many characteristics in common. The focus on filmmaking conventions is central to the shot-for-shot remake, given the form necessitates paying careful attention to how an existing work is constructed. In the shot-for-shot remake the actions of actors are reenacted but also those of the crew. The filmmakers study the formal and technical dimensions of the original films in order to be able to reproduce and interrogate their aesthetic decisions. I illustrate how in both cases, the remakes keep in time with their counterparts, a strategy facilitated by the fact that the original films are available to be replayed. While Hitchcock's *Psycho* is well known, widely accessible and highly influential, *What Farocki Taught* was an effort to increase attention and access to the ideas and techniques associated with *Inextinguishable Fire*. I investigate how the different circulation of the original films influences the production and reception of the remakes, including the salience attributed to the repetition of their techniques.

In Chapter 5, I explore the role of reenactment in the courtroom as a site of rhetorical contests over the past where conflicting interpretations of events are under scrutiny. I interrogate debates within the legal community about the admission of computer-generated reenactments as in civil and criminal trials in the United States. I explore how a growing body of guidelines developing around what can be admitted and how it should be presented build on long-standing concerns about the inclusion of media in trial proceedings. I turn to the infamous retimings of George Holliday's video of four Los Angeles police officers assaulting Rodney King in the trial *California v. Powell, Koon, Wind and Briseno* (1992), which showed how a familiar media event could be made to perform differently. Building on the extensive discussions by film and media scholars about this trial, I contend that control over the technical timing of film and media events makes it possible to replay events in ways that can reenact them. I consider how strategies associated with the use of digital and replay technologies in the courtroom can expand the range of events being examined and contested during a trial.

1

'To do; to perform': In-person reenactment, remediation and documentary performance

Resurgence in the use of reenactment in documentary-based film, television and video has been conceptualized by scholars such as Kahana (2009), Margulies (2003, 2019), Nichols (2008) and Winston (1999) as a 'comeback': a return to, and rethinking of, strategies that were prominent during 1930s to 1950s. For Winston (1999: 164), for example, it was the first decades of sound documentary, from the mid-1930s to the late 1950s, which marked what he describes as 'the classic period of re-enactment' in documentary. The filmmakers of this era, he argues, were already 'heirs to a persistent tradition of re-enactment' that included igloo building in *Nanook of the North* (Flaherty 1922); construction of fishing trawler cabins for *Granton Trawler* (Grierson 1934); and strategies associated with the first decade of the cinema, as discussed in the introduction to this book, such as table-top miniaturizations of battles and uprisings. For Kahana (2009: 46–7), the current popularity of reenactment in documentary marks a 'return of techniques of historical restaging' common in 'social realist films' of the 1950s such as the works that George Stoney made for the Georgia State Department of Health like *All My Babies: A Midwife's Own Story* (1953). Kahana (2009: 52) describes the reenactment as 'a hidden foundation within the history of documentary, one that, excavated by historians or filmmakers, might be employed in the remaking or deconstructing of the contemporary concept of documentary'. Indeed, it has become quite common to connect the current interest in reenactment with efforts to expand the definitions of documentary.

The marginalization of the reenactment, it is argued, was directly connected to the championing of a specific referential relationship for documentary filmmaking. Kahana (2009) and Nichols (2008) have argued that from the late 1950s and early 1960s, with the rise of direct cinema in the United States and Canada, and *cinéma vérité* in France, the reenactment lost currency as a form of documentary representation. The expectation set up by direct cinema that documentary filmmaking should capture the unstaged, unrehearsed, pro-filmic event is one that the reenactment was unable to meet. As Nichols (2008: 72) puts it, the techniques of observational and direct cinema became considered 'the "most" documentary of styles', the reenactment came to look more and more 'inauthentic'. Nichols and Kahana both argue that, although the reenactment has re-emerged in a vital role in documentary and has to some degree become 'once again taken for granted' (Nichols 2008: 73), the prejudice against the reenactment that came with the rise of direct cinema has persisted. Consequently, the resources available to analyse the reenactment remain quite scant, making the reenactment what Kahana (2009: 47) describes as 'one important but largely overlooked branch of the documentary tradition'. Therefore, these scholars have made the use of the reenactment across a range of film and television documentaries the focus of renewed critical discussion.

Even so, reenactments continued to be employed, sometimes unacknowledged, during the reign of direct cinema and *cinéma vérité*. It is Winston's (1999: 160) contention that, with the arrival of the 16mm synch-sound camera, while proponents of direct cinema thought they could dispense with reenactment, it persisted, 'even more hidden than it had been. It lurked, lurks, behind the observational, hand-held, available-light, long-take style of direct cinema where it was, and is, more or less invisible'. Winston (1999: 163) points to a broad range of directions that documentary makers can give to subjects in an effort to stage their actions that can be, as he puts it, 'considered legitimate documentary practice'. These include requests 'to repeat or delay an action' and 'to re-enact actions witnessed during the research process' – actions 'witnessed by the subject or others in the past' or 'witnessed elsewhere during the research process performed by other people of the same type as the subjects'. Such strategies are employed much more self-reflexively within the framework of *cinéma vérité*. Corner (1996: 43–4) characterizes the distinctions between direct cinema and *cinéma vérité* in terms of their different modes of address: 'Far from wishing to render the camera "invisible" and to project what happens before it as some magical capturing of the spontaneous', *cinéma vérité*, he argues, 'showed the filmmaking process intervening in the events filmed, with participants not only looking at, but also addressing, the filmmakers'. Margulies (2003: 229) positions Zavatinni and Antonioni's use of reenactment within a neorealist framework as part of the lineage of the intention in *cinéma vérité* 'to stage a transformative process on camera' (Margulies 2019: 113). Renov (2004) points to the concern in *cinéma vérité* with the encounter between the cinematic apparatus and participants, as a laying the groundwork for a shift towards greater emphasis on performativity and subjectivity in documentary filmmaking from the 1970s onward. The ideas and practices associated with *cinéma vérité* can be considered an ongoing influence on filmmakers working with reenactment.

That a reenactment declares itself the performance of a pre-existing event is essential to its acceptance in documentary film, television and video, even if this results in a mixed mode of address where some moving images in a work demonstrate a direct link to a pro-filmic reality and others do not exhibit this kind of indexical bond. In 2005, for example, controversy around the Academy Award-winning short documentary *Mighty Times: The Children's March* (2004), directed by Bobby Houston and Robert Hudson, centred on whether the audience was provided with enough information to enable them to distinguish reenacted scenes from archive footage. Frieda Lee Mock, the Executive Committee chairwoman of the Academy's documentary branch, warned that 'the failure to disclose their use of re-enactments called into question the nature of reality implied by the use of the term documentary' (cited in Morris 2008). The requirement that they be clearly signalled does not mean that reenactments necessarily need to stand out explicitly from other kinds of imagery. As Kahana (2008) points out, the documentary *Man on Wire* (2008), which investigates the events surrounding Philippe Petit's illegal high-wire routine between the twin towers of the World Trade Centre in 1974, was praised by some critics for its successful interweaving of reenactments, interviews and archive footage.

The self-reflexivity associated with the reenactment arises out of the necessity to make clear its specific temporal and referential status. 'Reenactments occupy a strange status', Nichols (2008: 73) explains, 'in which it is crucial that they be recognized as a representation of a prior event while also signalling that they are not a representation of a contemporaneous event'. He draws on Gregory Bateson's account of how representations can take on new meanings that shift their signification, quoting Bateson's example of how fighting among animals can be distinguished from play fighting: 'These actions in which we now engage, do not denote what would be denoted by those actions which these actions denote.' For Kahana, the challenge of signalling this kind of temporal and referential status is magnified for film reenactments because of the associations between the film image and the idea of inscription. In Kahana's (2009: 52–3) account of the etymology of the term 'reenactment' outlined by the *Oxford English Dictionary*, he proposes, that 'enactment is itself already a concept in which the problems of staging and mediation figure quite significantly, even before the addition of the prefix re-':

> The enmeshment of the two actions of enactment – to *do*; to perform – is a centuries-old problem, captured in its etymology and revived over a century ago in the birth of the moving image. Filmed reenactments – which date more or less to the origin of cinema – reopen the gap between the two original senses of enactment. It would, of course, be a mistake to claim that film single-handedly revived this problem, or that there were no institutional, public, or collective practices of reenactment prior to or beside cinema. ... But with cinema, the ontological ambiguity in the concept of enactment is practically unavoidable. Because the moving image comes to us with an effect of immediacy built in, one that installs itself in and as an authoritative record of the past simply because of the technical conditions of its production and its exhibition, the medium already seems to have the effect of public history, decreeing to audiences of any filmed event that *it was this way, this happened*. Under the conditions of these public displays of social recording, of a past that lives again before us, it can be very difficult to distinguish 'actual' actions from performances.

In the context of documentary this ontological ambiguity can become heightened by the complicated status of documentary subjects as performers. Nichols (1991: 121–2), for example, uses the term 'virtual performance' to describe the way documentary subjects perform as themselves through their habitual, 'normal self-presentation' during interviews. As Marquis (2013: 50) argues, conceptualizations of documentary performance involve the 'mediating presence of the film-making apparatus itself' and the interactions between mise-en scène, editing, cinematography, sound and documentary screen performers. Kahana's navigation of the etymology of enactment underscores how the issue of performance in documentary brings relations between mediation, staging and referentiality to the fore, drawing attention to some of the ways that performance is tied up with technical reproducibility.

The focus of this chapter is on what Margulies (2019) calls 'in-person reenactment', where subjects reenact events associated with their own lives. In-person reenactment necessarily involves negotiating what Kahana (2009: 52) describes above as 'the enmeshment of the two actions of enactment': doing and performing. Santas Aquino (2012: 51) points out that in the context of in-person reenactment (which she calls 'social actor reenactment'), documentary subjects take on the identities of both actor and social actor:

> At one level, they are actors because they reenact not only their past experiences and memories in front of the camera but also invented situations that nevertheless speak to these experiences. At another level, they are social actors because their reenactments take place in actual, sociocultural/political contexts and spaces.

Margulies's (2019: 14) summary of what she terms the 'dualities' associated with in-person reenactment – 'actor or person, past or present, representation or presentation, theatricality or authenticity' – aptly captures tensions central to the workings of the reenactment more generally but which are especially palpable with in-person reenactment.

In line with the evolving scholarship on documentary-based reenactment, the case studies span a range of media and cultural forms. *S-21: The Khmer Rouge Killing Machine* (Rithy Panh, 2003) returns former prisoners and prison staff to Cambodia's schoolhouse-turned prison (code-named S-21), now the Tuol Sleng Genocide Museum, where it is estimated that seventeen thousand people were photographed, interrogated, tortured and executed during Pol Pot's Democratic Kampuchea regime (1975–9). In the two-channel video installation *The Third Memory* (Pierre Huyghe, 2000), John Wojtowicz plays himself and directs a group of extras in a reenactment of his attempt to rob the Brooklyn branch of the Chase Manhattan Bank in 1972. *The Battle of Orgreave* (Mike Figgis, 2001), commissioned by ArtAngel and produced by Euphoria

Films and Channel 4, is a documentary about the collaboration between artist Jeremy Deller, hundreds of former coal miners, former police officers and members of British historical reenactment societies to stage a living history performance of a major confrontation between thousands of police and picketing miners in South Yorkshire in 1984.

Each of these case studies works with the idea that events are not discretely completed but continue to be remediated. In *The Third Memory*, for example, Wojtowicz negotiates between his memories of the heist and its representation in *Dog Day Afternoon* (Sidney Lumet, 1975) as well as his own performance for the television cameras: Wojtowicz's lengthy negotiations with police and the FBI during his twelve-hour siege became a media event. Deller, among others, points out in *The Battle of Orgreave* that the events associated with the 1984–5 Miner's Strike – a conflict between the conservative Thatcher government and trade unions over industrial relations and the decline of the coal industry – had been largely controlled by the government of the day. *The Battle of Orgreave* became a means to interrogate these contested events from the miner's perspective, bringing to the fore some of the inaccuracies that had preoccupied them.

For *S-21*, in contrast, there were very few people left who had lived through the events under examination. Of the thousands imprisoned at S-21, it is believed that only seven survived and three were still alive when Panh made *S-21*. Two, Vann Nath and Chum Mey, agreed to return to the prison/museum along with a small group of low-ranking former guards, an interrogator, clerk, photographer and medical officer (Boyle 2009: 96). While in *The Battle of Orgreave*, Deller and Figgis focus on the miner's perspective, cultivating a counter-narrative to the dominant perspectives of the government and media of the time, Panh actively includes the perspectives of the perpetrators. The idea to bring inmates and staff together emerged because of a chance encounter between Vann Nath (a former prisoner who survived because his paintings pleased the prison leadership) and Him Houy (deputy head of prison security at S-21) during another film Panh was making, *Bophana: A Cambodian Tragedy* (1996). When they met, Nath showed Houy his paintings – which depicted events he had witnessed or been told about – asking him to verify whether they had happened (Camhi 2004: 24; Oppenheimer 2012: 243–4). This encounter convinced Panh that, as he describes it, 'the testimony was not complete unless it was testimony from both sides of the situation' (Oppenheimer 2012: 244).

S-21: The Khmer Rouge Killing Machine

S-21 is primarily organized around episodic, self-contained scenes in which former prisoners and prison staff inhabit spaces inside and around the Tuol Sleng Museum. The decision to bring subjects back to the site where the events took place resonates with what Walker (2012: 270) calls the 'Holocaust documentary of return' in which 'filmed, situated testimonies' of refugees – who have returned to places they had previously survived, fled, were removed or rescued from – are 'delivered verbally and bodily from a significant site and in the presence of others', one of the most famous examples being *Shoah* (Claude Lanzmann, 1985). Actively responding to the site, the subjects of *S-21* gather together with the filmmakers to remember, reenact, recount, discuss, explain and even paint aspects of what happened during their time there. Their responses emerge from staged encounters with each other, the spaces and their contents, including documents contained in the museum's archive (such as photographs, administrative records, incident reports, arrest logs, prisoner's forced confessions, interrogation instruction guides and operational memos), mostly left behind when the Khmer Rouge fled in January 1979. The subjects' testimony is frequently in dialogue with, even verified by, details from these documents. Reading and explaining prison documentation facilitates the perpetrators' testimony, helping them describe events (and admit to participating in them) as well as corroborate and elaborate others' testimony. The documentation also inspires and verifies reenactments, which are interspersed throughout *S-21*. Sometimes several guards perform together or for each other. At others, they are solo. Whether subjects are giving testimony, participating in a reenactment or combination of these, the emphasis is on the bureaucracy associated with everyday life in the prison, its routines and documented incidents.

The earliest reenactments in the film are preceded by a scene in which Nath confronts the issue of the prison staff's humanity, agency and responsibility.

Having explained the torment that he and other inmates endured as depicted in one of his paintings, he asks them, 'How could you get used to seeing such suffering? ... You didn't think at all? ... Your ability to think as a human being, you lost it.' Huoy responds by emphasizing obedience: 'If they said this was the enemy, I repeated, this is the enemy.' Nath responds,

> I don't want to hear that: obedience to Angkar. If everyone only thinks Angkar, discipline, obeying orders, carry out orders or be killed, it's the end of our world, of justice. There are no more ideals, no more human conscience.

The issue of whether low-ranking former prison staff are responsible for what took place in the prison is a central question that resonates throughout the documentary. The reenactments that prison staff perform constitute the most palpable embodiment of this tension between accountability and indoctrination.

In one of these early reenactments, former prison staff demonstrate how they would collect a prisoner for interrogation. Prak Khan, a former interrogator, walks along a long outdoor corridor explaining, 'To find a prisoner, I have the cell number written on my palm.' His palm outstretched, he points into an empty room, 'Bring in Prisoner 13 for interrogation.' Khieu Ches, a former guard, walks into the room as the camera looks in from the doorway. Ches shouts, 'Number 13, get up! I order him up, blindfold him with a kramar.' He gestures as if blindfolding his own eyes. 'Handcuff him from behind.' He puts his own hands behind his back. 'Then I remove the bar.' He leans over removing an imaginary leg iron. 'I close the lock again and lead him out by the arm.' He walks back into the corridor as if holding a prisoner. Khan continues the narration, 'When I get the prisoner, I slip my arm under his and take him away.' He bends up his arm as if holding the prisoner and walks away from the camera.

Close to the midpoint of the film, we encounter Khieu Ches again as he becomes absorbed in the reenactment of his prison routines, pacing the large empty former prison cell and adjacent corridor. As in the previous reenactment, he oscillates between narrating his actions and shouting orders to absent prisoners: 'At 10 pm, the interrogator brings the prisoner back. Stand here! I unlock the door.' He acts out unlocking the door. 'I lead him in.' He walks into the middle of the former cell as if shepherding a prisoner. 'Stand there! I open the lock, put the irons on him.' He gestures putting on invisible leg irons. 'I take off the handcuffs.' He acts as if he is taking off handcuffs behind a prisoner's back. 'I remove the blindfold. I go out.' He walks out of the cell and back into the corridor. 'Be quiet! Don't make any noise! Otherwise, it's the club!' He shuts the door to the cell. 'I lock the door.' Once outside in the corridor again, he starts looking in through the windows, shouting at the prisoners and responding to unspoken requests: 'Rice soup? I'll bring it.' He opens door, picks up a bowl and walks back into the cell. 'Here, eat! That's all there is. And you, don't try to steal it. Or beware.' Ches paces in and out of the cell and repeatedly unlocks and locks of the door for almost five minutes, the longest reenactment in the film.

These reenactments are a variation of what Bruzzi (2016) describes as the 'animated' or 'active' interview in which subjects 'walk through the events they are recalling verbally'. They are the outcome of Panh's judicious observations, directions and staging. Panh 'set the stage' for Ches's testimony meticulously: Learning that Ches worked at S-21 at night, he filmed at night and tried to recreate the prison's neon lighting, playing revolutionary songs on the radio, as they did then. His crew found leftover items onsite and placed them outside the cell, including a water bowl and a bedpan and when Ches arrived, he incorporated them into his routines (Oppenhemier 2012: 244–5). Panh's approach emerged out of his interactions with a former guard who struggled to provide testimony:

> He could not speak to me. He would just give me a word here, a word there. It's very difficult to understand him, but he made a lot of gestures. I told him: 'You can complete your words by showing me what happened', and it became a re-enactment. I am not asking people to act. I just try to take the memory out of the body, what your body keeps, what your body feels. (Boyle 2016: 41)

Panh likewise told Ches: 'Show me your work, show me how you worked … you can use gestures, you can speak, explain it in any way you wish.' His approach enabled Ches and other prison staff to deliver their testimony as reenactment – to become performers in order to demonstrate what they did. Panh also asked his subjects to repeatedly go over actions that were difficult to express to cultivate 'the most favourable conditions' for their testimony (Oppenheimer 2012: 244–6). The reenactments performed by Ches and Khan, among others, are the outcome of a production process that emphasized repetition. As Panh explains, 'They start, stop, and start again ten or twenty times. Their reflexes return; I see what really happened. … The method and the truth of the extermination appear' (Panh and Bataille 2014: 91).

The guards perform tasks and drills for which they were trained and although the performances have an evidentiary value, the question of personal agency and responsibility remains largely ambivalent. Margulies (2019: 214, 216, 206), for example, proposes that the guards' 'inscrutable' and 'affectless' expressions may suggest 'the potential exchangeability of group members with other people' and that this 'further dilutes their personal responsibility' instead emphasizing what she describes as 'a broader machinery of killing'. In this respect, we could consider Khan and Ches's reenactments in relation to what Nichols (2008: 84–5) calls 'typifications', a category that includes examples like the igloo building and walrus hunting in *Nanook of the North* (Robert Flaherty, 1922), where 'there is no specific event to which the reenactment refers'. These are reenactments that are, as Nichols puts it, 'characteristic' rather than 'specific', emphasizing 'patterns, rituals and routines'. Nichols (2008: 85) describes reenactments in which an example becomes an exemplar as 'typical particulars'. He points to the mushrooming of this strategy in the era that Winston (1999: 164) associates with 'classic period of re-enactment' in documentary: the British documentary movement of the 1930s such as *Coal Face* (Alberto Cavalcanti, 1935) and *Night Mail* (Harry Watt, Basil Wright, 1936) where subjects reenact typical activities from their everyday working lives.

The mundane narration of repetitive actions contributes to the evidentiary value of the performances in *S-21* while bringing with it the heightened self-reflexivity that enables their actions to be declared as reenactments. This distinguishes the reenactments in *S-21* from those in *Nanook*, *Coal Face* or *Night Mail*, which, as Nichols (2008: 85) describes, 'possess a similar aura of present-day reality simply observed when they are, in fact, staged'. In the reenactments in *S-21*, Ches, Khan and other guards deliver the very literal narration of their actions in the present tense while testimony in other scenes is typically delivered in past tense. Even though they perform everyday actions and speak in the present tense, the events being reenacted clearly occurred in the past, the use of present tense contrasting starkly with the empty museum space in which they are performed. Prison staff address these spaces evocatively, their performances haunted by the spectre of their victims.

In this respect, the reenactments in *S-21* can also be considered in relation to Nichols's discussion of *Chile, Obstinate Memory* (Patricio Guzman, 1997). In this documentary, footage of President Allende's bodyguards protecting him from *The Battle of Chile* (Patricio Guzman, 1975–9) is intercut with the surviving men performing a reenactment of themselves guarding the presidential motorcade thirty-five years later 'on a deserted country road, with no crowd in sight' Nichols (2008: 77). This performance, Nichols (2008: 73) argues,

> clearly does not fulfil a state need this time; instead it gratifies a personal desire, it makes possible the enjoyment of going through the motions of guarding, as it were, when guarding itself remains squarely lodged in the past. ... but the camera's close-up view of his delicate grip, the rise and fall of his fingers, and the overt absence of an engulfing crowd attest to the psychically real but fantasmatic linkage of now and then.

While pleasure and desire are certainly not driving the reenactments in *S-21*, Ches and others do become immersed in their performances despite the similarly marked absence of others. Panh and his long-time collaborator, Prum Mesa (director of photography), also actively respond to the temporal and psychic complexity of these performances. As Panh explains,

> When the guard went inside to beat the prisoner, I don't know why I stopped Mesa, but I just put my hand on his shoulder, and he knew that he had to stop following him. You must have this kind of ethic in your heart, because when you are filming, things go too fast. I don't know, I see people. I see the prisoners. The room is empty, but I see people, so I just put a hand on Mesa's shoulder. 'Don't walk on people. We cannot walk on people who are lying there, who ask for help, who ask for water.' At that moment, I didn't know how important this was, but when I watched the rushes, I understood, okay, you can continue to make the film, because if you followed the guy, that means that you had become a perpetrator yourself. (Boyle 2016: 41)

Figure 1.1 The camera peers in through the window as Khieu Ches performs his routines in an empty cell. *S-21: The Khmer Rouge Killing Machine* (Dir. Rithy Panh, 2003).

Bruzzi (2006: 10) conceptualizes as performative those documentaries that emphasize encounters with their subject to stage a self-reflexive, 'multi-layered, performative exchange between subjects, filmmakers/apparatus and spectators'. Although Panh does not feature directly in his documentary, these kinds of exchanges between subjects and crew highlight how the performances are imbricated with their mediation and staging.

During these performances, we witness the guards threatening and beating prisoners, chaining and blindfolding them and escorting them away for interrogation but the extent of the violence associated with the reenactments is not nearly as graphic and horrifying as the testimony given in other scenes, where former prison staff describe interrogation methods or the disposal of dead bodies. But in the reenactments, the perpetrators go further than admitting or describing what they did. They show what they did. Boyle (2009: 98–100) goes as far as to argue that as Ches becomes swept up in reenacting his routines, he revives and relives the past, illustrating 'how alive

Cambodia's past is in the psyche of its survivors, both victims and perpetrators'. For Ranciere (2009: 101), the emphasis on routines, when combined with the use of present-tense narration, suggests something more sinister: that it is 'as if yesterday's torturer were ready to adopt the same role tomorrow'. Both accounts tap into the temporalities associated with reenactment.

When he decided to make *S-21*, Panh had been making films about the Khmer Rouge and the legacy of the genocide in Cambodia for almost two decades. He wanted to make a film confronting what happened at *S-21* because the Khmer Rouge claimed it did not exist. His film, which took more than three years to make, did provoke Khieu Samphan, former head of state for the Khmer Rouge, to admit the existence of the prison (Oppenheimer 2012: 250–1, 253; Boyle 2016: 40). The emphasis on staging, demonstration, haunting and authentication, brought together in *S-21*, makes these reenactments a potent strategy for working through otherwise supressed associations between past and present. Even though the museum space is empty, and those to whom the perpetrators speak are absent, having long since perished, the performances themselves are still important. By going through the motions, subjects in *S-21* bring the prison routines into the present, embodying them, making them felt, as they testify to the actions they performed that organized and maintained the prison.

The Third Memory

In *The Third Memory* John Wojtowicz reenacts guarding the bank employees he took hostage during his attempted robbery. Rather than reoccupying the original site, the space that Wojtowicz inhabits is a sound stage. The set for his performance is based on the inside of the bank in *Dog Day Afternoon*, the film based on his life, and to which he responds in *The Third Memory*. In contrast to *Dog Day Afternoon*, however, the mise en scène of *The Third Memory* is stark and non-naturalistic. The walls are bare and there is hardly any furniture. The set represents the idea of the bank schematically with only the basic props required. The setting outside the bank is even sparser and makes it more apparent that Wojtowicz is on a sound stage. Lighting equipment, boom mikes, cameras and the crew operating them are often visible in the frame, creating the impression that we could be watching Wojtowicz during the production process, working on-set, rather than watching a finished film. The juxtaposition, at times, of shots of the same scene from two different cameras angles even suggests that we could be watching rushes before the footage is edited together.

In a strategy that resonates with *The Act of Killing* (Joshua Oppenheimer, 2012) – a documentary inspired by *S-21* – it appears that Wojtowicz, a perpetrator, is given the means to stage, direct and star in his own story. While his crimes are not as heinous as many committed by those featured in *The Act of Killing* and *S-21*, his botched attempted robbery resulted in a hefty prison sentence and his accomplice, Sal Naturale, was shot dead by the FBI. As is apparent in *The Act of Killing*, but less so in *S-21*, Wojtowicz appears to be proud, even boastful, about what he has done. Like *S-21*, the reenactments in *The Third Memory* are an effort to show, explain and demonstrate what happened and Wojtowicz likewise narrates many of his actions as he performs them. His performances draw on the mode I argued is also central to *S-21* where subjects 'walk through the events they are recalling verbally' (Bruzzi 2016). In contrast to *S-21* where the victims being addressed are markedly absent, Wojtowicz's victims are played by actors, as is his accomplice. Wojtowicz directs the other performers, instructing them where to stand, how to move and what to say. The novice bank robber becomes a novice director.

Like the guards in *S-21*, Wojtowicz frequently narrates in the present tense, which often involves a mix of describing his own actions and giving orders, as is common in *S-21*. Margulies (2019: 190) describes the guard's narration of their actions in *S-21* involving the 'doubling of verbal and gestural information'. In *The Third Memory*, this doubling takes a different form as actors frequently repeat after Wojtowicz. Inside the bank, for example, Wojtowicz directs the actor playing his accomplice, Sal, on how to instruct the actor playing the bank manager they are holding hostage: 'Tell him to take his hand off the phone', says Wojtowicz, and the actor playing Sal says, 'Take your hand off the phone.' Out on the sidewalk in front of the bank, Wojtowicz says, 'Now a sergeant from around the corner comes around, stops right there.' As he describes the sergeant's actions, he also motions with his hand for the actor playing the officer to stop. He continues, 'Points the shot-gun at me and tells me "If you make a move, I'll blow your fucking brains out." OK, say it.' And the actor repeats, 'If you make a move, I'll blow your fucking brains out.' In these and other scenes throughout *The Third Memory* Wojtowicz takes on the role of narrator, performer and director, his narration sometimes also becoming his directions to the actors.

The combined roles of narrator, performer and director become especially complicated when Wojtowicz directs the actors playing his hostages at the same time as he plays himself as their captor. The two roles sometimes become conflated. When he instructs his actor-hostages to 'raise your hands slowly' and 'take a giant step back', for example, he is both instructing them as the director of the scene and performing a reenactment of his instructions to his hostages. Reenacting directions he gave to his hostages becomes a means to direct the actors' performances. His repetition and revival of past actions become connected to the production process. At one point, as he tells the actors to raise their hands, he begins by directing them as hostages, shouting, 'Let me see 'em! Let me see 'em! Don't touch any alarms!' This line, which suggests he is performing his role as captor, is followed by the direction: 'Now lower your hands slowly.' This subsequent direction has a much more ambiguous status as both a direction to the hostages and/or a direction to the actors. Wojtowicz's next instruction, 'Don't move but try to act natural', is clearly a direction for the actors rather than a reenactment of a direction he gave to the hostages. With these lines of dialogue delivered in close succession he moves between performing the role of captor, occupying the dual role of both captor and director, before assuming more distinctly the role of director, all within the same scene.

Wojtowicz had already become a performer during the original siege. He repeatedly came out onto the sidewalk and paraded in front of the bank, performing for the crowd who gathered, drawn to the spectacle, reporters, television cameras and the police officers surrounding the bank. He also became a director out on that sidewalk: successfully directing police officers to lower their weapons in front of the cameras. A snippet of footage from one of Wojtowicz's appearances outside the bank is included at the end of *The Third Memory* (coupled with the audio of Pacino shouting at the police from *Dog*

Day Afternoon). Erickson (2009: 111) quotes a hostage interviewed in a *Life* magazine article who suggests that Wojtowicz saw his performances during the siege as a 'means of survival'. The hostage described Wojtowicz saying, 'I want people out there, I want reporters out there, they're what's keeping me alive.' In *The Third Memory*, he proudly reflects on how television coverage of the siege interrupted the broadcast of President's Nixon's nomination. Wojtowicz's status as a 'media star' is affirmed by the subsequent coverage of his life, some of it displayed and incorporated in *The Third Memory* installation, including footage of Wojtowicz appearing on *The Jeanne Parr Show* (CBS, 25 January 1978), newspaper clippings related to the bank robbery as well as a response to *Dog Day Afternoon* that Wojtowicz penned while in prison.

Now 28 years older and dressed in a suit for *The Third Memory*, the sense that time has passed, and cannot be revived, is already conveyed by Wojtowicz's aged body. Margulies (2003: 220) argues that 'reenactment creates, performatively speaking, another body, place and time'. Of the three case studies in this chapter, it is in *The Third Memory* that this dynamic is expressly foregrounded, especially because of the existing media coverage of his younger self. His performance in *The Third Memory* resonates with Margulies's (2019: 5) claim that, with in-person reenactment, the subject is

> at odds with the time it represents, the real/actor is an active and disturbing revenant whose surplus presence generates a deep uncertainty regarding its status, its performative effectiveness, and its relation to an original experience.

That Wojtowicz's aged body becomes an incongruent double for his younger self underscores Margulies's (2003: 230) broader proposal that reenactment is grounded in the idea 'that one cannot change the past but can merely, and barely, reproduce its appearances'. The stylistic choices made for *The Third Memory* underscore this, the setting and performances conjuring an unrefined, partial self-reflexive sketch of past events rather than trying to recreate them. Nichols (2008: 80) argues that the

> partialness and constructed quality of the reenactment can be the source of a sense of dissatisfaction; the view is too incomplete or too cluttered (it may contain a body too few or too many as contemporary figures fill in for their historical counterparts).

The Third Memory involves both too many and too few bodies in different scenes. Wojtowicz is ever present; his accomplice and the hostages are played by actors but the police are largely absent. Sometimes, as occurs in *S-21*, Wojtowicz describes seeing people who are not there. As he performs going out onto the sidewalk to speak with police, he says, 'I see cops all over the place. Across the street. In the windows. Cops coming around this way. Cops coming around that way.' But there are no actors representing them. The set is dark and empty. Only one actor playing a police officer appears.

At the opening of *The Third Memory*, Wojtowicz introduces himself by referring to the character based on him in *Dog Day Afternoon*: 'My name is John S. Wojtowicz. I am the real Sonny Worzik and I'm the one that you see in *Dog Day Afternoon*.' His statement sets up a dialogue between his performance and that of Pacino, the actor who plays Worzik. Remarkably, Wojtowicz was already thinking about emulating Pacino before the heist. In *The Third Memory*, he talks about going to watch *The Godfather* (Francis Ford Coppola, 1972) for inspiration before his attempted robbery. *Dog Day Afternoon*, released in 1975 just a few years after Wojtowicz's heist, was already twenty-five years old when *The Third Memory* was made in 2000. And yet the way that Wojtowicz refers to it here does not suggest that passage of time, but rather refers to the temporality of the viewing experience ('the one that you see in *Dog Day Afternoon*'). This suggests that, as the film continues to circulate, Wojtowicz's engagement with the cinematic representation of these events from his life is ongoing. *The Third Memory* explores Wojtowicz's negotiation of what Erickson (2009: 120) describes as a 'tense dialectic' between his memory of his past actions and their representation in *Dog Day Afternoon*. As Huyghe explains it,

> His memory is affected by the fiction itself. He had integrated the fiction of *Dog Day Afternoon* into the fact of his life. He is always shifting between these two things, the memory of the fact and his memory of the fiction. (Dannatt: 2001)

The two-channel video format is used to juxtapose the reenactment of the bank vault being opened by the bank manager in *Dog Day Afternoon* with Wojtowicz's staging of his own reenactment of these events. Pacino performs side by side with Wojtowicz. (At other times Wojtowicz functions as his own double, appearing on both screens simultaneously from different camera

Figure 1.2 Two reenactments of the opening of the bank vault are juxtaposed as Al Pacino performs side by side with John Wojtowicz. *The Third Memory* (Dir. Pierre Huyghe, 2000) at the Renaissance Society at the University of Chicago, 2–30 April 2000. Photographer: Tom Van Eynde.

angles.) Pairing these two reenactments creates a doubling effect that allows audiences to compare the style, action, framing and mise en scène of each scene, which share similarities but do not match. The audio oscillates between Wojtowicz voice-over and on-screen narration, while *Dog Day Afternoon* mostly plays in silence on the other screen.

As Erickson (2009) and McDonough (2004) point out, there has been considerable debate about whether *The Third Memory* gives Wojtowicz the opportunity to 'speak back' to other media representations. Massera (2000: 95), for example, argues that the work is about 'reappropriating the representations that speak in our place and name' bringing Wojtowicz into 'the very heart of the spectacular machinery that has dispossessed him of his own identity … to regain his own image'. In this sense, the reenactment becomes a means for Wojtowicz to share his perspective on what happened and to fulfil his desire to 'set the record straight'. At the opening of *The Third Memory*, he disputes the implication that he sold out his accomplice to the FBI, leading to his death. The standard FBI warning about unauthorized reproduction, distribution or exhibition of copyrighted motion pictures, videotapes or videodiscs appears on both screens, as Wojtowicz says in voice-over: 'I told the FBI to go fuck themselves because I don't betray my partner. It's me and him.' While Wojtowicz's attitude to *Dog Day Afternoon* is also often oppositional, Erickson (2009: 109) proposes that Wojtowicz's engagement with the film reflects his desire for 'an image and economic gain closely associated with stardom'. Indeed, in the same opening in voice-over Wojtowicz also discusses his conflict with Warner Brothers about the money he believes he is owed: 'Instead they keep giving it to the hostages and I'm a millionaire living on welfare.'

For McDonough (2004: 109), Wojtowicz's performance in *The Third Memory* highlights not Wojtowicz's agency but rather 'the ever-increasing conscription of the subject by the mechanisms of that culture'. This relates to a broader concern across much of Huyghe's work with the idea that, as Huyghe describes it, 'representation or images [have become] more important than real events'. Huyghe proposes, 'Today, an event, its image, and its commentary have become one object' (Baker 2004: 83). The major, life-changing events of Wojtowicz's personal life associated with his robbery attempt became mediatized as they were occurring, as well as subsequently, through continued coverage in their aftermath. The proliferation of media representations of these events means that numerous performances of Wojtowicz circulate across the media landscape, his reenactments in *The Third Memory* circulating among the performances by his younger self and his fictional counterpart. The mediation and remediation of the attempted robbery and siege have even transformed, as Huyghe proposes in this work, Wojtowicz's own memory. Their remediation continues, the work itself also participating in this process.

The Battle of Orgreave

Like *The Third Memory*, in *The Battle of Orgreave*, in-person reenactment becomes a means to engage with, and intervene in, an increasingly mediatized event culture. As artist Jeremy Deller describes in the documentary, he first encountered the confrontation between police and picketing miners in South Yorkshire on 18 June 1984, as a media event. Media coverage of events has, as Patton (2010) argues, 'become part of the unfolding of events themselves' and central to the 'actualization' of events such as a demonstration or protest 'as a certain kind of event'. Political struggles over the portrayal of events occur, he argues, because 'event attributions do not simply describe or report pre-existing events, they help to actualize particular events in the social field'. As I outlined in the introduction, it has primarily been in the fields of art history and performance studies that reenactments have been understood to facilitate exploration of the relationships between mediation, performance and the concept of the event. Deller's work is part of a broader trend of artists working with what Lutticken (2005: 60) describes as 'forms of repetition that break open history and the historicist return of past periods'. Both *The Third Memory* and *The Battle of Orgreave* tap into what Lutticken (2005: 46) describes as an especially potent power associated with the reenactment: the capacity to 'break open and recharge the past by duplicating and interrogating our event culture' while at the same time becoming 'part of this very culture'.

The documentary, *The Battle of Orgreave*, over which Deller had no editorial control, focuses on the planning and rehearsal process. This approach resonates with King's (2012: 166) focus on the infrastructures, industries and communities of practice that shape a reenactment. The documentary pays attention to various stakeholders involved in the project and how their different knowledge worlds and agendas influence the production, which suggests that the process of producing the living performance is part of the artwork. Although a range of perspectives are incorporated, the experiences of former pickets and miners, and the communities to which they belong, remain central. Even so, the documentary shows how the organization and realization of the performance relied heavily on two of Britain's largest reenactment societies, the Sealed Knot (founded in 1967) and the English Civil War Society (founded in 1980), under the direction of Howard Giles, managing director of EventPlan and former director of a massive events program at English Heritage. Giles was hired by ArtAngel, the organization that funded the project.

Staged on 17 June 2001 (just one day before seventeenth anniversary of the clash), the performance could not adhere to the timescale of the original conflict, which lasted eight hours, instead condensing a portion of the events into two phases performed over two and a half hours. The first phase involved a stand off between pickets and police broken by charges from mounted police clearing the way for pickets to be pursued on foot by short shield police units. This was staged on a field close to the site of the original events with an area demarcated for three thousand spectators (including residents, friends, family and colleagues) and a master of ceremonies narrating and contextualizing the action as it was occurring. The second phase involved a reenactment of the police charge that pushed pickets over the local railway bridge and through the village streets to its outskirts.

By working with historical reenactment societies, Deller sought to draw a parallel between the English Civil War (a common focus for these societies) and the Miner's Strike. His intention was to position the conflict as 'part of the lineage of decisive battles in English history', proposing, 'It would not be an exaggeration to say that the strike, like a civil war, had a traumatically divisive effect on all levels of life in the UK' (Deller 2002: 7). The confrontation between police and pickets was chosen because the miners' loss on that day is symbolic of long-term political and social transformations that dramatically impacted the welfare of the British working class. David Douglass (National Union of Mineworkers branch secretary for Hatfield and mining historian) proposes in an interview in the documentary that the strike was 'a crossroad of history where a whole generation could have went a different way'. The decision to work with historical reenactment societies and a former director of events for British Heritage is also significant given the politicized emphasis on heritage and the heritage industries in Britain during the era of Thatcher's leadership. Hewson (1987: 9) argues that the Thatcher government used the heritage industry politically to encourage a culture of nostalgia to mask the 'climate of decline' in Britain and the neoliberal agenda to privatize public utilities. *The Battle of Orgreave* lives up to Hewson's (1987: 146) provocation to artists to instigate a 'dialogue between past and present' to challenge the delusions conjured by the heritage industry under Thatcher.

The documentary shows how the project facilitated this dialogue by bringing in-person reenactment into the world of living history. Deller gave members of Britain's historical reenactment societies – who typically perform much more distant pasts – the opportunity to stage a contested event within living memory, intermingling them with hundreds of former miners and pickets for whom that past was not remote or over. Wyatt, an ambulance driver at Orgreave, reminds the visitors that they are performing within and for a community dramatically impacted by the events being staged:

> I'd like to say welcome to South Yorkshire to all the reenactors. I hope you can share some experiences that those of us who live here, these events are actually burned into our folklore. They're burned into our community memory and our consciousness and we'll never forget them. ... There are very often events which things never seem the same afterwards and I think Orgreave on that day, things really could never be the same after that.

While the opportunity for historical reenactors to perform within such a community was quite unique, historical reenactment societies can also engage with the idea that the past continues to be remediated. As I discussed in the introduction, Schneider (2011: 11) shows that many hobbyist reenactors do acknowledge that the events they reenact are politicized and contested. She points to the belief among some hobbyist reenactors that the American Civil War continues 'to be fought through commemoration'. Deller wanted to take this further by having the reenactors 'fighting with and against men that were part of an unfinished messy history' (Slyce 2003: 78).

The documentary reveals some of the interactions between the knowledge worlds and agendas of these different stakeholders that emerged during the production process. Some historical reenactors, who are typically very focused on safety, were concerned that former pickets might get too swept up in reliving their past and become violent. A reenactor playing a picket says,

> I've been reenacting for seventeen years, up against guys with swords, maces, axes, horses, guns, you name it, and I haven't had butterflies for an awfully long time ... It's a bit ultra-realistic today so we'll see how it goes. And these maniacs, I've got to look after them and make sure they don't get hurt so my job is cut out for me.

As one reenactor in police uniform puts it during rehearsals, 'We've got a few concerns about some of the extras ... A few of us are a bit worried. Some of the extras don't really know when enough's enough.'

Giles explains in the documentary that the responsibility of staging an event within living memory strengthened his resolve to ensure the performance was 'as accurate as possible', an approach already known to be central to the work of historical reenactment societies, where there is a great emphasis on detail, minutia and 'mastery' (Agnew 2004: 330). The documentary provides insights into some of the ways that precise attention to detail, such as distinctions between police baton use on the field verses in the village, became a way to connect many locals to their memories and emotions. During rehearsal, a riot police trainer, PC Lister Worthington, instructs those playing officers:

> We're going to try some intimidation tactics that they did used to use then. Along the lines of Zulus. So, all you've got to do again is shout and just bang the shield at the front. If you get a whole unit doing that you will see the results.

Cutting to former pickets listening on the other side of the field, one says to the camera, 'Springs back in the memory. I mean it were a very frightening time when the police started charging and when they were doing the Zulu chant.' Others, feeling agitated, respond with: 'That's what we recognize. ... That's what made you move.' Scenes like this, along with many of the interviews, suggest that the actions and emotions that former miners and pickets express during their performances reflect not just their memories of their struggles at the time but also their feelings about the ongoing effects of the strike, including lost jobs, homes and families and the long-term depression of the region. This is exemplified in a statement by former miner Malcolm Bray during rehearsals: 'Personally I lost a lot during the Miner's Strike. I lost me home, I'm getting emotional now, me family to a certain extent. And, you know, now to be here and bring it all back.' As with *S-21* and *The Third Memory*, we have a strong sense here that time has passed. While those performing events associated with their own lives cannot go back and change what happened to them, the documentary shows audiences that these events are, as Bruzzi (2016) puts it, still being 'worked through', embracing the idea that an historical event 'is an "open" text that can be revisited'.

The emphasis on accuracy, embedded in the ethos and skillset of historical reenactment societies, was also well-suited to facilitating the intention of the local community to redress some of the inaccuracies in the media reporting of the events at the time. In the documentary, Tony Benn, MP for Chesterfield, 1984–2001, describes a famous instance of footage aired by the BBC that reversed the sequence of events captured by journalists on the ground, showing miners throwing stones and then a police cavalry charge when in fact the opposite had occurred: the police had charged and the miners threw stones in response. The edited events created the impression that the miners had initiated the confrontation. Benn argues, 'Whoever gave the orders actually destroyed the truth of what they reported.' A quote from an apology issued by the BBC in 1991 acknowledging this error is included in the documentary but in it the BBC allege that the reversal was inadvertent and a by-product of the haste in which the coverage was assembled. The mounted police charge became a central feature of the living history performance to highlight and challenge this reversal, with the events staged in their actual, original order.

Significantly, discussion in the documentary about the fact that police charged first, and that this was covered up by the BBC, relates to the view held by many participants that the Thatcher government had been planning the clash. As Hoyne (2009: 96, 116) describes it, the conflict between police and miners was highly mediated and staged: an 'intricately scripted and choreographed performance of power and authoritarian control' instigated by Thatcher and supported by the media. Several former miners interviewed in the documentary refer to the 'Ridley Report', published in 1977, in which Conservative MP Nicholas Ridley proposed how a conservative government could fight and defeat a major strike by a nationalized industry. Former police officer and local, Mac McLoughlin, explains,

> We were highly trained in tactics most police officers wouldn't use. ... I don't think I'd been there four weeks when we got issued our own personal riot gear. ... Looking back now in retrospect it seems like we were being trained up for a specific role.

Douglass even describes signs set out by police on the day of the clash with arrows pointing out to the miners where to go: 'All you needed, I thought, was an official starter with a flag and a whistle to set us off.' Agnew (2004: 335) argues,

> Rather than eclipsing the past with its own theatricality, reenactment ought to make visible the ways in which events were imbued with meanings and investigate whose interests were served by those meanings.

The inclusion of these interviews with those involved in the original clash highlights how the living history performance is understood by many of those engaged in in-person reenactment to restage a series of events that were already staged.

Mainstream media representations of the events at Orgreave reflected a generally antagonistic relationship between miners and the media at that time. Douglass points out during the documentary: 'Because we didn't trust the media – this was our own fault – we didn't let them on our side. So, they were only ever filming from the other side. If they ever came on our side, they got beat up.' The coverage of the reenactment reflects a different relationship between camera crews and participants, one that was collaborative rather than antagonistic, producing a counterpoint to the pre-existing media representations of the events. The staging of the original events was an attempt to produce images that promoted the idea that the Thatcher government had control over aggressive unions. The reenactment, on the other hand, teamed up with those participants whose actions had been unwillingly co-opted into the Thatcher government's production. The five cameras used to cover the performance often position audiences much closer to the action than the coverage of the events of 1984. Without the threat of real violence, and because the performance was so meticulously planned, cameras could be positioned in carefully chosen vantage points to capture the unfolding action in collaboration with participants. Cameras are embedded in the action, running across the field and through the villages with the pickets as they are pursued by mounted police. Cameras follow alongside the short shield units as they engage in combat, beating down pickets. A camera tracks rapidly down police lines in close up as they bang their shields and shout. As the two sides push against each other, a camera positioned just behind the police line rises, giving an aerial view of the conflict as both sides struggle to hold their positions.

Figure 1.3 Cameras are embedded in the action, influencing decisions about the staging of the performance. *The Battle of Orgreave* (Dir. Mike Figgis, 2001).

Lutticken muses (2005: 5), 'Like other performances, reenactments generate representations in the form of photos and videos. Is it the fate of the reenactment to become an image?' Indeed, Lutticken (2005: 51) says about the documentary *The Battle of Orgreave*: 'Once again flat, screen-based representation emerges as the destiny of the reenactment.' But Lutticken's focus on the documentation of the performance overlooks the significance of the fact that the planning for the performance involved the crew, the intentions of the documentary influencing some of the decisions about its staging. Margulies (2003: 230) argues, 'One cannot change the past but can merely, and barely, reproduce its appearances' but in the case of *The Battle of Orgreave*, collaboration between the different stakeholders involved in the production of the reenactment, including the documentary crew, could be considered to have produced a *better* performance of the events, with much greater coverage of the action.

Conclusion

The capacity to interrogate how the past is understood and to challenge pre-existing and official versions of events is central to the use of reenactment in each case. Margulies (2019: 5) argues that films involving in-person reenactment

> push us to ask how the gap between past and present is configured within the work, what the force of the citation is in the political present, and how reenactment contributes, through embodied experience, to a future archive.

Emphasis on the relationships between past, present and future, along with the use of the term 'archive', reminds us that the self-reflexive, performative dimensions of these reenactments, essential to their recognizability and acceptability in documentary, do not preclude their capacity to hold evidentiary value. However, as Schneider (2011: 39) argues,

> If we have become somewhat comfortable with the notion of bodily memory (if not bodily history), and comfortable with reading bodies engaged in ritual or repeated actions as carriers of collective memory, we are not entirely comfortable considering gestic acts (re)enacted live to be material trace, despite the material substance that is the body articulating the act. We do not say, in other words, that a gesture is a record, like a photograph or a written document or a tape-recorded testimony or a footprint – capable of registering the annals of history.

Schneider (2011: 33) challenges this thinking about referentiality and material traces by proposing,

> If the past is never over, or never completed, 'remains' might be understood not solely as object or documentary material, but also as the immaterial labor of bodies engaged in and with that incomplete past: bodies striking poses, making gestures, voicing calls, reading words, singing songs, or standing witness.

In-person reenactment offers an exemplary strategy for this negotiation between trace and performance. The performances in *S-21* especially suggest that some events that took place in the prison 'remain' in the bodies of the perpetrators who are inscribed by the actions they retrace. Attention to the reenactment of specific actions and gestures in front of the camera becomes a means of documenting prison routines. Subjects even perform among, and sometimes with, the records and remnants of the prison held by the museum.

All three case studies show how the production of reenactments involves the contextualization of traces associated with an event's manifestations. Subjects' performances become part of this process of citation, remediation and reconfiguration. The performances are not live (as is the case in the examples discussed by Schneider); rather, they are intertwined with their documentation, sharing in the materiality (as well as the reproducibility) associated with the production and distribution process. In-person reenactment in documentary involves subjects actively participating in the staging, mediation and documentation of their lives: Their performances cannot be separated from their mediation. The actions and bodies produced in these interactions remain entangled with the fluctuating referential status of reenactment in documentary and evolving conditions of media production and distribution shaping documentary-based film, television and video works.

2

Between document and diegesis: Reenactment and researched detail in the biopic

Across different historical periods in cinema and television, the performance and theatricalization of details uncovered in the research process has been central to the ways that reenactments claim their authority. As such, investigation and evaluation of other media representations has long been a part of the process by which a reenactment's historical accuracy is constructed. The documentation of a whole range of events, both public and private, is becoming ever more accessible as our capacity to circulate photographs, film, television and video footage (as well as reports, transcripts, artworks and other materials) grows. Today, much documentation previously difficult to access is available at the researcher's fingertips and to the wider public. Peirce's original conceptualization of the indexical trace has also been transformed not only by the recording capacities of the photochemical process, but also by the circulatory capacities of technical media. Doane (2007: 2) argues that it was the dominance of photography and cinema during the late-nineteenth and early-twentieth centuries that first facilitated this:

> The imprint of a moment, a person, an object, a movement could now be detached and circulated, repeated without perceptible difference far from its original time and place. Both the intimacy of that relation to a unique and contingent reality, and the detachability and circulation of its representation, have had enormous cultural consequences.

Television, DVD, Blu-ray and the internet have accelerated and diversified this circulation. With the increasing detachability of the indexical trace, the referencing of historical documents that are already in moving-image form is intensifying in the reenactment in response to the growing capacities of media technologies to readily circulate moving imagery. The reenactment of traces of persons and events circulated far from their original time and place has become a means of making referential claims.

In this chapter, I consider the relationship between the increasing detachability and circulatability of the trace and the production and reception of researched details in the biopic. The biopic is a subgenre of the historical film distinguished by its explicit emphasis on depicting the life, or portion of a life, of a documented historical person, past or present, whose real name is used (Custen 1992: 6) and whose life is deemed to be distinctive, usually because of his or her prominence, fame or infamy (Vidal 2014: 3). With its investment in researching and performing the material traces of a life, the biopic summons the reenactment. Vidal (2014: 3) even describes the genre as 'underpinned by reenactment'. For reenactments employed in the biopic, and the historical film more generally, it has traditionally been investment in the theatrical dimensions of the pro-filmic field, especially mise en scène, that has fortified a reenactment's claims to historical accuracy, claims that are usually made by putting researched details – which emerge out of the research undertaken in preparation for a film and are based in securing the referential claims of fictional narrative – in front of the camera. Rosen (2001) proposes that researched detail constitutes one of two main forms of referentiality associated with cinema. As I argued in the Introduction, however, it is the other view of referentiality that has primarily occupied film theory debates. Rosen (2001: 149) defines the historical film precisely in terms of its relationship to researched detail, constituted by the combination of

> a 'true story' (or elements of a 'true story') plus enough profilmic detail to designate a period recognisable as significantly 'historical', that is, as signifying a generally accepted minimum of referential pastness.

With this focus on incorporating replicas of details uncovered in the research process, the referentiality of the reenactment, the biopic and the historical film more generally typically emerges from an emphasis on verisimilitude – on the skill with which the filmmakers have manufactured a pro-filmic field that resembles verifiable details of a known event or historical period.

In the biopic, the actor portraying the main subject is a central site for the accumulation of researched details: not only the settings, props and costumes that s/he inhabits, or even the details of their resemblance, manufactured or actual, to the real person s/he is portraying, but also the actions that s/he undertakes. All are part of the pro-filmic field and its *mise-en-scène* that must embody and exhibit vital researched details of the life being represented, if the biopic is to be deemed faithful and accurate. This explicit emphasis and reliance on performance and action makes biopics especially rich in alliances between reenactment and researched detail. In this chapter, I focus on three biopics released between 1998 and 2008: *Milk* (Dir. Gus Van Sant, 2008), *Monster* (Dir. Patty Jenkins, 2003) and *Boys Don't Cry* (Dir. Kimberly Peirce, 1999). In each case, the subjects being represented have passed away and yet their bodies are still circulating and accessible through their media representations. Essential to the perceived veracity of these three biopics is the capacity to make comparisons between the performances of the actors and the recorded actions of their subjects.

Reenactments of events of ranging scale and complexity are intricately woven into the fictional worlds of *Milk*, *Monster* and *Boys Don't Cry* and become a means to contextualize traces of each subject's life within the biopic's narrative. Sometimes documented events are reenacted more than once, from multiple perspectives, or condensed to serve the needs of the story being told. Details conjured from telephone calls, tape recordings, police reports, courtroom testimony and television news, among other sources, are fused into the unfolding drama. The performances of the actors are central to this process as they deftly integrate the documented words, mannerisms, emotions and intentions of their deceased counterparts into the universes their characters inhabit, their performances reviving and sustaining salient details associated with their subjects' lives.

Milk focuses on Harvey Milk (Sean Penn), California's first openly gay elected official. Having lived a closeted life, Milk 'came out' in his early 40s and moved to San Francisco's Castro District in 1972. After three unsuccessful campaigns for office he was elected as a city supervisor in 1977. While in office he sponsored a successful civil rights bill that outlawed discrimination based on sexual orientation and lead a public campaign against John Brigg's unsuccessful Proposition 6 initiative for California, which would have required public school employees who were known to be gay to be fired from their jobs. Eleven months into his first term in office he was assassinated on 27 November 1978, along with Mayor George Moscone, by fellow city supervisor Dan White.

Monster is about Aileen Wuornos (Charlize Theron), a sex worker who lived in Daytona Beach, Florida, and who, at the time of her arrest in 1991, had accumulated a long history of charges for assault, armed robbery and forgery. After a series of high-profile court cases that began in 1992, she was convicted of killing six of her clients and became publicly known as America's first female serial killer. Wuornos claimed that she committed the crimes in self-defence because these men had either raped or attempted to rape her but later recanted this claim in 2001 after twelve years on death row. Despite concerns about her capacity to meet the requisite competency evaluation, she was executed by lethal injection on 9 October 2002.

Boys Don't Cry explores the life of Brandon Teena (Hilary Swank), who moved to Falls City, Nebraska, in 1993 at the age of 21 after getting into trouble with the law for theft and forgery. In Falls City, he found a new girlfriend, Lana Tisdel, and passed successfully as male before his transgender identity was discovered and he was raped by John Lotter and Tom Nissen, two men from Tisdel's circle of friends. He reported the rape to the police but several days later was shot and killed on New Year's Eve (along with Lisa Lambert and Phillip DeVine) by Lotter and Nissen, who had tracked him to Lambert's house in Humboldt, Nebraska. Teena's rape and murder have become an enduring symbol in public mobilization against transgender hate crimes in the United States.

All three films can be considered what Bingham (2010a: 18) terms 'minority appropriation' biopics. These are biopics that 'own the conventional mythologizing form that once would have been used to marginalize or stigmatize' their subjects. As minority appropriation, *Milk* is an example of Bingham's (2010a: 6) neoclassical, celebratory biopic, a form that revives what Custen (1992) terms the 'Idol of Production' – visionaries and heroes, typically a 'Great Man', who 'made great things for society' – a fixture of the genre during the Hollywood studio era. *Boys Don't Cry* is described by Bingham (2010a: 27) as queer appropriation and female biography, although Brandon Teena's transgender identity certainly complicates the latter categorization. Bingham (2010a: 8, 24) argues that biopics about women are commonly 'weighted down by myths of suffering, victimization, and failure' and typically chart their subject's 'downward trajectory'. *Monster* offers a variation on this trend and, like *Boys Don't Cry*, is also a queer and feminist appropriation biopic.

Minority appropriation biopics are part of a shift in contemporary biography towards the idea that all lives are worthy of the genre. Along with the researched detail and the indexical trace, the concept of fame is not static. As Custen argues (2000: 137), fame is affected by fluctuations in the ways that communications technologies record and disseminate our lives that have continued to transform the category of fame itself. Custen (2010: 137) conceptualizes fame as

> a set of potential relations among individuals and their worlds – a person who does something which is recorded and then disseminated to audiences – rather than a set of standard practices or stable intrinsic qualities. Any shift in the weight or priority accorded to one of these elements that make up the 'fame relationship' – and especially the means of mediation, and the means by which it is controlled – will dramatically alter the nature of the film biography product.

Vidal (2014: 21) argues that the rise of digital media has provoked an 'appetite for historicizing the present' and a focus on subjects who have recently entered collective memory. *Boys Don't Cry* and *Monster* are also connected to this trend. *Milk* reaches somewhat further into the past but is still focused on a relatively contemporary public figure.

Custen (1992: 228) proposes that 'notoriety has, in a sense, replaced noteworthiness as the proper frame for biography'. *Monster* and *Boys Don't Cry* reflect what Custen (1992: 216) describes as the 'enshrinement of the ordinary subject as victim', a key trait of a new subgenre of biopics that emerge in the era of television. By contrast to *Milk*, whose career required it, public attention was not sought by Wuornos and Teena. They became celebrities when the tragedies in their lives were first brought to public attention by the media. It was Wuornos's arrest on the charge of multiple murders that led to her life becoming widely publicized and sensationalized. Only after he had been murdered did Teena achieve celebrity status as a victim and the focus of public debate about transgender-hate crimes, with coverage ranging from tabloid television to true-crime paperbacks to intellectual analysis of Teena's cultural meaning. All three subjects suffered violent and untimely deaths – assassination, execution and murder – and in each case, their fame was closely connected to their deaths. That Teena lost his life because of he dared to live out his preferred gender identity is the tragedy that dominates his representation across media. The public image of Wuornos was tied to her trial, her years or death row and her execution. Assassinated at the height of his popularity, Milk became an enduring icon for LGBTQ lives, rights and politics.

Milk most explicitly, but also *Monster*, draw on their subjects' participation in activities that were designed to be, or became, media events, such as press conferences, interviews, courtroom trials, protests and televised debates. These televised events became central to how Milk and Wuornos were known publicly before and after their deaths and the televisual versions of these events typically become the source from which the biopics' reenactments are constructed and cross-referenced. Each of these films not only reenact, but also interrogate media representations of the lives they depict, reflecting on the ways in which their subjects' fame circulated and what it represented. *Milk* deals with its subject as a public figure, focussing on the values and ideals he stood for, attempting to 'revive' and instil in popular memory a significant figure of the 1970s. It incorporates many reenactments of television appearances and speeches Milk made during his campaigns that highlight his courage, conviction and vision. *Monster* and *Boys Don't Cry* are both used as a means of 'getting inside' the lives of people who were vilified and abused for failing to adhere to the expectations prescribed to their gender. Jenkins made *Monster* in part out of a desire to challenge the way in which the mainstream media sensationalized Wuornos's life, especially their labelling of her as the first female serial killer. The title of the biopic refers to the image the media made of her (Jenkins 2003). In the Press Kit for *Boys Don't Cry* released by Fox Searchlight Pictures, Peirce describes what drew her to Teena:

> Here was a character who was already becoming an icon within months after being killed. Brandon Teena represented so many strands of our culture – he was a female to male, he was a petty thief, he was the victim of a hate crime – he was being written about by true crime writers, journalists and feminists. There was no disputing that his story was dramatic and tragic, but the real challenge in

telling it was finding the human being underneath it all, discovering what it was like to be inside Brandon's skull the very first night he passed as a boy. When you think about who he was and begin to see how extraordinary what he did was, just how powerful his spirit, imagination and creativity had to have been.

The makers of *Milk* also reveal the 'private person' behind the 'public figure', though are less anxious to investigate how Milk interacted with the prevailing gender expectations of his era.

Bingham, Custen and Vidal have challenged the impression of the biopic as a 'static and unchanging' genre (Bingham 2010a: 22), working to address the lack of critical attention to transformations in the biopic over time. Vidal (2014: 9, 22) even points to the challenge for contemporary biopics of negotiating a media environment characterized by 'veritable visual-media saturation' where 'available archival materials (and their digital reconstructions) often crowd the screen, standing side-by-side or blending with dramatic reenactment'. The reenactments employed in the biopic must navigate increasingly complex referential, temporal and spectatorial relationships with researched detail. With the rapid circulation and widespread accessibility of audio-visual imagery, the biopic's fictional world increasingly depends upon convincing reenactments of events that are well known or accessible to its audiences. I propose that in this environment what often certifies a reenactment in the biopic as historically accurate is not so much the events it reenacts, but their media representations, making the most important events those that have already been well documented or widely circulated in the public domain as film, television and media events. The reenactment of a well-known or accessible media representation helps a reenactment to declare itself as the performance of a pre-existing event, the veracity of which can be easily measured.

As I have outlined, aspects of the lives depicted in *Milk*, *Monster* and *Boys Don't Cry* circulated at different times in books, photographs, television coverage and news reports. The reenactments in these three biopics cross-reference audio recordings, television footage, film footage and photographs. But I have chosen to focus on these three biopics because when each of the films was released, feature documentaries about the three lives in question were either currently in circulation or had recently been produced and screened. More than twenty years before the release of *Milk*, Rob Epstein won the 1985 Academy Award for Best Documentary for *The Times of Harvey Milk* (1984). Telling Pictures also released a new 'collectors' edition' DVD of Epstein's film to mark the twentieth anniversary of the documentary in 2004. Nick Broomfield's first documentary about the exploitation of Wuornos, *Aileen Wuornos: The Selling of a Serial Killer*, was released in 1992 and his second documentary, about her life on death row, *Aileen: Life and Death of a Serial Killer* (2003), was released in the United States just a few months before *Monster* appeared on the nations' cinema screens. The Teddy Award-winning documentary, *The Brandon Teena Story*, directed by Susan Muska and Gréta Olafsdóttir was released in 1998, while *Boys Don't Cry* was in production. Each documentary offers unique access to documents, experts and eyewitnesses that are not otherwise available to general audiences. They also include more readily accessible documents and testimony from archives, police reports, coroner's reports and media reports. The commercial circulation of these documentaries on DVD, Blu-ray and online has served to increase the availability of the testimony and documentation that they incorporate. This makes these three biopics very potent case studies for exploring how reenactments engage with, and are shaped by, pre-existing and extra-textual accounts of the events they depict.

Though in many cases audiences can now access the researchers' sources, for themselves, it remains one of the functions of promotional materials, including press kits, advertising, media interviews and film reviews to do it for them. Even with the much wider circulation of audiovisual materials, reenactments are not always self-evident to an audience and can often only be 'seen' thanks to promotional materials that draw attention to them. Doane (2002: 160) maintains that in the early years of the cinema:

> the requirement of external spectatorial knowledge was not atypical, but rather, constituted something of a norm. The spectator was often expected to have knowledge of another text (for example, newspaper accounts of a current event).

This expectation, crucial to early film reenactments, has continued to be important for the reenactment throughout the twentieth century and into the twenty-first. Explicit emphasis on the labour of producing pro-filmic detail became pre-eminent in the historical films of the Hollywood studio era once research departments became integrated into the Hollywood studios' division of labour during the 1920s. Rosen (2001), Custen (1992) and Sobchack (1990) draw attention to the way in which, at the height of the Hollywood studio era, the press materials for the studios' historical films emphasized the lengths to which research departments would go: 'Extravagant research efforts became, for the biopic, a way of reassuring consumers that every effort had been expended to bring them true history in the guise of spectacle' (Custen 1992: 41, 35). Nowadays the discourse of research in the marketing of biopics occurs not only prior to and during a film's initial theatrical release (as was the case in the Hollywood studio era), but also subsequently through the work of the DVD extras, where directors' commentaries, documentaries and additional interviews with filmmakers, cast, crew, friends, family and historical consultants can explain and alert audiences to research and research material.

In the examples discussed in this chapter, each biopic refers to and draws on its respective documentary (or documentaries in the case of *Monster*) in different ways. The differences are attributable to a variety of factors. These include the degree of popularity and level of critical attention the documentaries and the biopics received; the degree to which the materials used in the documentary were already in wide circulation; the significance of the new materials researched by, or created for, the documentary; the length of time that had elapsed between the subject's life and its representation in documentary and dramatic form; whether the documentary was released before – or concurrently with – the biopic; whether or not either film had been circulated or promoted in relation to the other; and whether or not either film explicitly acknowledges the other. These factors shape the kinds of referential and temporal relationships that researched details take on in the reenactments performed in each of the biopics.

The closing credits for *Milk* begin: 'Special thanks to the Academy Award-winning film *The Times of Harvey Milk* for its enormous contribution to the making of this movie. And to Rob Epstein', thereby not only making clear and unequivocal acknowledgement of its debt to, but also inviting dialogue with, *The Times of Harvey Milk*. The statement also implies that the makers of the biopic had a working relationship with the documentary's director, Rob Epstein, who made a personal contribution to the biopic independently of his film. Such acknowledgement is only proper, given *Milk*'s heavy reliance on the research materials uncovered and collected by *The Times of Harvey Milk* and given that *Milk* reenacts many of the events contained in it. Epstein and his team began making their documentary while Harvey Milk was still alive. It was released just six years after his assassination, a mixture of their own video and audio recordings of events in his life; archived television footage; interviews conducted with colleagues and friends after Milk's death; photographs they found or were given; and even the will that Milk had recorded, a tape of which was only entrusted to them by his attorney as the documentary was nearing completion (Epstein 2004). *Milk* includes reenactments based on all these different kinds of documentation including reenactments based on Epstein's own video and audio recordings of Milk's public debates and speeches; his participation in the 1978 Gay Freedom Parade in San Francisco; and the candlelight march that followed his assassination. As I will discuss, it also reenacts verbatim some of Milk's tape-recorded will and many of the speeches, debates and interviews contained in the television footage uncovered by and incorporated into *The Times of Harvey Milk*.

In contrast, neither in the promotion of, nor in the credit sequence for, *Boys Don't Cry* is there any explicit reference to the film's relationship with the documentary *The Brandon Teena Story*. The DVD commentary for the film emphasizes Peirce's independent research efforts, reporting that she 'set off on a five-year journey researching the life of Brandon Teena' (Peirce 1999). *Boys Don't Cry* and *The Brandon Teena Story* were being made at the same time and were each the result of separate research, but they do draw on much of the same research materials and subjects. *Monster* also has an ambivalent relationship with Broomfield's two documentaries about Wuornos, one of which preceded, while the other followed fast upon, the film's release. In the DVD commentary on *Monster*, Jenkins (2003) imagines herself as unique in her desire to create a sympathetic portrait of a 'monster', one that delves deeply into her story. She makes no acknowledgement of Broomfield's earlier, 1992 documentary, *Aileen Wuornos: The Selling of a Serial Killer*, which represented Wuornos as the victim of media frenzy and deals head-on with the grotesque way Wuornos was exploited by those whose object was merely financial, desperate to sell her story to the media. What is more, eleven years later Broomfield's second documentary, *Aileen: Life and Death of a Serial Killer*, released in the same year as *Monster*, painted a nuanced and sympathetic portrait, having added to its research materials interviews with her friends and supporters, focussing on the struggles Wuornos had faced in her childhood. Broomfield also argued vehemently against the execution of Wuornos because she could not meet the necessary mental health requirements. Despite Jenkin's own ambivalence, both *Monster* and *Aileen: Life and Death of a Serial Killer* were regularly cross-promoted and discussed together. One of the ways to access *Monster* is now as a DVD box set with the 2003 documentary.

In contrast to Jenkins, actor Charlize Theron acknowledged her debt to Broomfield's documentary in some of the interviews she conducted with the press to promote *Monster*, stating that Broomfield had sent her an early cut of *Aileen: Life and Death of a Serial Killer* (Cavagna 2004). Significantly, both of Broomfield's documentaries, especially *Life and Death of a Serial Killer*, became very important for validating Theron's performance as Wuornos in the critical reception of *Monster*. Horeck (2007: 147) argues, for example, that many scenes in the documentary of 'Wuornos raging against the world, shouting to reporters as she is bundled into cars' as well as two freeze-frame shots of Wuornos, her head tilted back and her handcuffs framing her face, which were extensively used in the promotion of *Life and Death of a Serial Killer*, are central to the visual iconography on which *Monster* draws. Horeck (2007: 151) points to a review of the film by Roger Ebert, in which he claims that:

> There were times, indeed, when I perceived no significant difference between the woman in the documentary and the one in the feature film. Theron has internalised and empathised with Wuornos so successfully that to experience the real woman is only to understand more completely how remarkable Theron's performance is.

The critical reception of both *Life and Death of a Serial Killer* and *Monster* became 'reliant not only on how they relate to actuality but also how they relate to each other' (Horeck 2007: 142). Not only is the '"real" Wuornos found on Broomfield's documentary scrutinised to see how the performance of the stunning actress in *Monster* matches up' but also, vice versa, 'Wuornos is found to be as good or less good and either more or less real than Theron'

(Horeck 2007: 150, 153–4). This statement suggests, intriguingly, that Theron's performance can be compared to Wuornos's own performance as herself, and as a celebrity in her own right – 'the first female serial killer' – in front of the cameras at her trial and in front of Broomfield's camera in both his documentaries. Wuornos shows her awareness that she is performing for the camera in *Life and Death of a Serial Killer* when she stops in the middle of an interview with Broomfield to brush her hair.

The biopic and the 'body-too-much'

Comolli (1978) argues that the interplay between absence and presence between subject and performer is a common feature of the historical film. It is especially so in the biopic, which has constantly to manage the tension that is generated by a performing body whose presence cannot help but signal the absence of the historical body it represents. Focussing on the example of Pierre Renoir as Louis XVI in *La Marseillaise* (Jean Renoir, 1938) Comolli (1978: 44) proposes that there is

> interference, even rivalry between the body of the actor and that other body, the 'real' one, whose (historical) disappearance has left traces in images other than cinematic ones which have to be taken into account.

This tension is felt increasingly strongly as the circulation and documentation of our public and personal lives multiplies – and will continue to exist in accessible form long after we die.

For Epstein, the documentary *The Times of Harvey Milk* gives Harvey Milk an afterlife, enabling him to circulate and touch new audiences. As Epstein (2004) describes it, 'Harvey Milk lives in the film now.' This is certainly how Epstein's documentary worked for Dustin Lance Black (2009), who wrote the screenplay for *Milk*:

> In one speech in [*The Times of Harvey Milk*] he [Milk] says 'Somewhere out there there's a kid from San Antonio, Texas' – which is where I'm from – 'who's going to hear that a gay man was elected to public office and it's going to give him hope.' And I remember just losing it. I broke down crying because, you know,

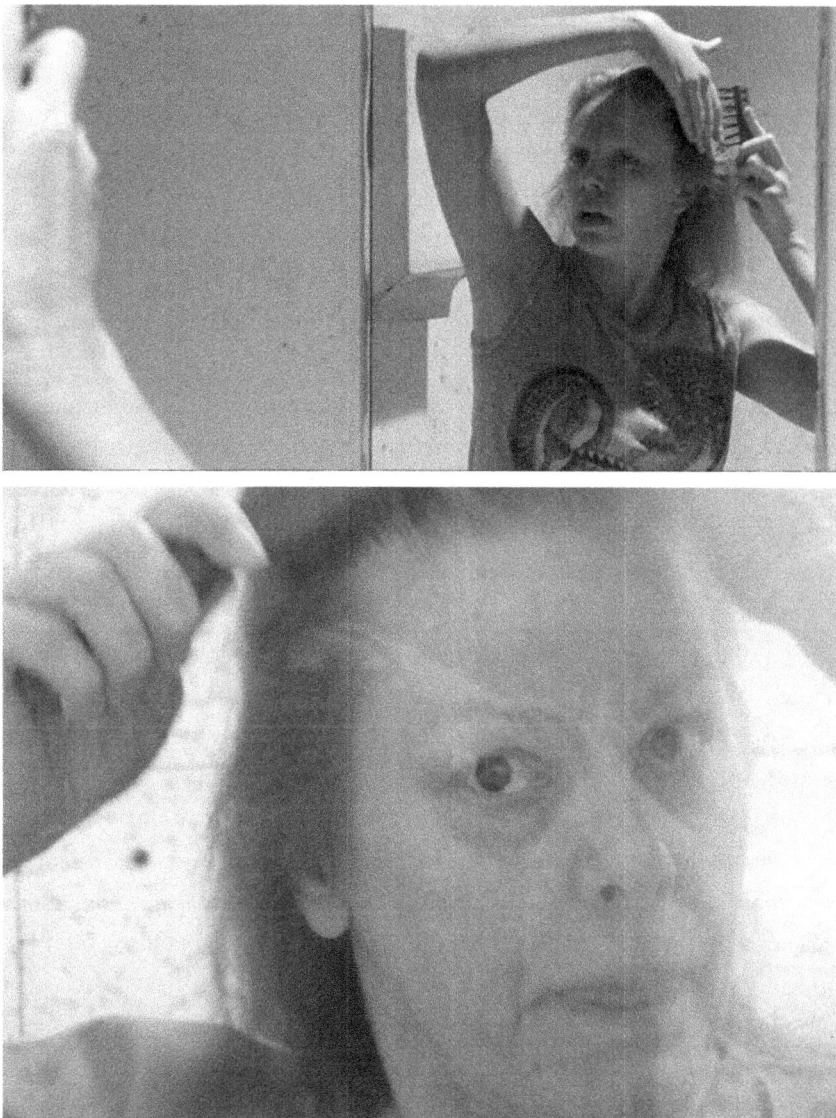

Figure 2.1 a, b Theron's performance in *Monster* (Dir. Patty Jenkins, 2003) can be compared to Wuornos's own performance as herself in *Aileen: Life and Death of a Serial Killer* (Dir. Nick Broomfield, 2003).

I was very much that kid. That's probably the moment that I thought, 'We've got to get this story back out there.'

In this interaction with *The Times of Harvey Milk*, Black felt personally hailed by Milk's speech many years after it was delivered. It is this connection with Milk through the documentary that prompted Black's desire to 'revive' Milk in a biopic that would itself facilitate a new circulation of Milk's presence and message to emphasize the continuing relevance of what Milk stood for. As Ebert's review of Theron's performance demonstrates, the circulation of Broomfield's documentary works to facilitate and intensify the kind of rivalry that Comolli conceptualized. Even after her passing, Wuornos continues to live before us in Broomfield's documentary, alongside Theron's performance in the biopic. While Ebert's account celebrates Theron's ability to disappear her own body as she cultivates Wuornos's, he also paradoxically suggests that in the rivalry between their two bodies it is Theron's performance that eclipses Wuornos's.

Comolli's argument makes clear that the biopic's focus on the life of a historical figure makes the actor portraying that figure central to the accumulation of the pro-filmic researched details that lend authenticity to the film. As I have argued, inevitably, actors in the biopic will perform reenactments of well-documented actions, but also, more broadly, they will attempt to perform the behaviours that characterize the historical persons they depict. Milk and Wuornos had very distinctive physical gestures, mannerisms and intonations that were extensively documented and were readily available because of the documentaries that had been made about their lives. The television, video and film footage of them enabled Penn and Theron to research, rehearse and ultimately demonstrate their successful embodiment of the unique actions, sentiments, behaviours, gestures and postures of their deceased counterparts. Vidal (2014), Bingham (2010b) and Carolyn Anderson and Jon Lupo (2003) all point to the biopic as a genre closely associated with star-making performances and award worthiness. In both films, audiences' capacities to assess these actors' performances of their subjects during significant, public and well-documented events in their lives contributed significantly to the positive critical and popular reception given to the actors' work. Theron's portrayal of Wuornos won her the Academy Award for Best Actress in a Leading Role for *Monster* in 2004, launching her career, and in 2008 Penn's performance as Milk earned him his second Academy Award for Best Actor in a Leading Role.

It is important to note, however, that Theron and Penn employ quite different performance styles. Bingham (2013: 240) considers Theron's performance in *Monster* as one of many examples of a category of biopic performance that he terms 'embodied impersonation'. He argues that most of the Oscars awarded to performers in the biopic have been for embodied impersonations (2013: 240). Penn's performance, on the other hand, is closer to Bingham's (2010b: 80) category of 'stylized' performance which is characterized by a reliance on suggestion and 'less on a full impersonation'. Penn remains much more visible and audible himself, even though he demonstrates his ability to research and perform Milk's distinctive mannerisms. Comolli (1978: 49) argues that it is a common strategy in the historical film to 'try to ensure that the actor's body is forgotten, to cancel it, to keep it hidden, at least, between the supposedly known and intended pre-eminent body of the historical character to be represented'. Penn's performance emphasizes craft over disappearance and is closer to what Comolli (1978: 49) describes as making the 'surplus visible' where the actor

> brings this body, his own, to the fore: he emphasises its reality and presence, multiplies its effects. Far from making the spectator forget it, he points it out to him: henceforth this body will not be something automatic. It begins to count, to weigh.

Penn's body, star persona and presence are apparent. He still 'revives' Milk, but does not, in the process, disappear and reappear in the ways that Theron does.

Penn calls Milk as the 'the movie star' of *The Times of Harvey Milk* (Passafuime 2008). He describes the process of transforming himself into Milk as an ongoing effort to keep reaching for Milk's 'electric warm personality'. Penn did not anticipate achieving a wholesale transformation into Milk but rather, proposes: 'You never assume you're going to get all the way there, but you figure that with the help of a director and a screenwriter and all the things that a movie is that you can get the spirit of it out there the best you can.' Articulating his vision of the oscillation between presence and absence at work in his body, he says that while he found the documentary and archive footage very helpful, his intentions were to be in conversation with them rather than try to replicate what he saw and heard in them:

> With that sort of thing, the best way you could use it was that you watch a lot the same way you'd play music all day in the background and not necessarily be thinking about it. But just I kept it on all the time and all the synapses start to connect and, if you listen carefully, you can hear the music of that and you kind of dance with it.

Here Penn conceives of his efforts to embody Milk's own on-screen presence as a dialogue rather than a makeover.

Swank also won an Academy Award for Best Actress in a Leading Role in 2000 for her performance in *Boys Don't Cry*, which, like Theron, launched her career. There was considerably less footage of Teena than of Wuornos and Milk. In the absence of film, video and television footage, the sources upon which Swank was obliged to rely for her performance as Teena included audio recordings and still photographs made available by friends and family members and circulated in the media reports about his murder. Pidduck (2001: 98) notes, for example, that the close up of Teena looking in the mirror in the opening scene of *Boys Don't Cry*, which mimics the framing of a photo of Teena frequently used in media reports, both positions the audience in a traditional relationship of identification and simultaneously 'rubs up against the residue of photographs widely reproduced in news reports, on the internet, or in the documentary *The Brandon Teena Story*'. And one of the photographs that Brandon carries in his duffle bag in the *Boys Don't Cry* is of Swank dressed as a gangster in imitation of a photograph of the 'real' Brandon Teena that appeared in the media after his death. These examples highlight the level of attention paid to the incorporation of specific researched details in the *mise-en-scène* of *Boys Don't Cry*.

Bingham (2010b: 80) places Swank's performance in the category of stylized performance rather than embodied impersonation. However, I argue that Swank's performance, like Theron's, is an example of embodied impersonation. The success of Swank's performance hinges primarily on her ability, through her cultivation of Teena's mannerism, to pass as male, a feat that marked Teena himself as a successful performer. This is a double disappearance because

Teena himself first 'performed' that radical disappearance of his female body into a male identity. In this sense Swank's performance is measured against Teena Brandon's own performance as Brandon Teena. Swank spent six weeks doing vocal training to deepen her voice, worked with a personal trainer to sculpt her body into Brandon's lean shape and strapped her breasts with tension bandages. As she explains in the press kit produced by Fox Searchlight Pictures (12), she also spent four weeks before production started trying to live and pass as male. This research experiment helped her to better understand what it was like to be Brandon Teena:

> Sure enough, people talked to me as if I was a boy. I was fascinated by their reactions, always looking into their eyes to see how they were reading me, if they were seeing through me. It was intense. It gave me a real insight into Brandon because this wasn't just a role for her. It was her life.

As Swank's account reveals, her efforts to transform herself for her role was not only designed to achieve an accurate physical likeness to her subject. Both Theron's and Swank's physical transformations were also closely associated with their emotional and psychological connections to Wuornos and Teena.

Figure 2.2 The success of Swank's performance hinges on her ability to pass as male, a feat that marked Teena himself as a successful performer. The close-up in the opening scene of the film references a widely publicized photo of Teena. *Boys Don't Cry* (Dir. Kimberly Peirce, 1999).

For Theron, there were lengthy preparation times in hair and make-up throughout the twenty-nine-day shoot to achieve many of the details of Wuornos's appearance. This included liquid latex applied to her face and dried with a hair dryer to achieve a leathery texture, as well as layers of tattoo paint with a spray gun to give her skin a mottled look. Gelatine was applied to her eyelids to make them droop, her eyebrows were plucked and bleached, and she was fitted with sculpted fake teeth. Gaining thirty pounds in three months to play the role, she reportedly maintained a diet of potato chips, soy sauce and miso soup to attain a bloated look during filming. Theron (Blackwelder 2003) describes her concerted efforts to gain weight for her role as driven by her desire for empathetic engagement with the suffering Wuornos had endured throughout her life:

> She'd lived a homeless life, so nutrition was the lowest thing on her priority list – whatever food she was going to get, that's what she was going to eat ... It wasn't about getting fat. Aileen wasn't fat. Aileen carried scars on her body from her lifestyle, and if I'd gone to make this movie with my body – physically I'm very athletic – I don't know that I would have felt the things Aileen felt with her body. It was about getting to a place where I felt closer to how Aileen was living.

Theron's efforts in weight gain not only helped to attain recognizable details of Wuornos's physicality but also enabled Theron to experience living with that physicality. The physical transformation created a likeness that Theron could inhabit.

In both cases, the emphasis on the veracity of the actress's performances did not stop with accurate or even empathetic reproduction of their subjects' physicality. The promotion of both *Monster* and *Boys Don't Cry* also sought to imply that the truthfulness in Theron and Swank's performances was directly connected to their capacities to make empathetic connections between their own personal experiences of transformation and suffering and those of Wuornos and Teena. Theron saw her mother shoot dead her physically abusive alcoholic father in self-defence (Horeck 2007: 149). Swank, who was born in Lincoln, Nebraska, the same town as Brandon Teena, explained in interview how growing up poor in a mobile home in the Pacific Northwest of the United States attracted her to playing outsiders 'who have to struggle against the odds' (Palmer 2001). By emphasizing the similarities between Theron's and Swank's personal experiences and those of the women they were portraying, the promotion of *Monster* and *Boys Don't Cry* sought to imply that Theron and Swank could reenact the struggles of their subjects authentically, contributing to the perceived veracity of each biopic. In a somewhat similar vein, Penn's frank and passionate political activism was an aspect of his star persona discussed in the media coverage of his performance in *Milk* with the suggestion that his own involvement in activism enhanced his capacity for empathy with his subject and lent authority and authenticity to his performance.

Significantly, the personal experiences that Swank and Theron drew on to gain closeness with Teena and Wuornos are also connected to the stories that have been central to the construction and promotion of them as stars. For Swank, especially, *Boys Don't Cry* marked the beginnings of an ongoing narrative central to her star persona. Stories about her rise from poverty to success in Hollywood were also prominent in the promotion of *Million Dollar Baby*, based on the life of Maggie Fitzgerald, a working-class woman who tried to turn her life around through her boxing career, which won Swank a second Academy Award for Best Actress in a Leading Role. They also featured in the promotion of *Conviction* (dir. Tony Goldwyn, 2010) in which Swank plays Betty Anne Waters, a high-school dropout and single mother who put herself through law school to try to overturn her brother's murder conviction. As Dyer (1986: 3) writes, 'Star images are always extensive, multimedia, intertextual and particular elements of a star's image will predominate at particular moments in that star's career.' Swank's and Theron's performances in *Boys Don't Cry* and *Monster* interact with, indeed contribute significantly to, narratives of personal transformation, suffering and empathy that have been integral to the production, continuity and success of their own star personas. Typically, stories about Swank's and Theron's rise to stardom imply that their achievements are the result of their ability to overcome the great hardships that they endured early on in their lives.

Swank is acutely aware that while the revelation of Teena's 'performance' as male was punished with rape and murder, her own successful transformation to 'pass' as male earned her accolades. In an interview with 'The Movie Show', she points out this contrast, stating, 'Here I am living my dream. ... I wanted to be an actress, and I'm accepted for it. She went off to pursue her dream and she's condemned for it.' In the case of *Monster*, the remarkable physical transformation of Theron into Wuornos was reinforced by Theron's reappearance and performance, like Swank, as a glamorous Hollywood star on the award circuit after the film was released. This other self-conscious and conscientious transformation into beautiful and graceful film stars is perhaps as important to the success of each film as their capacity to transform themselves into Wuornos and Teena. This oscillation in the bodies and performances of these two actresses drew attention to and helped to promote the accuracy of both biopics.

The performance of Christina Ricci, who plays Wuornos's girlfriend in *Monster*, was not recognized by the Academy in the way that Theron, Swank and Penn were or the other actors who played supporting roles in these biopics. Chloe Sevigny was nominated for Best Actress in a Supporting Role in 2000 for her portrayal of Lana Tisdel in *Boys Don't Cry* and Josh Brolin was nominated for Best Actor in a Supporting Role in 2009 for his depiction of Dan White in *Milk*. Although Ricci's performance was generally well received, unlike Theron, Swank, Penn, Brolin or Sevigny, she did not receive any major award nominations for her performance. Ricci plays a character called Selby, who looks nothing like Wuornos's actual girlfriend, Tyria Moore. Unlike Tisdel, who had cooperated with both the documentary and the biopic about Teena, Moore did not want to participate or be depicted in either: to dissociate herself from Wuornos and avoid incrimination, she had collaborated with the police. Accordingly, she is hardly visible in any of Broomfield's documentary footage or the television footage of Wuornos and the love story at the centre of *Monster* (as with *Boys Don't Cry*) is largely fictionalized. Ricci's performance as Selby was therefore not substantiated or measured by the documentation, participation or association of Moore. Her performance did not require the same strategies of research and rehearsal as Theron because her performance was not required to cultivate authenticating and measurable details of her character within the film.

Hybridized temporalities: Integrating television and audio events

Selby, a character who is for all intents and purposes fictionalized, is integrated into one specific reenactment of a well-documented event in the

Wuornos-Moore relationship: the recorded telephone call that Moore made, in collaboration with the police, to try to get Wuornos to confess. The events related to the phone conversation are reenacted on two occasions in *Monster*. The conversation (for which there is only audio documentation) is reenacted, with Selby in a hotel room, surrounded by police, and Wuornos on a prison pay phone in police custody. In Ricci's performance as Selby, she repeats several of the words and phrases spoken, as well as the emotions and sentiment expressed, by Moore in the actual phone call, saying, 'They've been up to see my parents asking all kinds of questions' and 'You're going to let me go down for something you did'. The reenactment of this exchange on the phone plays an authenticating role in *Monster* but it also draws attention to Moore's absence from the film because it suggests that Selby stands in for Moore in this reenactment, even if the differences between them are significant.

Reenactment sequences are woven into the narrative structure and fictional world of the biopic, entering relationships with more generalized historical dramatizations in the narrative and with a film's fictional scenes. Rosen (2001: 179) proposes that the researched detail embodies a hybridized temporality because it both 'claims to have its own previously documentable "reality", that of researchable historiography', but is also organized in relation to the 'virtual time' created by the narrative hierarchies and temporality of the fictional world of the story. Consequently, the researched detail manifests a complex referential and temporal tension by being able to 'simultaneously propose some extra supplement of referential truth, but one that can only be signified as diegesis'. The same can be argued for the reenactments employed in the biopic. Researched details are pervasive in these biopics, but not all dramatizations in these films are reenactments. Sequences that incorporate performances of specific, documented events and actions can be recognized as involving reenactments, interlaced within the biopic's fictional world.

The telephone call in *Monster* is integrated into the temporality of the fictional narrative but at the same time resonates very strongly with the documentation and circulation of Wuornos's life. The call is a key moment in Wuornos's private life that was made public because of her trial. While listening to the recorded conversation as it replayed in the courtroom, the 'real' Wuornos broke down and wept in front of the cameras, an incident that is included in both Broomfield's documentaries and was also shown on television in the United States at the time of her trial. What is more, Jenkins (2003) has described how watching Wuornos weep in court during the playing of this tape recording was the television event that first touched her emotionally and inspired her to make *Monster*. This suggests that Jenkins includes a reenactment of this breakdown in the film in part to encourage the audience of the biopic to recognize precisely what this television footage made her feel in the first place – that there is a different, more sympathetic 'monster'. While Jenkins experienced this breakdown as a television event, most audiences will now experience the breakdown through Broomfield's documentaries.

In *Monster*, Wuornos's breakdown is more closely connected to Selby visibly identifying Wuornos in the courtroom (in a brief reference to Moore's own courtroom appearance), than to the playing of the phone conversation. This breakdown is also linked to another set of events: Wuornos's documented courtroom outbursts upon receiving her death sentences. Her breakdown in *Monster* leads directly into a sequence in which the judge announces her death sentence. The outburst in response to the sentencing in the film is a combination of two such outbursts from Wuornos that were captured by television cameras. The film contrives to treat as one Wuornos's retorts after receiving her first death sentence that the judge and the members of the court were 'scumbags', with the statement 'may you rot in hell for sending a raped woman to death', which comes from a much lengthier outburst at a later trial in which she received additional death sentences. The footage of both outbursts is played at length in both of Broomfield's documentaries. In *Life and Death of a Serial Killer*, which reflects on these events twelve years after they occurred, they are shown close together as part of a recap of events covered in Broomfield's first documentary. In the earlier documentary, *Selling of a Serial Killer*, they appear further apart. Brought together in *Monster*, they constitute the final reenactment that plays an especially important authenticating role in the biopic. By ending the film with the courtroom outbursts, *Monster* links its more fictionalized dramatic world (focused on Wuornos's romantic relationship with Selby) to the events in Wuornos's life that were circulated after her arrest and trials in court. This helps to position *Monster* as an in-depth insight into Wuornos's personal life before the media frenzy surrounding her began.

There is one specific reenactment that is incorporated into *Monster* early in the film: Richard Mallory's rape of Wuornos. Mallory was her first victim, and the scene is based on Wuornos's courtroom testimony, captured by television cameras and included in both Broomfield's documentaries. In *Selling of a Serial Killer*, the footage of Wuornos's testimony is only about a year old and presented during the lead up to Broomfield successfully obtaining an interview with Wuornos for this documentary. In *Life and Death of a Serial Killer* the testimony is inserted almost like a flashback immediately following an interview with a much aged, wearied and more cynical Wuornos who has since spent twelve years on death row. The connection to this courtroom testimony is not self-evident in *Monster* because the giving of the testimony is not reenacted. The reenactment occurs in a scene in which she breaks loose and shoots Mallory dead after he has tied her to the front seat of the car, raped her with a tire iron and poured cleaning fluid over her genitals. Horeck (2007: 157) rightly describes this rape in *Monster* as the 'defining trauma of the film'. It works to set up a commonly held argument that this rape was the 'primal scene' for Wuornos's subsequent murders. This line of reasoning proposes that the trauma that she experienced by being so brutally and humiliatingly raped by Mallory, and her shooting him as he prepared to rape her again, was triggered and lived out in her subsequent shootings of later clients who either raped or attempted to rape her.

Horeck (2007: 157) contends that this rape scene in *Monster* 'derives its dramatic charge from its close association with Wuornos' powerful testimony'. Drawing attention to the ways in which the scene emphasizes specific details from Wuornos's testimony, she writes: 'The testimony is rendered here in visual detail and offered up to us as a truthful spectacle of the real.' In *Boys Don't Cry*, in contrast, Teena's charged testimony about his rape *is* reenacted and this testimony frames the reenactment of the rape itself as a flashback. In my view, the combination of the two reenactments in *Boys Don't Cry* is a much more effective integration of the documentation of Teena's testimony and lends this testimony a more potent veracity. But the examples from *Monster* and *Boys Don't Cry* both constitute prime examples of the kind of hybridized temporality described by Rosen (2001: 179) where researched details are connected to a 'previously documentable "reality"' and organized in relation to the 'virtual time' created by the narrative hierarchies of the fictional world. In *Boys Don't Cry*, the interaction between the two reenactments (testimony and flashback), based on the same document, successfully incorporates the audio recording into the dramatic world of *Boys Don't Cry* and frames the rape from the point of view of Teena, his testimony becoming the narration for the reenactment of the rape. I agree with Horeck (2004: 112) that the emphasis on flashback in *Boys Don't Cry* is designed to 'echo the trauma of the rape itself'. It foregrounds the trauma for Teena of testifying to police and being obliged to name his female genitalia in violation of his own gender identity, and it connects this with Nissen's and Lotter's desire to violate Teena's gender identity as a motivation for the rape itself.

The reenactment of the testimony Teena gave to police about his rape is one of the most significant reenactments in *Boys Don't Cry*. Not only because of it the successful integration of this documentation that is available to audiences through the documentary, *The Brandon Teena Story*, but also because Teena's rape was such a major turning point in the most widely publicized aspects of his life. It violated the gender identity he had been living out since his arrival in the town and the failure of police to prosecute the rape case quickly is also what ultimately put his life at risk. This failure has been central to the criticisms raised by those who use his life story in campaigns against transgender hate crime. It meant Nissen and Lotter were free to track Teena down on New Year's Eve and murder him, ostensibly to punish him for reporting the rape to the police. The incorporation of the audio recording of the same testimony in *The Brandon Teena Story* provides audiences with a point of comparison for Swank's performance of it in *Boys Don't Cry*. Swank speaks the testimony word-for-word and reenacts very closely Teena's intonation. Sheriff Laux, the officer who interviewed Teena at the police station and the other voice on the recording, is also interviewed in *The Brandon Teena Story*, sharing his thoughts, feelings and responses to the events described. These comments provide us with further material by which to corroborate Lou Perryman's performance as the sheriff in *Boys Don't Cry* and the reenactment of the report of the rape.

Milk reenacts many of the television news reports that were sourced by, and incorporated into, *The Times of Harvey Milk*. This decision is significant because the documentary filmmakers chose to incorporate television news reports because they wanted to give their audience an impression of the public reception of the events of Milk's life and death at the time that they were occurring. The emphasis on television news reports in the documentary works to suggest that, after his election to the Board of Supervisors, Milk's participation in political life became more regularly recorded and widely broadcast and many of the events central to his life in public office were televised events. Several of the televised events included in *The Times of Harvey Milk* could even be considered what Boorstin (1961) terms 'pseudo-events', such as his press conferences, staged and manufactured for media consumption. The makers of *Milk* repeatedly arrange for the verbatim reenactment of the audio of television news footage from *The Times of Harvey Milk* to take place in a location other than that in which the documentary shows it to have happened, placing it in a narrative context that suits the film. Consequently, it is often the literal repetition of the words spoken on television, and the actions that accompanied them, that gives the reenactments their authority. In this respect, the reenactments attest to Dayan and Katz (1992: 100) argument that televised events offer 'not just an unobstructed view of "there," but a wholly different experience that is available only to those who are *not* there'. The fact that the audio of Milk speaking on television is frequently treated as a more important source for reenactment than the location in which he is speaking suggests that these television interviews, debates and speeches were important as mediated public events – staged and performed to be broadcast – rather than as events that took place in a specific time and place.

Using this strategy *Milk* condenses multiple broadcast television events. For example, the reenactment of statements from a public debate between Milk and State Senator Briggs about gay teachers in schools, which was held at Walnut Creek School District gymnasium in Fullerton, Orange County, are combined with those from a television debate, on the same issue, that took place in a brightly lit blue and orange KQED/9 television studio and which had included other participants, such as Sally M. Gearhart and Belva Davis, who disappear from the reenactment. Both televised debates were part of the coverage of Proposition 6 in California, known as the Briggs Initiative, which was designed to have gays and lesbians fired from public schools. Milk was a central force in the campaign against the proposition, which was rejected at the ballot box on 7 November 1978. Key moments of the two debates are presented as if they were all part of the Briggs-Milk confrontation in Orange County. The *mise-en-scene* mimics, but does not replicate exactly, the setting of the gymnasium in the Orange County debate, with Briggs and Milk sitting at a fold-out table either side of a moderator, wooden seating behind them and the cords from their microphones visibly trailing onto the floor in front of them. From the KQED debate, Penn reenacts Milk's challenge to Briggs that his statistics on child molestation are a farce and combines this with a verbatim reenactment of the speech Milk gave during the Orange County debate challenging Briggs's assertion that gay teachers are a bad influence on children and would try to convert them to their lifestyle. In *The Times of Harvey Milk*, in contrast, while the television footage of both debates has been incorporated, it is the KQED debate that is given more prominence, as is Gearhart, who is interviewed about working with Milk on the campaign against Proposition 6. Both debates are covered in the section of the documentary focusing on the campaign. An interview with Gearhart is inserted immediately after the television footage from the Orange Country debate which is then used to contextualize the footage of the KQED debate and functioning at as a voice-over narration for it.

As well as the audio of public speeches, debates and interviews from *The Times of Harvey Milk*, excerpts of a will that Milk had recorded privately a year before his death, which was incorporated in the documentary, are also integrated into the biopic. The documentary includes a statement from the will in the opening section of the film before the title sequence. Over slow-motion footage of Milk marching with his peers and in the 1978 Gay Pride Parade in San Francisco we hear Milk speaking softly into his tape recorder. In contrast to his televised public speeches, interviews and debates, the will was recorded by Milk alone in his own home. As I mentioned previously, a copy of the recorded will was only entrusted to the documentary filmmakers by Milk's attorney as *The Times of Harvey Milk* was nearing completion. They had unique access to this recording. It was a private document not in circulation and was otherwise unavailable to general audiences. But the excerpts from the will that were chosen for the documentary still emphasize Milk's public life and his dedication to public service with statements like, 'I have never considered

Figure 2.3 a, b Key moments from two debates between Briggs and Milk about Proposition 6 shown in *The Times of Harvey Milk* (Dir. Rob Epstein, 1984) are brought together in *Milk* (Dir. Gus Van Sant, 2008), the mise en scène mimicking the gymnasium used for the debate in Orange County.

myself a candidate. I have always considered myself part of a movement.' The incorporation of statements like this serve the argument put forward by the documentary that Milk's vocation was intertwined with the historical moment in which he lived.

Some of the phrases from the will used in *The Times of Harvey Milk* are reenacted during *Milk*'s opening sequence. Penn mimics the mood and tone of Milk's delivery in the original recording, adopting a similarly low sombre voice and intonation. But rather than a disembodied voiceover, we see Milk sitting at a dining table as he turns on the tape recorder and picks up a microphone in the act of recording of the will. This scene is intercut with short dramatized scenes of him giving speeches as well as archive and documentary footage of the aftermath of his assassination at City Hall. In *The Times of Harvey Milk*, we do not hear from the will again after the opening sequence. It is the actor Harvey Weinstein who provides the voiceover narration for the documentary. In contrast in *Milk*, the reenactment of the recording of the will becomes a device that sets up Penn's Milk as the narrator of the biopic. As the biopic progresses, the voiceover serves the biopic's narration rather than offering us a verifiable connection to the documentation of Milk's life. Throughout the biopic we periodically return to Milk, sitting at his kitchen table, holding onto the microphone as he recounts events in his life, from his arrival in the Castro to his multiple attempts to run for office and his fight against Proposition 6. The will becomes a device for summarizing aspects of Milk's life. This is a significant example of how, as with *Monster* and *Boys Don't Cry*, verifiable reenactments in *Milk* are hybridized with narrativized diegesis and organized in relation to the 'virtual time' of the fictional world.

Since only the opening statement from the will is used in *The Times of Harvey Milk*, it is not possible to utilize the documentary to verify if Penn's other statements in *Milk* where he is shown speaking into his tape recorder are part of the will. The rest of the will remains a privately held document that is not in the public domain. At the end of the biopic, however, after his assassination, we return one last time to Milk sitting at his table with the microphone. Here we can confirm that the phrases he speaks are not from his will because they are part of a famous speech he gave about giving people hope, now blended with the narrative device of the recording of the will. The speech, delivered in the low sombre tone associated with the will rather than with the actual intonation in the delivery of the speech, continues over a scene which involves the reenactment of the candlelight march organized in the aftermath of Milk's assassination. Penn's delivery of the speech subsequently becomes the voiceover for actual footage of the candlelight march and vigil recorded by the documentary filmmakers for *The Times of Harvey Milk*. From this we cut back one last time to Milk, sitting at his kitchen table as he turns off the tape recorder before the film moves into the closing credit sequence and an overview of the lives of the real people depicted in the film.

Conclusion

Neither the concept of the researched detail nor the indexical trace is static and each of these two forms of referentiality have been influenced by transformations in the other. Their manifestations and conceptualizations are historically specific and have been affected by the media environments in which they are operating. Of the three biopics under discussion, only *Milk* regularly includes television and documentary footage with reenactments, historical dramatizations and fictional scenes – playing with the idea that the biopic is part of a crowded media landscape – but the production and reception of all three biopics has been impacted by the ways in which traces of the past increasingly exist side by side with their representation and dramatization. It is in the documentaries, though, that these subjects most vividly continue to 'live'. The televised debates and press conferences that Epstein and his team dug out of the television archives for *The Times of Harvey Milk* would likely still be languishing in those archives if they had not been included in the documentary. The filmmakers bring these into conversation with their own footage of Milk's involvement in the LGBT rights movement and with the sentiments Milk expresses in his privately recorded will. Broomfield organizes media events in Wuornos's life differently in his two documentaries, the structuring of this footage reflecting the passage of time and his evolving relationship with Wuornos. The ways in which all four documentaries weave together the research and documentation of their subjects' lives continues to influence how those lives are known.

Biopics engage with the concept of fame and respond and contribute to their subjects' reputation, status and recognizability. They negotiate with intertextual and paratextual sources associated with the lives of their subjects but also those of the actors. Fame always involves, as Custen (2010: 137) argues, the mediation of a set of relationships revolving around 'a person who does something which is recorded and disseminated to audiences'. Each of these biopics is engaged with subjects and actors who are caught up in evolving mediations of fame, celebrity and performativity. The ways in which Theron's and Swank's performances as aspiring stars were promoted in relation to *Monster* and *Boys Don't Cry* draw attention to this other register of performance associated with the culture of publicity, celebrity and public spectacle. The subjects of all three biopics were already media performers and the media representations of their life were already performative. Milk and Wuornos became performers by participating in (or being co-opted by) the publicity and public spectacle associated with their lives and deaths, while documentation associated with Teena's life and death was made to perform posthumously, his gender performance as male coming under widespread discussion and scrutiny. Wuornos performed for Broomfield and became the star of her widely televised court cases while Milk performed for television cameras as an activist, campaigner and politician. In this respect, many of the reenactments employed in these biopics can be considered performances of performances.

3

Dramatizing forensic crime reconstruction: Investigation, trace and deixis in police procedural television

Historian Alexander Cook (2004: 487-8) uses the term 'investigative reenactment' to describe a popular trend inspired by reality television where people are placed in simulated historical situations which 'set out not to dramatize a past that is already known, but to learn something about the past through the activity of reenactment and to communicate those findings to a wider audience'. In Cook's critique of the strategies commonly employed in examples such as *1900 House* (Channel 4, 1999-2000), *Frontier House* (PBS, 2002), *The Trench* (BBC, 2002) and *The Ship* (BBC, 2002), he proposes that television producers should turn to the detective genre, with its emphasis on the process of investigation and interpretation, as a model that would bring a greater self-reflexivity to this style of programming. Pickering, also an historian, points out that Collingwood (famous for idea of that 'the historian must re-enact the past in his own mind') suggests the fictional detective as a template for the historian: 'The hero of a detective novel is thinking exactly like an historian, he writes, when from indications of the most varied kinds, he constructs an imaginary picture of how a crime was committed, and by whom' (Collingwood [1956] 1994: 243, cited Pickering 2010: 123). Pickering (2010: 124) points out that Conan Doyle's Sherlock Holmes himself 'was not averse to a bit of actual reenactment to test a theory'.

What is being described here is the use of principles and procedures associated with crime reconstruction to determine the actions surrounding the commission of a crime. Chisum and Turvey (2000) see crime reconstruction as one of the most important responsibilities shouldered by forensic investigators, who can use physical evidence (as well as the statements of witnesses, suspects and victims) to provide investigative leads, draw conclusions about the circumstances of a crime and the behaviours of those involved, identify potential suspects and make links between victims, suspects and offenders. Gunning (1995: 22) argues that forensic investigation techniques introduced into criminology in the nineteenth century made an impact on detective fiction as early as the last decades of that century. He also points to Holmes, whose methods were characterized by scientific attention to detail:

> The nineteenth century witnessed a rearrangement of the hierarchy of judicial proof, as the value previously accorded to witness testimony was replaced by the scientific reputation of the analysis of indices. ... This new concept of evidence transformed both the narrative logic of signs of guilt and the methods of recognition. ... Detection was approached as a science, employing careful measurement and observation.

The creators of *CSI: Crime Scene Investigation* (NBC, 2000–15), one of the most ubiquitous, commercially driven detective series on television, claimed their explicit emphasis on forensic scientists and forensic crime solving as a new intervention in police procedural television, a popular subgenre of detective fiction focused on the cultures and subcultures of the police force. *CSI* follows a team of crime scene investigators, employed by the Las Vegas Police Department, as they collect and analyse evidence to solve criminal cases. Before *CSI*, the most popular American police procedural dramas on television from mid-1970s onwards had tended to focus on character-based narratives driven by psychological motivation, testimony and confession: *Police Story* (1973–7), *Hill Street Blues* (1981–7) and *Miami Vice* (1984–90) (Turnbull 2007). *CSI* reached 24 million American viewers by 2002 and became a truly 'worldwide television phenomenon' (Allen 2007a: 3). The initial success of *CSI* inspired a wave of forensic crime drama on television, including two high-ratings spin-offs, *CSI: Miami* (NBC, 2002–12) and *CSI: NY* (NBC, 2004–13). Its ratings dominance peaked between 2002 and 2005 (Byers and Johnson 2009), a period that marked the debut of another popular American police procedural television series, *Bones* (Fox, 2005–17).

Bones became the longest-running one-hour scripted drama for Twentieth Century Fox Television, tallying up 246 episodes over twelve seasons. Often critically distinguished from *CSI* by its emphasis on humour as well as character depth and development, *Bones* also differentiates itself because of its focus on investigative techniques associated with forensic anthropology. In each episode of *Bones*, forensic anthropologist Dr Temperance Brennan (Emily Deschanel) – a character inspired by novelist and forensic anthropologist Kathy Reichs – collaborates with FBI Special Agent Seeley Booth (David Boreanaz) and a team of scientists (known colloquially as 'squints') at the Jeffersonian Institute Medico-Legal Lab where they investigate potential homicide cases in which the corpses are so degraded by age or damage that they are less intelligible to regular medical examiners, coroners and forensic pathologists. Booth contributes to each investigation by undertaking what is framed as more traditional police work – pursuing and interviewing suspects – while engaging in regular, lively banter with Brennan about the interactions between his investigative techniques and her forensic approach.

CSI, and subsequently *Bones*, actually marked the genre's return to forensic investigation, previously popularized by *Quincy, ME* (1976–83), in which a medical examiner (played by Jack Klugman) uses forensic medicine to solve cases with greater accuracy than his police force colleagues with whom he is often in conflict. (See Byers and Johnson 2009; Dobson 2009; Jermyn 2007; Panse 2007). Panse (2007) positions the work of physician Dr Mark Sloan (Dick Van Dyke) who solves crimes with his son, a homicide detective, in *Diagnosis Murder* (1992–2001) as another important precedent. Turnbull (2007) goes back as far as the pioneering *Dragnet* (NBC, 1951–9; 1967–70), in which a single case is solved in each episode through the pursuit of evidence in close consultation with the crime lab. *CSI* and *Bones* renewed the emphasis on the crime-solving conventions of the genre, which had been somewhat overshadowed by the character-driven plots typical of series like *Hill Street Blues* and *Miami Vice*.

CSI and *Bones* both focus on investigation, investigative puzzles, problem-solving and crime reconstruction. The emphasis on deciphering the events of a crime from its traces is central to both series. In forensic investigative work the collection and documentation of physical evidence is the foundation for a crime's reconstruction. The narrative structure of every episode of *CSI* and *Bones* is built on the founding principle of forensic science: the idea that 'every contact leaves a trace'. This principle, established by the founder of forensic science Edmond Locard, is distilled from his proposition that 'a criminal always takes something to the scene of a crime and always leaves something there' (Locard 2002: 178, cited in Panse 2007: 157). As police procedural television dramas driven by the principles of forensic investigation, *CSI* and *Bones* are inspired by a form of scientific investigation that focuses on the analysis of indexical traces. Locard conceptualizes trace evidence as indexical trace, defined by a physical, material contact with a referent at a time in the past and remaining as a form of testimony to a past interaction. That the emergence of an indexical trace always depends upon 'certain unique contingencies' (Doane 2002: 92) makes such traces particularly valuable for forensic investigation, since it assures their direct relationship to the specific events under investigation. The idea of the indexical trace is essential to the diegetic world of the *CSI* and *Bones* investigators, who collect and analyse material traces left at crime scenes – bone fragments, specks of skin, hair follicles, broken nails, grains of dirt, particulates, residue from bodily fluids – and successfully identify victims, perpetrators, murder weapons and cause of death often from the tiniest of traces, focusing on the minutia of the crime scene. Many of the kinds of trace evidence commonly favoured in *CSI* as well as in *Bones* correspond closely to Peirce's own examples of the indexical trace which include not only the photograph, but also the bullet-hole, the footprint and the fingerprint. He describes the bullet-hole, for example, as 'a sign of a shot; for without the shot there would have been no hole' (1991: 239–40).

In Chapter 2, I considered the performance and theatricalization of researched details uncovered in the research process. In this chapter, I explore the role that reenactment can play in the investigation and verification of indexical traces. As I have already begun to outline, crime scene reconstruction constitutes a productive field for analysis of investigate approaches to reenactment. *CSI* and *Bones* dramatize the investigative processes associated with crime reconstruction in every episode. The physical, scientific reenactments, as well as the more spectacular, computer-generated reenactments in these series embody the idea that reenactments are not 'limited to teaching knowledges in entertaining ways' as King (2012: 12) puts it, but can also be involved in 'knowledge *making*' when communities of practice from similar and different knowledge worlds work through procedures and problem-solve together.

It is the central relationship between trace evidence and crime reconstruction in the narrative and investigative logic of these police procedurals that creates the conditions for the possibility of reenactment in the series. The combination of investigative puzzles, problem-solving, crime scene investigation, crime scene reconstruction and reenactment has enjoyed wide popularity on television across a range of fiction and non-fiction genres. The kinds of shows that are most typically associated with this phenomenon fall under the umbrella of documentary and factual television such as the global franchises associated with *Crime Stoppers*; *America's Most Wanted* (Fox, 1988–2012); *Seconds from Disaster* (National Geographic, 2004–18); and *Mayday* (also known as *Air Crash Investigation*, Cineflix, 2003–). Therefore, I appreciate that, at first view, it may seem odd to focus on police procedural television drama. As well, typically, we think about the use of reenactment in film and television in terms of the reenactment of pre-existing, real events, even when employed within a fictional narrative, like the examples discussed in Chapter 2. The events being reenacted in *CSI* and *Bones* belong to the diegetic world of these series and do not typically have any basis in an external reality. They are reenactments of fictional events within a fictional narrative. Occasionally, the scenarios explored in *CSI* are based on real-life events shared with the writing team by the forensic investigators who advise the series, or sometimes the writers take inspiration from crimes that have been reported in the media, but if a case is based on a 'true story', this is rarely signalled to the audience (see Mendelsohn 2004).

But as I have proposed, narrative emphasis on reenactment has long been part of detective fiction and police procedural television and I position *CSI* and *Bones* as innovations in relation to an existing convention. Reenactments in *CSI* and *Bones* serve an investigative function in the narrative, playing a role in the verification of indexical traces, and helping to lead the audience through the investigation. The reenactments provide demonstrations of various hypotheses by presenting and trying out provisional versions of the events of a crime from the perspective of multiple characters during the narrative, until what actually happened can be established. They constitute examples of an approach to reenactment that Bruzzi (2020: 187) describes as 'acting out ... speculative, hypothetical, maybe even merely imagined' events. I have chosen to focus on the early seasons of both *CSI* and *Bones* here as this is where the foundation for the distinctive approach of these long-running series is established. I focus on the original *CSI: Crime Scene Investigation*, rather than address the whole *CSI* franchise, because *CSI: Miami* and *CSI: NY* take a different approach to the relationship between forensic science and traditional police work, featuring more characters working in policing and criminalist roles rather than scientific roles (Dobson 2009).

The formulaic, predominantly episodic, narrative structure of *CSI* and *Bones* relies on the status of the indexical trace as a form of testimony to a past event, foregrounding not only the physicality of the indexical trace, but also the temporality of the indexical trace, which is of crucial narrative significance. The narrative emphasis on indexical traces as residues of past interactions serves to emphasize that the events of the crime in each episode took place in a narrative past. As is common for the police procedural, the events under investigation in *CSI* often occur off-screen and are brought to light through the process of deduction, the audience participating in the investigative process with the police (Arntfield 2011). Typically, a *CSI* episode will open with a glimpse of the events of one of the crimes to be investigated in the episode or with the discovery of the crime scene by a member of the public. This is followed by a narrative ellipsis: in the very next scene the crime has taken place and a crime scene has been established; investigators have usually arrived and begun to make preliminary assessments of what happened. This narrative ellipsis typically occurs before the opening credits, so that by the time the credits roll, the longest period of time devoted to the narrative in the episode has already elapsed and the investigation has already begun. Arntfield (2011: 87) argues that this convention in the police procedural of presenting the central crime under investigation as a 'prologue' to an episode was solidified with *Law & Order*'s (1990–, NBC) characteristic 'cold opening', while in *Homicide: Life on the Street* (NBC, 1993–9), the revelation of a case begins with the act of writing the victim's name up on a white board.

Bones follows a similar structure. As with *CSI*, the convention of presenting the central crime as a 'prologue' is utilized regularly. However, in *Bones* the cases involve situations where the corpse has become so degraded that a regular Medical Examiner cannot perform the analysis and a forensic anthropologist is needed to identify and interpret trace evidence. As Stevens (2005) puts it, '*Bones* is Fox's version of *CSI*, but with more thoroughly dead people; unlike the gooey corpses on the CBS franchise, this show's skeletal remains are dry as dust.' This means that the events of the crime are often positioned even farther in the narrative past. Sometimes it is only a few days but more often weeks, months, sometimes even years have passed since the crime was committed. In 'The Man in the Fallout Shelter' (1:9), for example, the victim's body was sealed in a shelter for a period of fifty years. In *Bones*, it is even more likely than in *CSI* that the events of the crime occur off-screen, with few exceptions, one being 'The Man in the SUV' (1:3) where the crime is depicted before the credit sequence and the body of the victim is degraded instantaneously by a bomb blast. It is rare to see the body discovered by a member of the public, although occasionally this is the case, such as in 'The Man in the Bear' (1:5) where a veterinarian is examining the corpse of a dead bear to determine cause of death. Instead, at the beginning of an episode, a case is typically referred to Agent Booth who brings it to Brennan. Often they go to inspect a crime scene. Most commonly, although there are variations, once Brennan confirms the basic details of the victim's identity and declares the death a murder, remains and physical evidence from the crime scene are sent back to the lab for examination and the credit sequence begins. After the credit sequence, Brennan is typically back in the lab directing her team in the analysis of the remains on their examination tables.

The central relationship between trace evidence and crime reconstruction in the narrative and investigative logic of *CSI* and *Bones* is often represented with reference to advanced forensic technologies and spectacular visual effects as well as by more prosaic investigative techniques. As investigators try to establish what certain traces reveal about a crime, they are often depicted staging and performing physical investigative reenactments to help them reconstruct events and establish the reasons why a trace might have been left at a crime scene. These reenactments are typically designed to try to produce a replica of a trace that has been discovered. In the *CSI* episode entitled 'Burked' (2:1), for example, Gilbert Grissom (William Petersen) has a hunch that a victim has been suffocated. He positions a dummy on the floor and he and his colleague Catherine Willows (Marg Helgenberger) put the victim's shirt on it. Willows presses down with her knee on the dummy's chest, acting out her and Grissom's hypothesis about how he was suffocated. She opens the shirt and finds three mysterious round marks on the dummy's chest similar to those found on the body of the victim. Willows agrees with Grissom: 'He was burked.' It is this agreement, confirmed by the fact that their reenactment produced traces like those found on the corpse, which establishes the meaning of the original trace.

In *Bones*, similar strategies are regularly employed. In 'The Man in the Wall' (1:7), for example, Jack Hodgins (T. J. Thyne) and Zack Addy (Eric Millegan) attempt to determine if a similar indentation found in the skull of two different victims was created by being struck by the head of a distinctive walking cane owned by one of their suspects, which they believe might be the murder weapon. Zack puts on a protective body suit and holds a circular mould. On Brennan's instruction, Hodgins attempts to strike the mould Zack is holding as hard as he can. Comparing magnified photographs of each indentation on their computer they can confirm a match and identify the cane as the murder weapon. A similar strategy is used by Brennan in 'The Woman at the Airport' (1:10). Brennan identifies the murder weapon by striking and scraping moulding material using the unique, specially designed tools of a plastic surgeon, who is a suspect, in an effort to find a match with markings found on the victim's skull and identify the murder weapon.

In *Bones* these reenactments are often presented as scientific experiments, and are most often performed by the Hodgins, an entomologist by training, and Zack, Brennan's protégé. In 'The Man on the Fairway' (1:14), for example, a bone fragment is found at a crime scene and the team determine from this fragment that the victim was frozen, dismembered, fed into a wood chipper and spread over a golf course. They identify the brand of wood chipper from the cuts on the bone. The wood chipper is brought to the Jeffersonian and Zack and Hodgins run a dispersal pattern test on the chipper by feeding a frozen pig into it (the morphology of pig bones being similar to humans). Comparison of the dispersal pattern from their test with the bone fragment confirms that the woodchipper brought in was the one used on the victim. In 'The Titan on the Tracks' (2:1), Zack and Hodgins create an artificial skeleton and cover it in spam before setting it alight to determine if additional accelerant was used to burn a victim. These kinds of reenactments depict investigators performing procedures associated with 'the scientific method' employed by forensic scientists: they make an observation; theorize a hypothesis; design experiments to test this hypothesis; and conclude their hypothesis is true when the experiments support it (Chisum 2002). In these kinds of investigative reenactments, the reenactments performed do not necessarily resemble the original events. Instead the focus is on simulating conditions associated with the original events to produce an outcome that verifies specific aspects of what happened.

CSI and *Bones* are obsessed, at the level of narrative, with producing the truth claims of the indexical trace, which, as testimony to and a remnant of a past event, is unable to speak for itself, but must be deciphered in order that the events of that crime be understood. Each trace must be analysed, its causes 'replayed' and interpreted by investigators to establish its relationship to its referent. This is a defining characteristic of the indexical sign, which, in all its formations is understood by Peirce as having no meaning in itself, but simply attesting to the existence of something else. These physical, scientific reenactments, as well as the more spectacular, computer-generated reenactments in both series, which I will turn to in a moment, are tightly bound up in what Barthes ([1972] 1992: 17) has described as the hermeneutic code of narrative, the function of which 'is to articulate in various ways a question, its response, and the variety of chance events which can either formulate the question or delay its answer; or even constitute an enigma and lead to its solution'. They perform significant formal functions pivotal to the narrative structure of each episode. They are employed as highly self-conscious narrative mechanisms that pose questions about the nature of a crime under investigation as well as providing delayed answers to those questions. They are narrative events that help to establish the meaning of the indexical traces under investigation. The certification by the forensic investigators of material traces as indexical traces is central to the resolution of every crime investigated in *CSI* and *Bones*. Not until the investigators can verify the story told by the bits and pieces of trace evidence as the true story of the events in question can the episode be given narrative resolution.

What initially distinguished *CSI* as an innovation in police procedural television was its emphasis on forensic procedure and the technologies of forensic investigation, elaborately displayed in the series for their remarkable visual effects. *CSI* brings back an emphasis on forensic investigation to the police procedural and combines it with an emphasis on the spectacle of forensic procedure, its technologies and visual effects. Police procedural television has continued to respond to what Arntfield (2011: 76) describes as 'paradigm shifts in law enforcement technology'. *CSI* is a series that makes spectacular what Panse (2007: 153–4) describes as 'the procedures of processing'. The creators of *CSI* foreground the use of new specialized scientific equipment, such as chemicals like luminol which, when illuminated with a special blue light, causes invisible blood traces to glow.

In *Bones*, too, there is explicit emphasis on forensic procedure and the technologies of forensic investigation. In every episode, investigators examine X-rays and microscopic images showing audiences everything from organic particulates to the chemical composition of metals. Specific technologies are showcased in individual episodes. In 'A Boy in the Bush' (1:6), for example, the camera is positioned inside Zack's helmet at a crime scene as he uses thermal imaging technology to detect heat residue released from a decomposing body. In the same episode, Hodgins identifies the chemical compound found on a victim's jawbone by placing it in a methyl oxide chamber where we observe a colour change on the bone before he examines bone scrapings using a mass spectrometer. In 'The Man in the Wall' (1:7), Brennan dismembers and rehydrates a mummified hand, peeling the skin off the victim and wearing it like a glove to obtain a fingerprint. In 'The Graft in the Girl' (1:19) Hodgins uses Laser Induced Breakdown Spectroscopy (LIBS), projecting lasers onto a fragment of a bone graft to analyse its composition to identify where the suspect lived and worked. In 'The Woman in Limbo' (1:22) he uses laser scanning confocal microscope to identify mass produced cardboard in the soil with the remains of the victim. He uses Electron Dispersal Spectroscopy to identify what the cardboard was coated in and finds out that the cardboard was the remnant of a movie ticket before using UV analysis to identify the writing on it. A variety of strategies for cleaning bones in the lab are demonstrated across the seasons of *Bones* including using flesh-eating beetles and soaking skeletal remains in a giant tub of 4 per cent peroxide solution in 'The Woman in the Car' (1:11).

In both *CSI* and *Bones*, emphasis on the spectacle of forensic procedure is closely associated with the process of crime reconstruction and the use of reenactment. *Bones* features a distinctive investigative tool known as 'The Angelator' (or 'Angelatron'), a three-dimensional graphics and computer program designed to produce holographic projections that simulate virtual scenarios of a crime to help determine cause of death. The program, developed by resident forensic artist Angela Montenegro (Michaela Conlin), helps investigators visualize, hypothesize, try out and demonstrate their theories about specific events associated with a crime. Holographic simulations are created by incorporating what is known about the evidence from the crime into the computer program and analysing it according to scientific laws and theories. Most often, the focus is on the analysis of identifiable indexical traces, such as the damage done to a bone, as investigators try to determine how that specific trace was produced and thereby reconstruct an action or event.

The Angelator is inspired in part by the kinds of reenactments I discuss in Chapter 5 where a computer program is used to analyse data according to its rules (governed, for example, by the laws of physics or mathematics) to create computer simulations that help investigators and litigators reconstruct, and draw conclusions about, an event. As I will discuss, these computer simulations are becoming increasingly popular in trial proceedings in the United States, especially civil cases, subject to specific admissibility tests and the attainment of appropriate scientific verification. In *Bones*, it is rare to see the investigators participate in trial proceedings. The focus is on the lab. Once Angela has prepared a simulation, a group of investigators typically gather around the projection space to view and discuss the scenario and analyse what is depicted in each reenactment. Most commonly, the reenactments will be narrated by Brennan or Angela who explain and interpret what the audience is seeing. The scientific and investigative validity of the Angelator is supported by Brennan who challenges Booth's initial scepticism about the Angelator, which he describes as a 'holographic crystal ball' in the pilot episode, telling him, 'It's not magic. It's a logical recreation of events based on evidence.'

In every episode of *CSI*, material traces found at crime scenes participate in computer-generated reenactment sequences that draw attention to their status as trace evidence of that crime. These sequences, known as the series trademark '*CSI*-shots', typically follow the path of a fragment or bullet into an orifice or wound to reenact the formation of the trace of a crime or accident inside the body, as it is being proposed by a pathologist, coroner or forensic investigator. If they do not enter the body through a wound or orifice, they often spectacularly simulate the proposed impact of violence, illness or disease on the internal workings of the body. The *CSI*-shot has marked the series as an innovation in police procedural television and is one of the most frequently discussed aspects of the series. *CSI*-shots have often been seen as a form of reenactment, even if the term has rarely been used to describe them. In the critical discussion, various synonyms for reenactment have been used to describe *CSI*-shots. One of the few exceptions is Lury (2007: 112), who describes *CSI*-shots as a 'visceral reenactment of the crime'. For others, these sequences are 'reconstructions' or 'simulations'. Allen (2007b: 66–8) describes them as 'virtual reconstructions', 'visualisations of hypotheses' and 'hypothetical "reconstructions" of what happened'. Gever (2005: 457) describes the computer-generated reenactment sequences as 'simulating the damage inflicted by the fatal weapon'. Tait (2006: 5) describes them as 'digitally produced shots which simulate bodily interiors and the effects of violence upon them'. Weissmann and Boyle (2007: 93–4) describe them as standing 'as an authentic recreation' and 'providing a visual model of the scientist's spoken explanation'. These descriptions are understandable given that terms like 'simulation' and 'reconstruction' are often used in connection with the kinds of imaging technologies employed in forensic and scientific investigation.

Jermyn (2007: 80–1) describes them as 'reconstructing a privileged point of view' in which a victim's 'death is reconstructed', but also describes reconstructions of the events of the crime as 'stylised flashbacks which take us back to the moment of physical impact'. I am particularly wary of regarding the *CSI*-shot as a 'flashback'. It would be wrong to call them flashbacks just because they occur within a fictional narrative. While the reenactment is generally associated with non-fiction genres, and the flashback with fiction, neither is necessarily tied to these categories. As well, flashbacks are more speculative than *CSI*-shots, which are attached to the science of forensic investigation. *CSI* employs flashbacks as well as *CSI*-shots, and each is distinguishable from the other. Occasionally, a *CSI*-shot is even employed *within* a flashback. In the episode 'Chaos Theory' (2:2), for example, scrutinizing some of the victim's hairs found in the suspect's car, forensics investigators note that it carries skin tags: it has been torn out. This discovery produces a flashback showing the victim's face in close up as she struggles with the suspect, followed by a *CSI*-shot reenactment of her hair being ripped out in extreme close-up, as if the hairs on her head are under the investigator's microscope. In *Bones*, too, there is a clear distinction between the reenactments created by the Angelator, which are displayed on a platform in the lab surrounded by an audience of scientists and investigators, and flashbacks, which are used infrequently.

CSI-shots and the simulations produced by the Angelator in *Bones* often create computer-generated reenactments of unstageable 'events' that are so small in scale, or occurring inside the human body, that no camera, even if it were 'on-the-scene' as the events were occurring, could easily hope to capture. In *Bones* the explicit focus on scientists and scientific analysis brings even greater emphasis to the idea of events that cannot be seen with a human eye and that can only be seen with specific technologies. Microscopes are a ubiquitous feature of the mise en scène and almost always accompanied and enabled by computers that identify, magnify and measure a wide range of bone fragments and particulates. What is more, as Weissmann and Boyle (2007: 90) and Tait (2006: 50) propose in relation to *CSI*, the digitally produced *CSI*-shot can make internal events of the body spectacular, when previously they had no real event-status at all. This is also often the case with the reenactments produced by the Angelator. It is quite common in *Bones* for the Angelator to show only a victim's skeleton as the holograph reenacts the damage done to their bones. In 'The Man in the Wall' (1:7), for example, Angela inputs details of a victim's skeleton into her computer program and uses the bone damage on that skeleton to create a holographic reenactment of the victim being attacked. As Angela and Brennan discuss what the bone damage indicates, the Angelator reenacts the attack, showing her skeleton being pushed into a wall followed by an animated box that is inserted within the larger projection showing a close-up of this damage. In 'The Man in the SUV' (1:3), the Angelator is used to simulate the impact of poison on a victim's body in fast motion and the scenario is used to approximate the date the poison was ingested. Across both series, in such examples we also often witness not just an expansion of the idea of what constitutes an event for the reenactment but also an expansion of the idea of performance as computer-generated virtual blood vessels and microbes perform for the investigators and the audience. By performing a reenactment of the impact of disease or toxicity on the internal workings of a computer-fabricated bodily interior, microbes can become, as Bazin (2001: 145) once put it, 'the greatest actors'.

In *Bones* and *CSI*, attention to details and events that human eyes, or cameras, could not capture reflects the emphasis in both series on the capacity of forensic science to work with the minutiae of a crime but also their exploration, and indeed celebration, of the possibilities opened up by emerging digital technologies. Both series dramatize and reflect on some of the emerging trends associated with the computer animations and simulations I discuss in Chapter 5. But unrestricted by the rules of admissibility and affordability that govern 'real-world' crime solving, computer graphics and special effects are used in *CSI* and *Bones* to dramatize ambitious computer-generated simulations of crimes that may be beyond the scope of what can be achieved in an actual investigation. Much has been made by scholars and legal commentators of the so-called '*CSI*-effect': an increased expectation among jurors of forensic evidence in criminal trials, reflecting the influence of television shows focused on forensic investigation (see Cole 2015). These immensely popular television series have also fed the popular imaginary in terms of the future of crime scene reconstruction and computer-generated reenactment.

In *Bones*, emphasis on imagining the future possibilities of forensic technologies is reflected in statements made by several characters about the immense resources of the Jeffersonian Institute Medico-Legal Lab in comparison with the resources available to regular crime scene investigators. When Brennan comments on the depressing basement building that houses the FBI morgue in 'The Man with the Bone' (1:17), Booth retorts, 'Not everyone gets to play in a multi-million-dollar lab.' In 'The Titan on the Tracks' (2:1), when pathologist Camille Saroyan (Tamara Taylor) takes over the Forensic Division she admits to Booth that she took the job at the Jeffersonian because it has better equipment. Brennan's former mentor, Dr Michael Stires (Josh Hopkins) is shown a simulation created with the Angelator in 'The Girl in the Fridge' (1:8), which illustrates the inflammation and degradation of a victim's joints, and comments, 'My department's still working with Polaroids.' This remark is particularly telling since it sets up a contrast between analogue and digital technologies.

The reenactments imagined in these series reflect an era marked by the declining importance of the pro-filmic field to image production. As I discussed in Chapter 2, the pro-filmic field has traditionally been the terrain in which the reenactment authenticates itself. It has been central both to the incorporation of historical details and to the reenactment's ability to stage an event. As digital image production becomes increasingly less dependent on recording physical spaces and performances, the significance of the pro-filmic field to moving-image production is correspondingly reduced. Although the pro-filmic field has been fundamental to the ways in which film and television reenactments make their referential claims and declare themselves as reenactments, *CSI* and *Bones* are responding to an era in which it has become possible to produce computer-generated reenactments that were never staged in front of the camera.

Panse (2007: 162, 158–9) points out that the narrative emphasis on the referential and temporal powers of the indexical trace in *CSI* takes place in a digital production environment:

> The indexical tracing by the CSIs within the diegesis is detached from the indexical images of its televisual representation and even further removed from the non-indexical images processed by the computer. ... It is as though the CSIs are emphasising what the absent trace is in computer-generated television – the older medium of the indexical trace, celluloid. The excessive references to trace and traces *in* the image might compensate for the absence of trace *of* the image: the content of the programme for the lack of its medium. ... The dead bodies with indexical traces on digitally processed sites might be those of celluloid.

She argues that we could read the obsessive emphasis on the truth claims of the indexical trace in *CSI* – especially in their frequent depiction in the series using computer-generated imitations of forensic technologies – as a compensatory acknowledgement of the waning truth claims of the image as indexical trace in the era of the photochemical image's decline. This sophisticated reading of *CSI* is reinforced by the correspondences that have already been drawn in film theory between the photograph and other examples of the indexical trace provided by Peirce. Wollen ([1969]1998: 125–6) was the first to draw attention to the fact not only that one of Peirce's own examples of an indexical sign is a photograph, but also that Bazin's analogies for the photograph's ontological relation to reality match several of Peirce's other examples of indexical traces, including the fingerprint, the mould and the death mask, defined by both thinkers in terms of an existential bond between signifier and referent. The association between the fingerprint and the photograph has a long history in film theory. As Bazin (1960: 15) observes, 'The photograph as such and the object in itself share a common being, after the fashion of a fingerprint.' Indeed, Gunning (1995: 34) points out that in police filing systems from the nineteenth century until very recently, fingerprints have been 'recorded and archived as photographs'. He argues that the conceptualization of the photographic image as indexical trace underpinned its centrality to nineteenth- and twentieth-century criminal identification systems, which archived not only fingerprints, but also other unique individual bodily features, now shown in *CSI* and *Bones* to be stored on computer databases.

CSI and *Bones* reinvest in the idea of the indexical trace, in both their narrative structure and their computer-generated reenactments, in the era when the idea of the image as indexical trace is waning. As the digital image becomes 'less and less anchored to the prior existence of things and people', says Rodowick (2007: 86, 74), not only the truth claims, but also the temporality bound up in the image as indexical trace becomes an experience that is 'already historical'. While it may seem somewhat inappropriate to discuss these television series in relation to what have primarily been film theory debates about indexicality, it is nonetheless the case that these highly formulaic series repeatedly engage relationships between reenactment, trace and deixis in response to complex shifts in media production. As has been widely discussed in analyses of *CSI*, its production values are broadly 'imagined from a cinematic metaphor', which for both Rodowick (2007: 97) and Rosen (2001: 309) is a defining feature of the legacy of cinema in and for the current media environment. Rodowick (2007: 97, 101) argues that in the transitional, hybrid media climate we inhabit, 'an idea of cinema persists or subsists within the new media as their predominant cultural and aesthetic model for engaging the vision and imagination of viewers' and that 'the qualities of the "photographic" and the "cinematic" remain resolutely the touchstones for creative achievement in digital imaging entertainment'.

One of the ways that the series signals itself as cinematic – rather than 'photographic' – is through the deployment of computer-generated special effects. The cinematic 'look' of *CSI* is realized through a combination of spectacular special effects, expensive Super 35mm film stock, cinematic lighting techniques and expensive digital post-production colour manipulation (Turnbull 2007: 27–9). This conceptualization of *CSI* as cinematic because of its use of techniques associated with both analogue and digital technologies is indicative of the transitions underway in image production, and the undoing of the medium-specific delineations and the conceptualizations attached to them. At the same time, it is important to note, as Turnbull (2007: 18–21) argues, that emphasis on cinematic production values is not unusual in television, even within the television crime genre. She cites the distinctive aesthetic of *Dragnet* (1949–59) – the genre's earliest example – which she describes as being characterized by a 'cinematic self-consciousness' marked by 'elaborate and carefully lit shots' that echoed 'the style of *film noir* in its artful lighting and placement of characters'. Likewise, Dobson (2009: 80) describes *Hill Street Blues* and *Miami Vice* as presenting audience with high production values and 'a cinematic approach'.

In *Bones*, the conceptualization of the Angelator evokes digital and cinematic aesthetics. Holography, originally an analogue practice, can now be computer-generated. The holographic projections of the Angelator, visually distinctive from the style that otherwise dominates the series, are created in post-production using digital special effects. A lot of dialogue in the scenes with the Angelator is dedicated to Angela explaining the design and development of the software and the nature of the data that she enters and manipulates. The sounds accompanying the animated images are non-naturalistic and computerized, accompanied by a generalized high-pitched electronic humming as well as clicking noises that denote Angela's manipulation of the computer simulation as it is being watched. The three-dimensionality of the simulations is emphasized by the way the investigators surround the projections on all sides and their digital origin is highlighted by pixelated vertical lines that permeate the projection space, illuminated top and bottom. At the same time, the emphasis on the projection of light and on the investigators as audience also suggests a cinematic experience. The *CSI* and *Bones* production teams are certainly not in mourning for the heyday of the photochemical image.

The emphasis on computer-generated spectacle in the *CSI*-shot suggests the series' creators have embraced the possibilities being made available in the complex transitions in image production. Created by special-effects production company Stargate Digital, and produced by combining prosthetics, slow-motion capture photography, periscope cameras, layered CGI effects, 3D animation and 3D modelling, *CSI*-shots maximize and celebrate the unprecedented manipulability available to digital image production. The initial production stages of a *CSI*-shot sometimes utilize a periscope camera that moves in and out of a custom-built prosthetic body in a manner that, in part, simulates the way an endoscopic camera might move through a real body. As I have described, *CSI*-shots often follow the path of a fragment or bullet into an orifice or wound and reenact the formation of the trace of a crime or accident inside the body. It is the movement of the endoscopic camera, designed to augment and extend the surgeon's ability to see inside the human body, that 'wound-cam' (Jermyn 2007: 80) *CSI*-shots often seek to mimic. As they reenact the inscription of a trace, these kinds of *CSI*-shots also invoke the endoscopic camera metaphorically. Computers have also been in use for some time in the medical-imaging industry to produce virtual endoscopies that simulate what the endoscopic camera can do using computer algorithms. José van Dijck (2001: 229–31) describes the extent to which virtual endoscopies can produce images of the internal workings of the body that far exceed the possibilities of the endoscopic camera:

> Virtual endoscopy offers viewing possibilities that exceed the potential of real endoscopy, so the surgeon's eye and the public eye can travel to places where the material camera cannot. … Unlike video endoscopy, virtual reanimations can make our eyes fly through walls of organs and take on any plane or perspective.

We can never verify these digital reconstructions within an experiential frame of reference because no physical or electronic eye can actually travel through organs.

The simulations of the virtual endoscopy provide a visual language that helps the *CSI*-shot to embrace computer-generated reenactments from the point of view of a bullet, a knife or some other object as it penetrates a victim's corpse. The *CSI*-shot puts the style and approach of the reanimations produced by computer-generated virtual endoscopy to work in its fictional television narrative. It mimics, not so much what Rosen (2001: 313) calls a 'virtual camera', as the computer algorithms of virtual endoscopy to illustrate a hypothesis proposed by the investigators about how a victim came to end up a corpse on their autopsy table.

Panse's astute analysis of the ways in which *CSI*'s obsession with indexical traces can be understood as a compensatory gesture in the face of the indexical trace in decline in image production is very much to the point. The *CSI*-shot explicitly re-invests in the idea of the indexical trace, even in its absence from the image, by deploying the series' distinctive computer-generated special effects. It is my contention that *CSI* also responds to the anxiety that the image as indexical trace has lost its potency by making ideas of the indexical trace a key thematic concern *and* by invoking deictic indexicality, the other primary subcategory in Peirce's conceptualization of the indexical sign. As I outlined in the Introduction, deictic indices direct and focus attention, setting up a co-present existential relationship between themselves and that to which they point, either literally or figuratively. Examples of deictic indices include shifters in language, demonstrative, relative and personal pronouns and the pointing finger. In the Introduction, I aligned the performative and demonstrative dimensions of the indexical sign, characterized by acts of showing and directing attention, with the idea that a reenactment must always draw attention to the fact that it performs a pre-existing event. *CSI* regularly performs the idea of the indexical trace through what I would describe as spectacular digital deixis. Digital deixis in the *CSI*-shot celebrates a computer-generated indexical trace on the computer-generated interior of a human body. The attention-grabbing deictic performance of the *CSI*-shot explicitly invests in the idea of the indexical trace, which is rendered digitally and performed by deixis, making the indexical trace spectacular too. Further, I propose that investment in spectacular digital deixis in the *CSI*-shot summons a 'cinematic metaphor' associated with the computer-generated effects-driven Hollywood blockbuster, a phenomenon with which Jerry Bruckheimer, *CSI*'s executive producer, has long been associated. By invoking digital spectacle, *CSI* does not pretend to look like cinema, but draws on Hollywood cinema's *theatrical* aspects as cinematic metaphor.

The *CSI*-shot typically begins with an accelerated, digitally produced 'snap-zoom' (Lury 2005: 45) inside a corpse. This act of deixis draws our attention to the indexical trace and to the reenactment. Preceded by a flash of bright white light (Weissman and Boyle 2007), these high-speed snap-zooms illustrate what Peirce means by a deictic index. The snap-zoom 'takes hold of our eyes' and 'forcibly directs them to a particular object' (Peirce 1992: I. 226). Deictic indices set up relationships between themselves and their referent by pointing. As I indicated in the Introduction, Peirce's conceptualization, the pointing finger, which he identifies as 'the type of the class', works in a similar way to the 'hailing' function of deixis in language including shifters such as 'here', 'there' and the demonstrative pronoun 'this', which he argues are 'nearly pure indices, because they denote things without describing them' (Peirce 1992: 226). For Doane (2007a: 4), who conceives of the close-up as a performative act that 'points to what is there', this ability to force our gaze and our attention is the most potent power of the index. And in a discussion of the relationship between the close-up and deictic indexicality, she quotes Metz's articulation of the close-up as deixis:

> A close-up of a revolver does not mean 'revolver' (a purely virtual lexical unity), but at the very least, and without speaking of the connotations, it signifies 'Here is a revolver!' It carries with it a kind of *here* (a word which André Martinet rightly considers to be a pure index of actualisation). (Metz 1974: 67, cited Doane 2007b: 138)

Green and Lowry (2003: 48) also maintain that a relationship between deixis and trace is already at work in the photographic image. They conceptualize photography as a 'performative gesture which points to an event in the world', arguing that the photograph contains 'two forms of indexicality, the one existing as a physical trace of an event, the other as performative gesture that points to it'.

Snap-zooms also appear in *CSI* as stand-alone, attention-grabbing extreme close-ups that work as acts of hailing, repeatedly and dramatically directing the audience's attention to trace evidence at a crime scene, on a dead or living body, or in the possession of investigators. Translated into sentence form, says Peirce (1932: III. 361), an index 'would be in the imperative or exclamatory mood, as in *Look over there!* Or *Watch out!*' The snap-zoom close-up is an act of deixis that says, 'There is an indexical trace of the crime!' Snap-zooms make the indexical trace perform narratively as evidence, explicitly alerting audiences that the trace being pointed to will be essential to solving the case. In 'Overload' (2:3), for example, as investigator Nick Stokes (George Eads) looks at a suspect's jacket, there is a sudden snap-zoom into an extreme close-up of some variously coloured fibres on it, before his colleague Catherine Willows uses tape to lift the fibres off.

Bones also makes use of close-ups to point audiences' attention to the significance of particular indexical traces. Significantly, in *Bones*, these close-ups are often of investigator's computer screens which display already magnified microscopic, digitally processed images of indexical traces, foregrounding the role of digital imaging technologies in making visible the minutia of a crime. In many of these close-ups the computer screen becomes a frame-within-in-the-frame that encloses the digital representation of the indexical trace, focusing our attention in on it. Occasionally, the camera also zooms into these close-ups such as in 'Superhero in the Alley' (1:11), where Brennan analyses a fragment of bone lodged in the victim's spine under a microscope. Following a series of close-ups as Brennan and Zack propose that the fragment could have come from the victim's murderer, the sequence ends with the camera zooming into a computer screen image of the magnified bone fragment, underscoring its narrative importance.

In *Bones*, investigators also regularly literally point their fingers to important indexical traces, often pointing directly in close-up to their computer screens. In 'The Woman in Limbo' (1:22), for example, Brennan and Zack are struggling to work out what happened to Brennan's mother whose body has been uncovered. Zack tells Brennan he cannot find the evidence of remodelling on the skull he is looking for. Brennan proposes that her mother's subdural hematoma started smaller than originally thought and grew overtime. On the computer screen the two of them examine the surface of the skull directly. When they look at the image at five hundred-times magnification in close-up, Brennan says to Zack, 'See here!' as she points to the circular pattern at the centre of the screen, her arm and hand in view reaching diagonally across the close-up of Zack's computer. Zack identifies these as 'microscopic fractures on the osteans', leading to a breakthrough in their investigation. In 'Woman in the Garden' (1:12), Zack announces to his colleagues that he's found something and quickly moves a microscope across the examination table so that an enlarged image of the victim's pelvic bone appears on the screen behind him. He explains that the bone started healing around the bullet. We cut to a close-up of the computer screen with Zack's gloved hand in the frame, his finger pointing to the bullet as Brennan declares, 'This wound healed years ago. He didn't die by being shot.' In 'The Solider on the Grave' (1:21), the camera zooms into an extreme close-up of a bullet wound as Hodgins's tweezers point to it. As he declares 'Got something!' we cut to a mid-shot of Brennan and Hodgins leaning over the body, the computer image of the magnified wound between them. The camera starts zooming out to reveal Zack and Angela also leaning over the body as all four turn their heads to the image on the screen where Hodgins's tweezers still point to the wound. Brennan concludes: 'Someone wanted to cover up the friendly fire incident', the realization prompting her and Angela to attempt a reconstruction of what happened.

We can compare two acts of deixis in *CSI* – the stand-alone snap-zoom and its use in the *CSI*-shot reenactment – in 'Ellie' (2:8), an episode in which both take place in quick succession. As a dead body lies before Dr Al Robbins (Robert David Hall) on an examination table, a stand-alone snap-zoom into a close-up of the corpse's bloodied ear accompanies Robbins's identification of it as the site of the cause of death, alerting the viewer to its significance. But a few moments later, as 'Doc Robbins' explains in more detail how a bullet entered the ear (and with what consequences), another snap-zoom triggers a *CSI*-shot deep into the ear canal, reenacting the path and the impact of the bullet. While the snap-zoom remains on the surface, pointing out the bloodied ear as indexical trace, the *CSI*-shot snap-zoom plunges the viewer inside the corpse

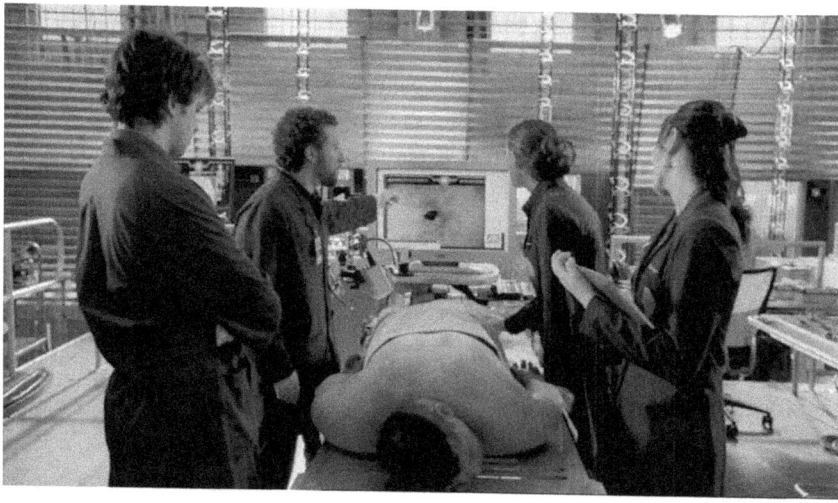

Figure 3.1 In 'The Soldier on the Grave' (1:21), Brennan, Hodgins, Zack and Angela lean over a body, Hodgins's tweezers pointing to a computer image of a magnified bullet wound, their discovery prompting Brennan and Angela to attempt a reconstruction of what happened. *Bones* (2005–17).

at high speed, in a computer-generated reenactment of the formation of the indexical trace, returning the trace to the moment of contact, hailing traces of the wound inside the body, the formation of which it has just reenacted. The deixis of the *CSI*-shot points to the indexical trace, establishing an existential relationship through co-presence, but also makes it – the residue of a past interaction – perform a reenactment of its own inscription, dramatizing the idea of the indexical trace by foregrounding the deictic. This act of hailing is not purely a visual act, but also activated by visceral, computer-generated sound effects that are in effect highly performative pointing gestures, directing and drawing our attention. These sound effects are integral to the ability of the *CSI*-shot to make the trace perform, reenacting the sounds of the movement, impact and inscription of the trace.

Doane (2002: 219) draws attention to the 'temporal tension' between the two forms of the index, one defined in terms of its relationship to the past, the other characterized by directness and immediacy:

> On the one hand, the indexical trace – the footprint, the fossil, the photograph – carries a historicity, makes the past present. At the other extreme, the deictic

index – the signifiers 'here', 'now', 'this', 'that' – are inextricable from the idea of presence.

By bringing the indexical trace to life, the *CSI*-shot as well as the Angelator, go even further, setting up a direct interaction between the temporality and contingency of the trace (which endures through time as testimony to its physical, material contact with a referent at a time in the narrative past); the temporality of deixis (where an existential bond is defined by co-presence); and the temporality of the reenactment, by making the indexical trace perform what has been positioned narratively as a pre-existing event. The *CSI*-shot and the Angelator make the trace legible by showing us not only what is 'there', but *how it got there*.

In *Bones* the Angelator makes indexical traces perform for an audience of investigators who stand around the simulation, narrate and commentate. Like the *CSI*-shot, the Angelator often makes an indexical trace reenact the event of its own inscription in a spectacular and highly performative fashion. As with the finger pointing close-ups described above, during the holographic simulations, Brennan and the other investigators regularly point to the production of traces of crucial significance by using the language of deixis, declaring 'here!' or 'there!' In the very first episode of the series, 'Pilot' (1:1), for example, Angela creates a reenactment of the struggle between a victim and perpetrator based on the defensive wounds on the bones of the victim's hand. Brennan and Angela show the reenactment to the rest of the investigative team who surround the holograph. Angela explains that the wounds 'suggest it wasn't until the third or the fourth penetration ... that Cleo stopped fighting back'. As they watch the holographic victim and perpetrator struggle, following the sound of the click of a button, Brennan suddenly declares, 'That's probably the fatal stab right there', pointing her finger at the projection, directing the audience's attention to a close-up three-dimensional simulation of a knife penetrating the victim's ribcage.

In both series, indexical traces can be made to perform multiple versions of their inscription. In *CSI*'s pilot episode (1:1), for example, Grissom, his latest recruit, Holly Gribbs (Chandra West), and the coroner discuss the bullet wound in a corpse being examined on the autopsy table. Grissom tells Gribbs that if the victim shot himself, the bullet hole 'would look like this' – at which point a *CSI*-shot follows the bullet's trajectory into the body, then pulls back to reveal a bullet wound in the chest. Doc Robbins, the coroner, responds by saying that the wound is too big for suicide and that it looks to him as though someone shot the victim as they stood over him. Again, a *CSI*-shot follows the bullet into the body on the examination table, pulling back to show the corpse with a larger bullet-hole than before. As provisional or hypothetical versions of the events of a crime, the *CSI*-shots themselves cannot resolve the anxiety about the truth claims of the indexical traces that they foreground. Instead, the existential bond between deixis and trace set up in the *CSI*-shot produces a scenario in which the authenticity of its digital deixis (which successfully embodies the definition of the deictic index as a denotative performance) works to disguise the inauthenticity of the digitally produced indexical trace (which has no real physical connection to an external reality) validating the indexical trace at the level of performance. The existential bond between the *CSI*-shot and the bullet-holes in the pilot episode produces a scenario in which the explanations provided by the investigators make the bullet-holes (which

Figure 3.2 In 'Pilot' (1:1), Angela creates a reenactment of the struggle between a victim and perpetrator based on the defensive wounds on the bones of the victim's hand. Brennan and Angela show the reenactment to the rest of the investigative team who surround the holograph. *Bones* (2005–17).

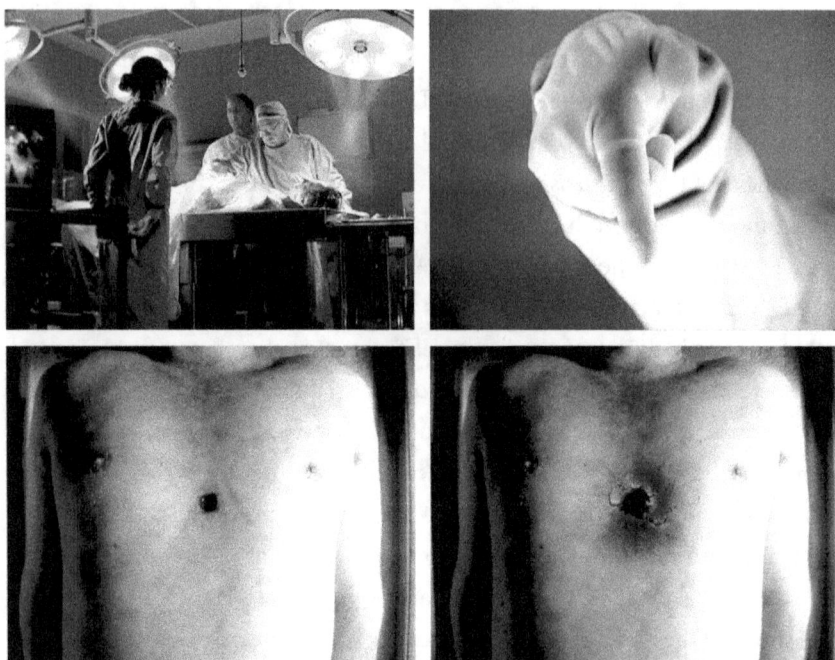

Figure 3.3 a, b, c, d In 'Pilot' (1:1), a snap-zoom reenacts the path and impact of a bullet *CSI*-shots and invokes an endoscopic camera metaphorically. Explanations by the investigators make the bullet-hole perform multiple accounts of its inscription. *CSI: Crime Scene Investigation* (2000–15).

have no real physical connection to an external reality) perform in *CSI*-shots that demonstrate multiple accounts of their inscription.

Here the *CSI*-shot offers a spectacular demonstration of a hypothesis, presenting provisional versions of past events from the perspective of multiple characters during the narrative, until what happened can be properly established. More generally as hypotheses, *CSI*-shots leave no traces on the bodies they penetrate, a point that the makers of the series are anxious to make from the outset, in the series' inaugural episode: despite the multiple routes the bullet *might have* taken through the body that Grissom, Gribbs and Doc Robbins are examining, traces of only one, the actual one, remain. Although given the point of view of the on-screen investigators, these shots exist primarily for the benefit of the audience. Yet the *CSI*-shots create a scenario where, in giving the audience these hypothetical scenarios, the forensic investigators themselves also acquire the knowledge they articulate in the *CSI*-shot scenarios.

In *Bones*, too, the Angelator is regularly employed to try out multiple hypothesis about how the events of a crime occurred. In 'Woman in the Garden' (1:12), for example, Angela and Brennan use the Angelator to help them think through how a victim's head was fractured by a bedpost. They try out a simulation of a conflict between one of their suspects and the victim, but their relative heights and the angle of the victim's fall do not match. Angela calculates that the suspect would have to be seven foot eight inches to fit the evidence, which is highly unlikely, and so they bring up a schematic of the bedroom and determine that the victim would have needed to fall from a height to explain the damage to her skull from striking the bedpost. Brennan hypothesizes that the victim could have been yanked off a ladder by a full-grown man. Angela tries out this hypothesis on the Angelator and it matches the evidence.

In 'A Boy in a Tree' (1:2) Angela and Brennan use the Angelator to test our different hypotheses about how the victim, who was found hanging from a tree, broke his hyoid bone to try to determine whether it was a suicide or if he was murdered. Angela tests out different possibilities for how the victim might have jumped from the tree. When Brennan discovers that the victim had consumed ketamine, she proposes that choking by the rope combined with the ketamine could have caused him to regurgitate, holding gastric juices in his upper throat, weakening the hyoid. She asks Angela to run some scenarios that consider the bone deterioration caused by the hyoid being digested by stomach acid. Angela applies a timeline to the simulation and runs it in fast forward. As they watch this version together with Booth, Brennan narrates the events being depicted: 'The body decomposes and the gastric juices, trapped by the noose and Nestor's oesophagus actually digest the hyoid over time.' As the simulation continues, Brennan watches, proclaiming suddenly, 'Wait. There! The hyoid cracked' as she points to the Angelator. Angela's simulation determines it would have taken eight days for this process to have taken place. Brennan tells Booth that the finding is congruent with suicide.

Interestingly, it is precisely because of its presentational value that Danny Cannon (2004) regards the computer-generated *CSI*-shot as a significant intervention in the television crime genre. While scenes in other crime series about the sifting of evidence might be 'all talk', he says, in *CSI* they are 'all about show':

> What's the best way to tell that story? If you're in an autopsy room, is the best way to just stand there and point or get some pictures out and do that or actually use the camera like they did in *Fantastic Voyage* and dive inside that body and that will tell the story for us.

Visual-Effects Supervisor for Stargate Digital, Larry Detwiler (2004), makes the same point when he explains that in the autopsy scene in the episode 'A Little Murder' (3:4), the writers put in a *CSI*-shot of an operation the victim had undergone to get his bones stretched 'because they wanted to show this event'. In *Bones*, as illustrated in the examples described above, there is an ongoing dialogue between explaining and showing that is especially heightened in the scenes involving the Angelator simulations. In the computer-generated *CSI*-shot and the computer simulations produced by the Angelator, the reenactment's theatricality has become characterized by acts of showing and drawing, directing and focusing attention.

As I have outlined, the reenactment's primary investment in theatricality lies in the fact that, to be recognized as a reenactment, it must foreground that it stages and performs a pre-existing event. Its openly presentational mode of address and undisguised emphasis on staging, performance and spectacle have always been its defining characteristics, essential to its ability to signal itself. This self-reflexive, presentational mode of address that has characterized the reenactment from the first decade of the cinema remains crucial to the recognition of a reenactment *as* a reenactment in the digital era even as the terrain of the pro-filmic field becomes increasingly diluted in contemporary image production. It is still possible to conceptualize theatricality in the reenactment without recourse to the theatrical dimensions of the pro-filmic field. It requires that we consider its presentational mode as based on showing rather than on staging. Deictic indexicality can enable a reenactment to draw attention to itself as a performance and an act of demonstration. In the Introduction, I aligned the reenactment with Gunning's (1990: 57) 'cinema of attractions', emphasizing the importance of direct address, spectacle and exhibitionism. I argued that the reenactment embodies what Elsaesser (2007: 211) describes as the 'reflexivity and self-reference, display and performativity that we have come to associate with the "cinema of attractions"'. Here I want to suggest that, in an increasingly digital media environment, the theatricality of deixis can take on a crucial role for the recognition of a reenactment *as* a reenactment and the activation of the indexical trace for reenactment. We have been too ready to see both the reenactment and the digital image as remaining outside the domain of the index. Now that the reenactment and digital imagery – both considered problematic to the idea of the indexical trace – have begun to work together, it becomes apparent that neither has been problematic to the idea of the index, only to that of the image as indexical trace. Deictic indexicality comes to the forefront, highlighting the capacity for indexicality that has always been present in the reenactment and is readily available to digital media.

4

Restaging the cinema: Reproducibility and the shot-for-shot remake

Central to the discussion of the reenactment in this book is the contention that for a reenactment to be recognized as a reenactment, it needs to foreground that it is staging and performing events that have already taken place. In this chapter I extend this conceptualization to thinking about the workings of the film remake, specifically the shot-for-shot remake. The shot-for-shot remake foregrounds repetition in the remake directly, drawing attention to itself as both repetition and performance, invoking the tension between the two agendas that I have identified as central to the reenactment. As Horton and McDougal (1998: 2) rightly say about the remake, a film that advertises itself 'as a reworking of an earlier film' always 'forces us to read in a different way, by considering its relationship to the earlier film'. The self-conscious emphasis on staging, performance and literal repetition in the shot-for-shot remake brings to the fore the self-reflexivity of the reenactment in the remake. Bruzzi (2020: 187) defines the reenactment as 'a copy, a repetition of something that has already happened, which it resembles (usually closely, sometimes critically), but from which it remains distinct'. Verevis (2006a: xii) defines the remake as a 'particular case of repetition', one that is 'stabilised, or *limited*, through the naming and (usually) legally sanctioned (or copyrighted) use of a particular literary and/or cinematic source which serves as a retrospectively designated point of origin and semantic fixity'. The shot-for-shot remake draws attention to this point of origin. As I discussed in detail in Chapter 2, a range of different sources and research materials associated with an event can be consulted in the production of a reenactment. In Chapter 2 I explored some of the ways that biopics employ reenactments based on media representations of events as well as mediated events that were staged to be circulated. The shot-for-shot remake is also engaged in the reenactment of existing moving images that were planned and crafted by a production team with the intention of being circulated.

With the shot-for-shot remake, the focus is not only on *what* the original films represent but also *how* they represent it: aesthetic and technical choices are interrogated and repeated. Two examples that exemplify this approach are Gus Van Sant's controversial remake of Alfred Hitchcock's landmark suspense film *Psycho* (1960), released in 1998, and Jill Godmilow's *What Farocki Taught*, also released in 1998 in the lead up to the thirtieth anniversary of Harun Farocki's short experimental essay film, *Inextinguishable Fire* [*Nicht loschbares Feuer*] (1969), about the development of Napalm B by Dow Chemical. Godmilow begins and ends *What Farocki Taught* with scenes in which she explains in detail how she remade *Inextinguishable Fire* shot-for-shot because she was inspired by what the film had to say and 'the way it said it'. Van Sant's intentions and process are explained through the promotional and publicity materials, including the production notes and press kit, which make scarcely any reference to issues of theme and characterization, but instead, in extensive detail and with great self-consciousness, emphasize the work of the crew and the technical aspects of the production process. Through these materials we learn that original floor plans were used as well as the very Universal Studios lot on which the first *Psycho* had been filmed. Van Sant even tried to work as closely as he could to Hitchcock's original thirty-seven-day shooting schedule, virtually implying that the original production process itself was an event ripe for reenactment (see Universal 1998: 4–17). The focus on the cinematic grammar of the original films means that the actions being reenacted are constituted not only through the actors' performances but also those of the crew: the position and movement of cameras, lighting, blocking and so on. The crews repeat, with a remarkable degree of accuracy, a whole range of actions necessary to the production of a shot-for-shot remake. This occurs primarily in the production phase but also in post-production with the recreation of the edits, for example, and the rescoring of the soundtrack.

Various taxonomies have been developed to categorize different degrees to which remakes announce and perform their intertextuality (see Eberwein

1998: 28–31). Whatever the taxonomy, one of the principal distinctions to be drawn is that between the *uncredited* or *disguised* remake and the *acknowledged* or *direct* remake. Limbacher (1979: viii) defines the 'disguised or uncredited remake' as one in which the productions have failed to acknowledge significant plot similarities. The '*direct* remake', on the other hand, says Druxman (1975: 13–14), is one that 'doesn't try to hide the fact that it is based on an earlier production': it may make minor changes to dialogue, to narrative and even perhaps to the title, but is essentially 'the same film as its predecessor – with publicity campaigns not hiding that fact'. Greenberg (1991: 170) divides the *direct* remake, into two categories: *the acknowledged, transformed remake*, which acknowledges the original but makes substantial alterations, and *the acknowledged, close remake*, which replicates the original narrative with minimal or no change. Van Sant's *Psycho* and Godmilow's *What Farocki Taught* are both *direct* remakes that acknowledge and stay close to the original. As shot-for-shot remakes, they do more than replicate the original narrative: The filmmakers study the formal and technical dimensions of the originals to be able to reproduce them. They are what Forrest and Koos (2002: 20) term 'true' remakes, because they 'cop[y] the way the original's images are presented on the screen'. Indeed, Forrest and Koos's (2002: 21) explanation of the 'true' remake is closest among the existing taxonomies to a description of the shot-for-shot remake.

While the language of the distinction between the 'true' and 'false' remake might suggest a preference in the critical reception for the 'true' over the 'false' remake, in fact the opposite is the case. Forrest and Koos borrow these categories from the critical reception given the remake by Protopopoff and Serceau (1989: 37–45) who regard the 'false' remake, characterized by 'auteurist reworking and re-interpretations', as far preferable to what they call the 'shameless plagiarism' of the 'true' remake. This attitude to the 'true' remake echoes in the wider critical reaction to Van Sant's approach to *Psycho*, which proved very unpopular with critics and scholars. While many of Van Sant's other films have generally been well received by critics, his 'shameless plagiarism' of *Psycho*, deliberate and openly acknowledged, was the subject of often angry and negative reviews which widely considered it an irreverent and foolhardy insult to an original masterpiece, little short of 'cinematic blasphemy'

(Santas 2000). Because Van Sant's *Psycho* is an *acknowledged, close remake* of a film that has stood the test of time and was considered *ahead* of its time, no one regarded it as an improvement on the original. Van Sant was 'simply asking for bad reviews', says Naremore (2002: 388), proposing that some films have 'such artistic prestige and historical significance that remaking them, as opposed to quoting them or borrowing their ideas, seems crass and pointless'. The original theatrical run of Hitchcock's *Psycho* was so successful that it was reissued into cinema theatres in 1965 and 1969. A landmark of suspense cinema, it is considered one of cinema history's most 'critically saturated' (Schaeffer 2000) films. In 1992, judged by the U.S. Library of Congress to be of cultural, historical and aesthetic significance, *Psycho* was selected for preservation in the National Film Registry.

Psycho: Couldn't the original movie do?

Remaking, borrowing and referencing Hitchcock has long been a cinematic and televisual phenomenon, and in Verevis's (2006a: 68) view, Van Sant's very literal and self-conscious remake of *Psycho* is not so markedly different: it 'differs textually' from the multiple circuits of referencing, adapting, remaking and reworking of Hitchcock's classic 'not *in kind* but only in *degree*'. Even the sequels and prequel to *Psycho* made in the 1980s – *Psycho II* (Richard Franklin, 1983), *Psycho III* (Anthony Perkins, 1986) and *Psycho IV: The Beginning* (Mick Garris, 1990) – remake aspects of Hitchcock's original film (see Verevis 2006b). As McDougal (1998: 52–3) points out, 'The notion of a remake becomes complex with a filmmaker like Hitchcock because he was continuously and obsessively remaking his own work.' In 1956, Hitchcock famously released a *direct* remake of his own 1934 film *The Man Who Knew Too Much*. While this 'autoremake', like Van Sant's *Psycho*, is a *direct* and *acknowledged remake*, it differs drastically from Van Sant's approach. The 1956 film is an *acknowledged, transformed remake*, which makes substantial changes to the original film. Since it is driven by 'auteurist reworking and re-interpretations', it could be characterized as a 'false' remake (Forrest and Koos 2002: 21–2). Although it retains the title and structure of the 1934 original, it has different characterizations. It also has what McDougal (1998: 59–61) terms 'different social, political and geographical dynamics'. In the eyes of critics and historians alike, Hitchcock had improved on the original, and the 1956 version is commonly favoured. In the director's own judgement, 'the first version is the work of a talented amateur and the second was made by a professional' (cited Druxman 1975: 20). McDougal (1998: 52–3) points out that not only was it Hitchcock's practice to return compulsively to his themes, but he also 'often remade a single shot or a transition between shots' as well as 'entire sequences'. It is this focus on remaking at the level of the shot, the sequence and the transition between shots, that is central to Van Sant's remake.

Van Sant proposed to approach *Psycho* in the spirit of the tradition of restaging classics works in theatre:

> There is an attitude that the cinema is a relatively new art and therefore there's no reason to 're-stage' a film. But as the cinema gets older, there is also an audience that is increasingly unpracticed at watching old films, silent films and black and white films. (Universal 1998: 5)

Van Sant draws on the tradition of the theatre through a reflection on the shifting status of spectatorship in the cinema. It is his sense that the cinema was ageing, and that film spectatorship had transformed over the lifetime of the cinema, that inspired him to restage *Psycho*. The emphasis on restaging infers the theatrical cinema experience as a specific historical formation of the cinema. Joseph Stefano, who wrote the original screenplay for Hitchcock and returned to it for Van Sant, was enormously gratified to see his work treated like a classic American play. He was enthusiastic about the idea of restaging *Psycho*:

> I don't know of any screenwriters who have had their work remade in the same sense that say, Arthur Miller, has seen his plays redone. Even though the opportunity to see my work brought to life again is something I simply never expected, I thought it was a wonderful thing to happen. (Universal 1998: 7)

Naremore (2002: 390) points to a fundamental difference between a script intended for the stage and one intended for the screen, when he argues that Van Sant's remake is 'not simply a re-filming of Joseph Stefano's script, but an elaborate quotation of things that were *literally printed on another film*'.

By bringing the theatre's age-old tradition of restaging plays to the cinema, Van Sant's remake highlights the ways in which technical reproducibility has produced certain ideas and forms of repetition.

No other remake of Hitchcock has generated the same degree of critical outrage. In 1998, the year in which Van Sant's *Psycho* was released, Santas (2000: par. 2) points out that two other *direct* Hitchcock remakes reached the screen: Andrew Davis's *A Perfect Murder*, based on *Dial M for Murder* (1954), and a TV-movie version of *Rear Window* (1954), starring Christopher Reeve. Neither attracted the outrage levelled at *Psycho*. The critical dismissal of Van Sant's efforts was especially fuelled by the fact that in a major contrast to earlier historical times, when a film had limited currency beyond its initial release, by 1998, when the remade *Psycho* was released, the home video market had already effected a marked change in the relationship between originals and their remakes. The television rights were originally purchased by CBS in 1966 and the film is now accessible on VHS, DVD, Blu-ray and online. When 'the old film is available alongside the new for video rental', writes Leitch (2002: 39–40), remakes are often in competition with their originals and will typically 'attempt to supersede [them] for all but a marginal audience watching them for their historical value' with 'the goal of increasing the audience by marginalizing the original film, reducing it to the status of the unseen classic'. 'The true remake', he continues, 'admires its original so much it wants to annihilate it'. The story of MGM's purchase of the negatives of Thorold Dickinson's original *Gaslight* (1939) in 1944, as George Cukor was preparing his remake for the studio, is part of cinema lore (see Leitch, 2002: 50). MGM wanted to wholly obliterate access to the original, destroying even the possibility that the original might again become available for viewing.

The shot-for-shot remake, by contrast, typically works, not to annihilate the original but rather to draw our attention to it. Van Sant's *Psycho* is a version of what Leitch (2002: 47, 50, 49) calls an *homage*, the primary purpose of which, he says, is 'to pay tribute to an earlier film rather than usurp its place of honor'. It has not been a particularly common category for the remake and in Leitch's view, 'Homages deal with the contradictory claims of remakes – that they are just like their originals, only better – by renouncing any claims to be better.' Leitch (2002: 47) argues that 'a faithful homage would be a contradiction in terms (the most faithful homage would be a re-release)'. But Van Sant deliberately engages in this 'contradiction in terms' at a time when, as Mulvey (2006: 12) describes, the 'new availability of old cinema through new technology' had become a commonplace, everyday aspect of film spectatorship. As I discussed in Chapters 1 and 2, the growing circulation of moving images has facilitated an increased co-presence of multiple representations and performances of the past and both shot-for-shot remakes engage with this phenomenon. Mulvey (2006: 24–5), reflecting on Jean-Luc Godard's *Histoire(s) du cinéma* (1998), which intertwines cinema history with the recording of the history of the twentieth century, has suggested that 'cinema will increasingly become a source of collective memory of the twentieth century for those who missed living through it'. Mulvey (2006: 181) imagines the cinema at the end of the twentieth century as a kind of 'parallel universe', a 'recorded film world' that, like the recorded events of the 'real' world, can be 'halted or slowed or fragmented'. As long ago as 1982, Cavell (1982: 78) maintained that cinema's 'evanescence' was becoming less and less inevitable, that emerging distribution technologies were drawing attention to the historical specificity of the experience of movies as exhaustible, disappearing objects. Rodowick (2007: 26–8) tells how his sudden discovery in 1989 that Pasolini's entire *oeuvre* was available at his local video store marked the moment at which he recognized that film-watching had truly begun to shift from being something rare, requiring the pursuit of unique and specific circumstances, to becoming a customary aspect of his daily life. For Rodowick, this realization changed his sense of cinema's relationship to time and with it the realization of 'profound consequences for the phenomenology of movie spectatorship'.

Many of the film's critics in the aftermath of its release argued that the widespread accessibility of the original created the conditions for the redundancy of a shot-for-shot remake. This is certainly the view of Santas (2000: par. 13), who asks rhetorically, 'What can an exact copy do for a viewer, especially a viewer to whom the original is so readily available?' Ebert (1998), however, argues that Van Sant's remake is, perversely, 'an invaluable experiment', because 'it demonstrates that a shot-by-shot remake is pointless; genius apparently resides between or beneath the shots, or in the chemistry that cannot be timed or counted'. Verevis (2006a: 16) points out that while

Martin Scorsese's critically acclaimed 1991 version of *Cape Fear* circulated happily with J. Lee Thomson's 1961 version on a collector's edition DVD box set, Van Sant's emphasis on shot-for-shot repetition summoned the boundary between remaking and replaying too closely. The questions the remake raised for critics generally coalesced into a consensus on a question that captures well the spectatorial conditions into which Van Sant's *Psycho* was released: 'Couldn't the original movie do?' (Santas 2000: par. 7). But the reasons for which Van Sant's remake has been dismissed as redundant are the very reasons why the film is useful to this book.

Verevis (2006a: 1) asks two related questions about the nature of the film remake: 'How is film remaking different from the cinema's more general ability to repeat and replay the same film over and again through reissue and redistribution?' and 'how does remaking differ from the way every film is "remade" – dispersed and transformed – in its every new context or re-viewing?' Because remaking overlaps with other forms of repetition available to the cinema, Verevis (2006a: 74) argues that a

> 'broad conception of the remaking of *Psycho*' would acknowledge 'any of the several re-releases of *Psycho* (from 1965 onwards) and its subsequent licencing by MCA for network and syndicated television screenings, and (later) sale to video tape and disc, as further revisions – or remakings – of the film'.

He goes so far as to suggest that remaking might extend to 'the cinema's ability to repeat and replay the same film over and again' (2006b: 15). In short, says Verevis, to reissue, rerelease, redistribute or replay *Psycho* can also be thought of as remaking it. This approach to Van Sant's *Psycho* highlights the problem of trying to think about repetition in the remake outside of a relationship with media time, specifically, the multiple kinds of repetition made increasingly available through redistribution, reissue and replaying. Taking my cue from Verevis, I ask, what can be gained from thinking about the remake as imbricated with these multiple forms of repetition, from replaying to redistribution? Rather than argue, as Verevis does, however, for an extension of the idea of remaking to include reissue, rerelease and redistribution, I propose that Van Sant's *Psycho* can help us to understand the shifting status of the cinema as a cultural institution and to think through intersections between technical repetition, the remake and the reenactment, especially as they relate to the changing conditions of film spectatorship.

The press kit issued by Universal describes how Van Sant had a DVD of Hitchcock's *Psycho* with him on the set, approaching the replaying of the DVD as a tool to facilitate its refilming (Universal 1998: 10). Indeed, it is hard to see how, without such an aid, he could have realized his intentions to take the idea of the remake as a repetition literally. It was the range of temporal manipulations associated with the DVD player – the ability to pause, rewind, fast forward, speed up, slow down and replay the film in DVD form – that facilitated this unique attempt at a shot-for-shot remake. Actively manipulating the temporality of the original *Psycho* over repeated viewings of the DVD even enabled Van Sant to hone in on continuity mistakes he and his team had identified in the original and carefully replicate them. What is more, with the DVD version of the original playing alongside the shooting of each scene, Van Sant required his cast and crew to keep time with Hitchcock's original. He timed the duration of each scene to coincide precisely with that of the earlier film, trying literally to reenact *Psycho* at the same pace as the original film (see Universal 1998: 10). Van Sant attempted to replicate almost exactly, with a few minor variations, the narrative, framing, blocking and editing of the original *Psycho*, right down to the length of the shots and the timing of the actors' performances. By contrast to the accolades heaped on the actors who perform in the biopics I discussed in Chapter 2, however, the performances of those who played in Van Sant's remake of *Psycho* were almost universally panned as inadequate to their 'originals'. By bringing the DVD player onto the set, Van Sant set up a direct interaction between restaging, replaying, refilming and retiming and all forms of repetition were central to the successful production of his shot-for-shot remake. By heightening the degree of repetition in the remake with the help of the DVD player, Van Sant created a remake of *Psycho* that was enabled by, and entangled with, the new forms of technical repetition made available by the DVD player.

The kinds of technical repetition made increasingly available by video, DVD, Blu-ray and online distribution have made a variety of approaches to replaying available to film spectators. Mulvey (2006: 22, 26), for example, investigates a 'new interactive spectatorship' orientated around the act of replaying. Now

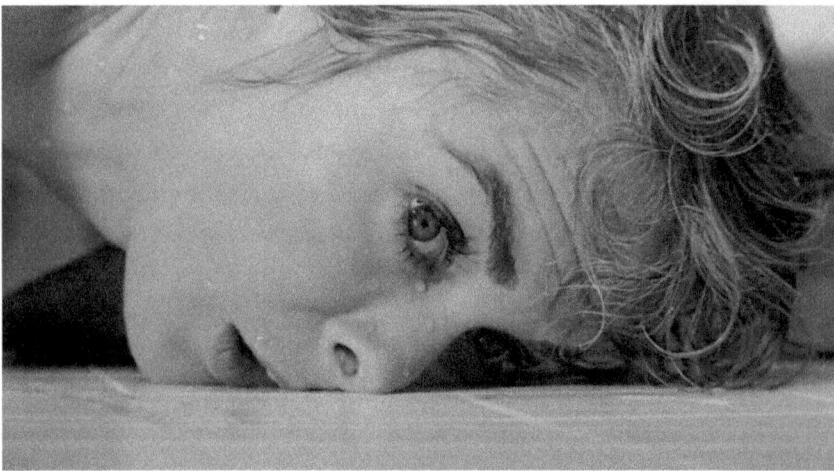

Figure 4.1 a, b In *Psycho* (Dir. Gus Van Sant, 1998) the filmmakers attempted to replicate the narrative, framing, blocking and editing of the original *Psycho* (Dir. Alfred Hitchcock, 1960).

that we can watch specific scenes over and over; fast forward, rewind, pause, slow down and speed up any film; or stop at any moment in a film as we please, there is an increasingly ubiquitous engagement with cinema that uses electronic and digital technologies to slow, halt, delay, repeat and return to images, moments or sequences in a film. She focuses on how engagement with films by means of delays, repetitions, returns and other forms of retiming made available through domestic viewing technologies can produce different kinds of spectatorial encounters with cinema as well as different transformations of the films themselves. Her analysis serves to emphasize that the conditions of film spectatorship are tied up with shifts in technical reproducibility.

A key figure in Mulvey's (2006: 11) discussion of the shifting nature of film spectatorship is that of the 'pensive spectator', who is 'engaged with reflection on the visibility of time in the cinema', and this figure has emerged with these new conditions of film spectatorship. Mulvey (2006: 195) derives her notion of the pensive spectator from Bellour's (1987) discussion of the way in which freeze-frame analysis explores relationships between movement and stillness in the cinema, maintaining that Bellour anticipated the kind of reflection on the film image that is now readily available. Mulvey (2006: 8, 144) argues that the interruptions and delays imposed on the flow of a film through return and repetition expose 'the cinema's complex relation to time'. The temporalities inherent in film include not only stillness and movement but also a multiplicity of different speeds – kinds of time that video, DVD, Blu-ray and online distribution make readily available to the film spectator. As the pensive spectator manipulates the temporality of a film, s/he not only transforms her/his relationship with that film but also transforms the film itself as 'hitherto unexpected meanings can be found hidden in the sequence'. Pensive spectatorship of the original *Psycho* – a mode of viewing that is attentive to and shaped by repetitions, returns, temporal delays and freeze-frame analysis – enabled the making of the shot-for-shot remake, underpinning the attempt at literal repetition. With Van Sant's *Psycho*, new ways of consuming old movies become a new way of remaking movies that offers a reflection on film consumption and on the complexities of film time. Pensive spectatorship enables Van Sant to create out of his *Psycho* a critical reflection both on cinema's past and the complexities of cinema's present.

What Farocki Taught: To find an image is to refind it

In *What Farocki Taught*, Godmilow emphasizes dialogue with *Inextinguishable Fire* and explicitly signals the status of her film as a reenactment. Scenes from *Inextinguishable Fire* are periodically superimposed into the remake, reminding audiences that the original film is available to be replayed. These double exposures, interspersed throughout the film, facilitate co-presence between pairs of bodies, filmed almost thirty years apart, who exist together in the remake in their different settings, briefly cohabiting. With this strategy audiences are reminded that the shot-for-shot remake requires the actors to perform pre-existing performances. The actors' bodies in these scenes are not exactly aligned but rather slightly offset, existing side by side, working together as a pair. Small variations become apparent such as different hairstyles, body types, gait and gestures. At the same time, the exactness of the shot-for-shot replication becomes apparent, showing how closely the remake imitates the framing, blocking and editing of *Inextinguishable Fire*. Like Van Sant's *Psycho*, the cast and crew perform in time with the original. In some instances, such as a scene that takes place in the reception of the offices of Dow Chemical, it is the camera position and movement, rather than the actions of the actors, that is the most important performance being doubled, reminding us that the shot-for-shot remake involves reenactments that are performed by the crew.

The relationship between *What Farocki Taught* and *Inextinguishable Fire* is influenced by the very different historical status and circulation of *Inextinguishable Fire*. While the place of *Psycho* in the cannon is undisputed, Godmilow tried to elevate the status of *Inextinguishable Fire* for cinema and television history, pointing back to the original to create new interest and curiosity about it and the context in which it was made. Godmilow (Godmilow and Shapiro 1997: 101) conceives of her remake as 'a way to re-publish the original, and this time, to make sure it's distributed and paid close attention'. More so than Van Sant's *Psycho*, *What Farocki Taught* is an example of Leitch's (2002) *homage*: the intention of the remake is to 'pay tribute' to the original. While Farocki's work and life may not have been studied and valorized to the extent of Hitchcock's, he was nonetheless a prolific, highly regarded and influential filmmaker and artist. *Inextinguishable Fire*, Farocki's first surviving film, marked the beginning of a forty-five-year career in which he produced over one hundred film and video works, some of them reworked and adapted across cinema and gallery contexts. *Inextinguishable Fire* initiates some of the enduring themes and concerns of his career including his focus on war and the workplace. Farocki worked with a very different economy of production to Hitchcock as his approach was associated with low-budget, independent production and circulation. Represented by Green Naftali Gallery, major exhibitions of his work have been mounted at MoMA and Tate Modern and his work is housed in their collections. Farocki continued to work with a variety of forms and techniques across his long career ranging from agitational films like *Inextinguishable Fire* to multichannel video installations such as *Workers Leaving the Factory in Eleven Decades* (2006) and *Deep Play* (2008).

Godmilow explains during the epilogue to *What Farocki Taught* that when she first saw *Inextinguishable Fire* in the early 1990s she felt angry that it had never been shown in the United States (although several of Farocki's films are distributed in the United States by Noon Pictures), especially given its focus on the production of napalm for American forces during the Vietnam War. Godmilow says that she was 'shocked that someone else had made it, someone whose country wasn't even implicated in the war'. While the *Inextinguishable Fire* was in German, indeed it was made for German television, the setting was a chemical factory in Michigan in the United States. Godmilow remakes the film in the United States and uses American actors who speak in English. As she explains in the prologue, 'In the original, German friends of the filmmakers played the parts. That is, they played Americans. I use Americans for Americans.' This transition offers a parallel with Michael Haneke's *Funny Games*. Originally filmed in German in 1997, Haneke remade his film in the United States and in English shot-for-shot in 2007. Loock (2017: 181) argues that Haneke's insistence on remaking his film shot-for-shot was a means to resist the trend of foreign films remade in Hollywood being given a 'substantial makeover' to appeal to American tastes and habits, which typically extends to the way they are shot and edited. Haneke did so to bring the film closer to the source of his critique: to make it more accessible to an American audience because the film was responding to the ways that American cinema can make violence consumable (see Jeffries 2008). *What Farocki Taught* likewise brings *Inextinguishable Fire* closer to the source of the original film's critique. The makeover of *Inextinguishable Fire* likewise extends to the casting and aspects of the mise en scène but not to the composition or duration of the scenes. This is because, like *Funny Games*, the significance of *Inextinguishable Fire* for

Godmilow rests with its aesthetics as much as its subject matter: What matters is the ways that film language is deployed to make a critique.

While Van Sant's film is situated within the Hollywood studio system – and has been received and understood in relation to dominant traditions, trends and ideas associated with Hollywood remakes – Godmilow's remake is connected to gallery and museum contexts where the association between reenactment and remaking has already been established. Shot-for-shot remakes have achieved a notable salience among the body of work associated with a range of curated exhibitions organized around the concept of reenactment. *Service of the Goods* (Jean-Paul Kelly, 2013), for example, remakes shot-for-shot a selection of scenes from Frederick Wiseman's documentaries about state-run institutions: *Titicut Follies* (1967), *High School* (1968), *Law and Order* (1969), *Hospital* (1970), *Basic Training* (1971), *Juvenile Court* (1973) and *Welfare* (1975). Other examples include Paul McCarthy and Mike Kelly's *Fresh Acconci* (1995), which restages five works from the 1970s by multimedia artist Vito Acconci, and *Eat Fear/Angst Essen* (Ming Wong, 2008) in which the artist reenacts *Ali: Fear Eats the Soul* (R. W. Fassbinder, 1974), playing every role himself. In *Remake* (Pierre Huyghe, 1994–5), *Rear Window* (dir. Alfred Hitchcock, 1954) is remade shot-by-shot with amateur French actors in a Parisian housing project. *Shulie* (dir. Elisabeth Subrin, 1997) offers another variation on this trend, a shot-for-shot remake of an unreleased student documentary about Shulamith Firestone made in 1967 when she was a 22-year-old student at the Art Institute of Chicago. *What Farocki Taught* is part of this trend in experimental film and video works that involve remaking the work of earlier artists and filmmakers. *Inextinguishable Fire* and *What Farocki Taught* are now both in the collection of the Museum of Modern Art in New York.

Tomic (2013: 439) proposes that the curatorial focus on reenactment in art institutions follows on from the legacies of 'appropriation art' where the reuse, reproduction and reframing of existing imagery connects to a long and rich history. This development is also associated with a phenomenon that Bourriaud (2002) argues emerged in the 1990s characterized by an increasing number of artworks being 'created on the basis of pre-existing works' as 'more and more artists interpret, reproduce, re-exhibit, or use works made by others or available cultural products'. Godmilow's work is informed by these traditions as much as it is conventions associated with the film remake. The connection between practices of appropriation and reenactment in the art world also resonates with Farocki's own long-standing practice of reusing, reassembling, recontextualizing and juxtaposing existing footage, including home movies, discarded surveillance footage, videogames and workplace and military training videos in works such as *Videograms of a Revolution* (1999) and *Serious Games* (2009–10). 'For Farocki', Elsaesser (2005: 56) argues, 'to find an image is to re-find it'. Farocki's evolving practice responded to increasingly media-saturated environments in which the capacity to circulate photographs, film, television, video and online materials grew exponentially over his career. As he explains, 'Because so many images already exist, I am discouraged to make new ones; I prefer to make a different use of pre-existing images' (cited Fox 2014). It became Farocki's view that it was 'better to quote something already existing and create a new documentary quality' (cited Robinson 2015).

Godmilow undertook her shot-for-shot remake to think through not only Farocki's but also her own concerns about conceptualizations of documentary and its representational claims. When asked to describe *Inextinguishable Fire* in the epilogue, she says,

> Well, most of you would think of it as a documentary. It's got a very serious subject and you wouldn't recognize any of the actors in it. But actually, it's not a real documentary at all. … We don't have a name for this kind of film. We should get one, I think. Its inexpensive. Its direct. Its strong.

Godmilow says that she admired the way that *Inextinguishable Fire* replaced what she describes as 'documentary's "pornography of the real" with real analysis and real provocation'. She defines 'pornography of the real':

> As in the way we get off on war footage where there's blood and dead bodies flung all over the place. We love to look at the shame and suffering of famine victims, AIDS patients and unemployed workers. We're seduced by the realness of the horror. Turned on in a kind of sexual way.

In the epilogue to *What Farocki Taught*, Godmilow explains that when she first saw *Inextinguishable Fire* she 'was jealous. Farocki had got it right without finger pointing, without self-righteous hysteria, he'd gotten to the bottom of the thing.' She admired the film so much, she says, that she 'just wanted to copy it', as a means to study Farocki's aesthetic decisions and the thought processes that guided them. The remake of *Inextinguishable Fire* is a means for her to promote an approach to filmmaking that she strives for in her own practice and that she sees Farocki's work as embodying. *What Farocki Taught* advocates for the ongoing relevance of the aesthetic insights embodied in *Inextinguishable Fire* and promotes critical reflection on conventions associated with the documentary genre more generally. In this respect, *What Farocki Taught* is about studying and showcasing not only Farocki's techniques but also, as the film's title suggests, Farocki's philosophies and insights. Farocki, who taught at the University of California, Berkeley and at the Academy of Fine Arts Vienna, is known for his extensive writings about film and image-making, including the many pieces he published in *Filmkritik*, during his time as managing editor from 1972 to 1984. Like Farocki, Godmilow is also a teacher and she shot *What Farocki Taught* on the campus of the University of Notre Dame where she taught.

Godmilow's decision to explain her own practice at the beginning and end of *What Farocki Taught* can be understood as a reference to Farocki's own appearance at the opening of *Inextinguishable Fire*. A portion of this scene is superimposed into the remake. An actor sits at his desk, framed in mid-shot, and reads from the testimony given by Vietnamese napalm survivor, Thai Bihn Dahn, at the Vietnam War Crimes Tribunal. At the end of the testimony, footage of Farocki in the same role in *Inextinguishable Fire* emerges, his face ghosted over the actor's. Farocki speaks but we do not hear the audio from the original film, only the English subtitles appear. The double exposure continues as the actor and Farocki look at the camera and begin one of the film's most important speeches – 'How can we show you napalm in action. And how can we show you the damage caused by napalm?' – before Farocki fades from view as the actor carries on:

> If we show you pictures of napalm burns, you'll close your eyes. First, you'll close your eyes to the pictures. Then you will close your eyes to the memory. Then you'll close your eyes to the facts. Then you'll close your eyes to the entire context. If we show you a person with napalm burns, we will hurt your feelings. If we hurt your feelings, you'll feel as if we'd tried napalm out on you, at your expense. We can give you only an idea of how napalm works.

Burning his arm with a cigarette, as Farocki did in *Inextinguishable Fire*, the actor explains that a cigarette burns at 400 degrees Celsius while napalm burns at 3,000 degrees. Bringing Farocki into the remake here emphasizes his personal articulation of the challenge of how audiences understand, and are implicated in, the mediation of war and violence and the limits of our frameworks for their representation. Farocki is summoned to speak directly to the audience, imploring us to reflect on the concerns he has raised. Later in *What Farocki Taught*, as two scientists watch television footage of the war in Vietnam from the evening news, one takes off his mask and buries his head in his hands. As he does so, he is accompanied by his predecessor from *Inextinguishable Fire*, who is superimposed into the remake, performing this same despairing action almost thirty years earlier. As with the resurrection of Farocki, the scientists' parallel reactions, which take place almost thirty years

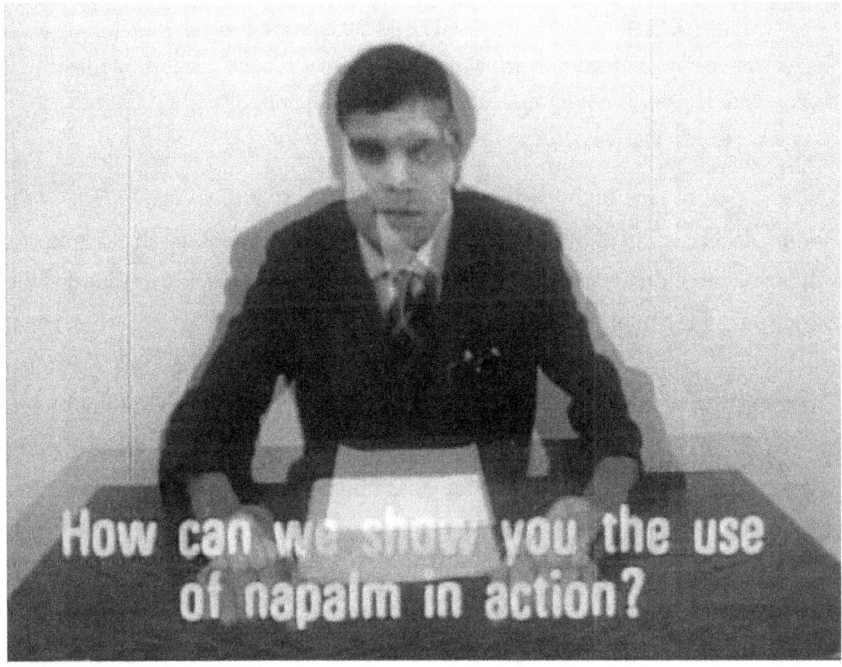

Figure 4.2 Farocki is ghosted into *What Farocki Taught* (Dir. Jill Godmilow, 1998), the double exposure facilitating his co-presence with the reenactment of his performance from *Inextinguishable Fire* (Dir. Harun Farocki, 1969).

apart but coexist together in the remake, underscore the longevity and salience of Farocki's concerns.

Godmilow says in *What Farocki Taught* that what she liked about *Indistinguishable Fire* was 'the way it treated its audience'. She summons Farocki to articulate what she has previously described as a central agenda of her own practice: the attempt to 'produce an audience of individuals who can learn some conceptual tools with which to articulate a critique' and who 'become active intellectual participants in a discussion of the social conditions and relationships represented' (1997: 83). In an interview about her filmmaking practice Godmilow (Godmilow and Shapiro 1997: 83) argues that filmmakers should put 'their materials and techniques in the service of ideas – not in the service of sentiment or compassion-producing identification'. The documentary films she most respects, she says, 'don't produce audiences of compassionate spectators of the dilemmas of others' and 'don't produce identification with heroics or sympathy for victims' because

> by producing their subjects as heroic and allowing us to be glad for their victories, or by producing them as tragic and allowing us to weep, the audience experiences itself as not implicated, exempt from the responsibility either to act or even to consider the structures of their own situation. (1997: 86–8)

These concerns are embodied in Godmilow's best known work, *Far from Poland* (1984), a film about her attempt to make a documentary about Poland's Solidarity movement after being denied visas to travel back to Poland. Like Farocki in *Inextinguishable Fire*, Godmilow features in *Far from Poland*, articulating some of the ethical dilemmas she faced in making the film. Challenged to rethink the traditions of documentary in which she had been trained so that she could continue with the film while based in the United States, Godmilow engaged with the possibilities and challenges of working with reenactment. She utilized American actors from New York's Mabou Mines group to perform reenactments based on interviews and transcripts of conversations that had been published in the Solidarity press during 1981. The range of subjects included a group of coal miners; a government censor; and Anna Walentynowicz, the worker whose firing inspired the Gdansk shipyard strikes that precipitated the Solidarity movement. The film is featured in

Nichols (2008: 85) taxonomy of documentary reenactment as a pioneering exemplar of the category that he terms 'Brechtian Distanciation'. The conceptualization and incorporation of the reenactments into *Far from Poland* helped Godmilow explore and articulate her views about the limitations of the classical conventions associated with the documentary genre, concerns which also inspired her engagement with *Inextinguishable Fire*. The decision to reenact interviews and transcripts in *Far from Poland* was driven by the desire to showcase the reinventions of socialist language emerging from the Solidarity movement. In contrast, it is Farocki's use of cinematic language in *Inextinguishable Fire* that is being showcased through its reenactment in *What Farocki Taught*.

Advocating for greater uptake of the style and approach that Farocki's work embodied, Godmilow describes *What Farocki Taught* as 'my gauntlet, thrown down to other American filmmakers to re-think their practice' (1997: 101). She describes her remake as 'my manifesto to the agitprop', positioning Farocki's film as an exemplar that 'seeks to agitate, to stir things up, and then to propagate, to plant some new seeds'. As Gunning (1999: par. 12–13) aptly describes it, Godmilow's remake can be understood as

> an act of remembering and honoring a moment, the moment of Farocki's clarity, insight and courage in making the original film. ... [I]t asks us: can we think as clearly, work as economically and as vividly in the future? If it does not inspire us to new work, this film will exist to embarrass us, to show what can be (once was) done.

But the emphasis on remaking the film shot-for-shot still raises the question: Couldn't the original movie do? One answer to this question lies in Nichols (2013: 25) conceptualization of the work that reenactment can do:

> Recognizing that what we witness is a reenactment, we also recognize that it carries a retrospective interpretation, one a record of the original events would have lacked. In this sense the reenactments do not mean the same thing as what the events they represent meant: they evidence the passage of time, the gaining or failure to gain, insight, and they do not carry the same consequences.

Made in 1969, *Inextinguishable Fire* responds to the issues emerging about the representation of the Vietnam War as the war was still unfolding. Thirty years after the release of *Inextinguishable Fire*, the war in Vietnam was well and truly over but mediatization of war has intensified significantly. Forrest and Koos (2002: 3) argue that remakes 'reflect the different historical, economic, social, political and aesthetic conditions that made them possible'. The shot-for-shot remake of *Inextinguishable Fire* creates an opportunity to reflect on the political, cultural and historical contexts in which the original film was made, initiating dialogue about what has and has not changed in the intervening years.

Psycho and delayed cinema

While Godmilow describes *What Farocki Taught* as a 'period piece', recreating the era of *Inextinguishable Fire* with old cars, sixties fashion and era-appropriate typewriters, Van Sant's remake inhabits a setting contemporary with the times in which it was released in the late 1990s. Druxman (1975: 24) argues a problem for film remakes is that in 'many cases, the moral values or situations in a once-exciting story have become so antiquated that even the best screenwriter cannot make the plot workable for contemporary audiences'. Updated fashions and furnishings sit uneasily in outdated narrative conventions, innovative and shocking in the original *Psycho*, but tired and clichéd when re-enacted nearly four decades later. As Cheshire (1998) observes, the original *Psycho*

> depended on narrative surprises that can't possibly be surprising now; on genre conventions that were superseded decades ago; and on material considered daring in 1960 that's long since lost its power to raise even an eyebrow.

Santas (2000) argues that while $40,000 in the original movie was 'enough to tempt, but not large enough to defy logic', even the upgrade to $400,000 in the remake 'seems far, far too much to carry in one's pocket even in today's world, where cash transactions are rare'. The updated opening scene, in which Sam Loomis and Marion Crane lie in a post-coital state of nudity, fails to conjure even a whiff of mischief out of what was originally a highly scandalous, but less explicit, scene. Druxman (1975: 24) argues that 'changes in production and acting techniques as well as the … maturing social attitudes of the public' have made many of the original films that were 'early classics' themselves into 'anachronisms'. Van Sant's *Psycho* embodies the anachronisms, updating 'the times' in which the film was set but simultaneously succeeding to make the narrative seem old-fashioned and out of date.

Rather than recreating the 'original experience', the remake of *Psycho* inhabits mixed temporal locations. New technologies are used to produce an experience that is at once updated and outmoded. Decisions about how to integrate the updated with the outdated are discussed in considerable detail in the film's promotional materials. The press kit reports how the original score was re-recorded and expanded under the supervision of Danny Elfman to take advantage of new sound-recording technologies. But these new technologies were used to reproduce an outdated experience. The score was re-recorded in stereo, rather than the original mono, but the sound designers tried to recreate the harshness of the original recording as it would have blared out of the speakers in the cinema without fidelity (Universal 1998: 13). Costumes and furnishings were remade based on the original designs and outlines and, with the aid of the original shooting script, the remake attempted to replicate Hitchcock's blocking. Hitchcock wanted the opening shot of his film to be a long, complete pan/zoom helicopter shot over the city into Marion's hotel room, but this was impossible, as the helicopter shot was newly invented and could not yet be perfected (Rebello 1991: 80; Krohn 2000: 234). Instead he had to make do with a combination of swish pans and dissolves. For the remake, taking advantage of the technological developments of the intervening thirty-eight years, Van Sant and his director of photography Christopher Doyle achieved the complete traveling helicopter shot. On the other hand, like Hitchcock, Van Sant used rear-screen projection – taking advantage of the latest rear-screen projection technology available – for the early driving sequences, even though by the late 1990s digital effects had largely superseded the old technique (Universal 1998: 11).

Druxman (1975: 18) refers to what he terms 'timeliness' as a common factor driving the decision to remake a film: The coming of sound, colour and wide screen, for example, prompted remakes of films that were liable to be enhanced by these processes. New screen techniques might have been perfected or the theme of a film becomes relevant again. The 'timeliness' to which Van Sant's remake refers is the changing nature of film production and reception.

Figure 4.3 a, b The traveling helicopter shot at the opening of *Psycho* (Dir. Gus Van Sant, 1998) achieved what Hitchcock had envisaged for *Psycho* (Dir. Alfred Hitchcock, 1960).

'Periods of intense technological change are always extremely interesting for film theory', argues Rodowick (2007: 9, 31), 'because the films themselves tend to stage its primary question: *what is cinema?*' The current transitions have also, he continues, made us 'suddenly aware that something *was* cinema', and prompt us to ask not only 'what is cinema?' but also 'what was cinema?' Van Sant's *Psycho* puts these questions into dialogue with one another. To watch his *Psycho* is to experience the relationship between the historical/cultural changes and technological changes of the intervening years.

Mulvey's (2006: 26, 23) term 'delayed cinema' describes an engagement with the cinema that participates in this dialogue between the cinema's past and its future. She argues that 'the coincidence between the cinema's centenary and the arrival of digital technology' created a false opposition 'between the old and the new' that fails to take into account that digital convergence has produced a complex dialectic between digital and analogue technologies. The delayed cinema, which engages directly with the realities of digital convergence, challenges 'patterns of time that are neatly ordered around the end of an era, it's "before" and its "after"'. Instead of establishing a relationship between 'before' and 'after', Van Sant's *Psycho* blends old and new, reflecting the period of intense technological change in which it was made, characterized by the convergence of outdated and updated technologies working together in the same media environment. The remake meticulously integrates these updated and outdated elements, playing with the temporalities of a so-called 'timeless classic' in such a way as to make the remake appear anachronistic and outmoded. With his redundant new remake, Van Sant managed to stage for us not only an idea of the cinema that is passing away but also the contradictory, changing times in which the cinema currently lives. It is the uneven temporality, set up through the tension between the outdated and the updated, that makes Van Sant's remake a version of Mulvey's politically charged delayed cinema and foregrounds this tension in the remake genre more generally. In Van Sant's *Psycho*, the mixed temporal locations of the remake produce a temporally dislocated spectator who witnesses a remake that uses new technologies to produce outdated experiences and updated fashions and furnishings and morals that do not match with the outdated narrative conventions. The remake performs a relationship to cinema history through a reflection on this marginalized, delayed and temporally dislocated spectator.

The *Psycho* press kit points out that 'like many film-watchers of his generation, Van Sant first saw Hitchcock's *Psycho* on television' (Universal 1998: 5). The television spectator is an especially important figure in relation to the original *Psycho* because the film was made within the Hollywood studio system at a time when the old Hollywood cinema was in crisis because of the rise of television and of independent film production in America. According to Rebello (1991: 26, 28, 84), because of Paramount Studio's reluctance to finance

Psycho, Hitchcock began to explore ways in which the film's budget costs could be trimmed. (Paramount merely distributed the final film.) His solution: to return to black and white, to low-budget, scaled-down production values and to 'shoot it quickly and inexpensively, almost like an expanded episode of his TV series, "Alfred Hitchcock Presents"'. He financed the film himself and made it at television pace with multiple set ups (between fourteen and eighteen a day) using some of his regular television collaborators and crew at MCA and Universal-International. Hitchcock also frequently used two cameras during production, a standard practice for television at the time but not for cinema. As Rebello (1991: 27–8) points out, the trailer of *Psycho* was even modelled on Hitchcock's introductions to *Alfred Hitchcock Presents* and scripted by James Allardice, who wrote the lead-ins for the television series. Kapsis (1992: 60) proposes that the trailer would have led television audiences to believe that '*Psycho* would be in the tradition of Hitchcock's macabre little teleplays'.

For Mulvey (2006: 85), Hitchcock's decision to return to black-and-white, to low-budget production values and to the studio acknowledges the emerging conventions of television production, but it also 'harks back to an earlier era of Hollywood'. In doing this, she writes, the film produces 'a sense of the "new" out of a rearrangement of the "old"'. Hitchcock responded to the complex transitions underway in film production – which manifested as a crisis for the Hollywood studios and a crisis of funding for Hitchcock – by employing production techniques associated with the 'threat' itself, creating hybrid of film and television production techniques. The 'look' of *Psycho* made it appear like a teleplay but also at the same time, like an old black-and-white Hollywood, a relic from cinema's past, which constituted a significant amount of the material being recycled and broadcast on US television at that time. *Psycho* is therefore marked by innovations that are also often anachronisms. The film responded to the unique historical moment in which it was made with a combination of the updated and the outdated. In other words, Hitchcock's *Psycho* staged the temporal dislocations that marked its own historical moment just as Van Sant's remake stages the temporal dislocations that mark its own historical moment.

Van Sant's approach to *Psycho* does not signal these historical specificities and temporal dislocations in the original. His decision to film the remake in colour is perhaps the most obvious violation of the historical specificity of the original since Hitchcock had already made *Dial M for Murder*, *Rear Window*, *North by Northwest* and *Vertigo* in colour before he made *Psycho*. However, in 1998, colour television having been selling in large numbers in the United States since the late 1960s, the use of black-and-white had an entirely different meaning from that which it had four decades earlier. Godmilow explains in the epilogue to *What Farocki Taught* that while she chose to remake Farocki's black-and-white film in colour, she used Kodachrome to give the film a 'dated ... period look for the sixties'. The frivolous, garish and bright colour choices for Van Sant's remake, in contrast, suggest instead the subsequent reformulation of *Psycho* by the slasher movie (Verevis 2006b: 23). Across this book I reflect on the operation of the reenactment in specific genres. The film remake has a unique relationship to the idea of genre, since it can be conceptualized *as* a genre and at the same can 'jump from genre to genre' (Forrest and Koos 2002: 6). As Frow (1999) suggests, 'Every remake simultaneously refers to and remakes the genre to which that intertext belongs.' The remake of *Psycho* reflects the changing status of the conventions *Psycho* pioneered and the new genres it subsequently inspired by making *Psycho* look like the kind of movies that have turned those conventions into clichés.

Conclusion

As I discussed in the early chapters of this book, scholars such as Bruzzi (2020) and Schneider (2011) have proposed that the practice of reenactment can draw attention to the idea that an event is always open, that its constitution, meaning and status is evolving, being made and remade. Eberwein (1998: 15) similarly proposes that the remake encourages us to consider the meaning of the original as 'still in process'. The burgeoning trend of fans creating shot-for-shot remakes collaboratively online also resonates with this conceptualization. The crowd-sourced shot-for-shot remake of *Shrek* (2001), titled *Shrek Retold* (2018), for example, which played at the same pace as the original so that the two could be watched together, draws on jokes about and reimaginings of *Shrek* circulating in online meme culture (see Stokel-Walker 2018). The group who filmed a shot-for-shot remake of *Star Wars Episode III: Revenge of the Sith* over five days in 2017, using a Samsung Galaxy A5, Microsoft PowerPoint and Rebaslight, did so to send up what is regarded by many *Star Wars* fans as a bad film (see Opam 2017).

For Schneider (2011: 121), this process becomes more apparent the more directly a work imitates its source. In her analysis of the reenactment of *Akropolis* in *Poor Theatre* (Elizabeth LeCompte, Wooster Group, Performing Garage, NYC, 2004), she proposes that 'the closer the re-enactment came to a literal or clone-like precision, the more "other" it simultaneously grew'. The shot-for-shot remake can be understood as engaged in an approach to reenactment that strives for 'literal or clone-like precision' that likewise reveals that a reenactment is not the same as what it repeats. Van Sant's remake cannot restage the historical specificities of Hitchcock's *Psycho*. It stages its own changing times instead. In doing so, the remake adds to the anachronisms embraced in the original. For most of the reviewers who wrote about the remake, the perceived banality of Van Sant's *Psycho* only served to solidify the place of Hitchcock's *Psycho* in cinema history as a superior masterpiece and a 'timeless classic'. Nonetheless, Van Sant's *Psycho* reminds us that the cinema is not timeless. Times change and with them so does the cinema. The circulation of this remake in the same marketplace as its original provides a vision, just as Hitchcock's *Psycho* did, of cinema in transition.

What Farocki Taught is about spectatorship: how cinema and television construct and engage audiences. Throughout his career, Farocki explored instructional scenarios, pedagogical role playing and the ideological dimensions of image-making, including, as Elsaesser (2002) puts it, 'the institutions that produce and circulate these images'. Elsaesser argues that Farocki's work was inspired by the insight that cinema had made the world tangible in new ways that extended to 'all spheres of life'. *What Farocki Taught* reflects on how evolving conventions associated with institutions like cinema and television might influence how we understand ourselves and interact with others. Shot-for-shot remakes like *What Farocki Taught* that are connected to the remediation and appropriation of cinema, television and other media in the art world move beyond notions of the film remake with which Van Sant's work has been associated. By focusing on the reenactment of image-making practices and their associated ideas (as opposed to events and their documentation), *What Farocki Taught* reminds us that media representations have real-world effects, that they impact our subjectivity, intersubjectivity and ways of being in the world. As the pervasive circulation of moving images continues to intensify, and the interactions between events and their mediation continue to become more complex, exploring connections between practices of reenactment, remediation and appropriation is becoming more and more important.

5

Trial by media: Fugitive testimony, demonstrative evidence and computer animation in the courtroom

Building on debates drawn primarily from disciplinary fields associated with film and media studies, I chose to work on the reenactment because of its mutability and success as a transdisciplinary form. The mobility of the reenactment, its capacity to traverse media and institutional contexts, is part of the value, but also the challenge, of studying this representational form. In this chapter, I shift my focus from film and television examples to the notable rise in the acceptance of computer-generated reenactments in courtrooms globally. Reenactments admitted into courtrooms function very differently, of course, from those deployed in film and television shows that circulate around legal proceedings and criminal investigations such as *Crime Stoppers* and *America's Most Wanted* (1988–2012), true crime documentaries or the E! News reenactments of the criminal trials of celebrities like O. J. Simpson (1995) and Michael Jackson (2005). But debates among legal and forensic scholars and practitioners about the incorporation of computer-generated reenactments into legal proceedings do frequently draw on long-standing conceptualizations of referentiality, mediation and spectatorship that have been circulating in the legal community since films were admitted into court proceedings in the United States in the 1920s (see Schwartz 2009). I consider how these conceptualizations are shaping the production, admission, reception and institutionalization of these computer-generated reenactments and how their status as reenactments is being regulated and communicated.

Debates about the use of computer-generated reenactments in legal proceedings illustrate very clearly that different institutions use media differently, their evolving practices creating different kinds of texts. It is an issue that came into stark focus for film and media scholars when George Holliday's video recording of four Los Angeles Police Department officers assaulting Rodney King, a 25-year-old Black man, became the centrepiece of the six-week court trial against the four officers in *California v. Powell, Koon, Wind and Briseno* (1992). My own interest in the courtroom context originated from thinking about how my understanding of reenactment intersected with debates about referentiality and technical reproducibility that emerged in film and media studies around the King video. Details associated with the production and circulation of this video have been widely reported. In the early hours of 3 March 1991, Holliday made a nine-and-a-half-minute recording on a cheap small-format home video camera from the balcony of his Lake View Terrace apartment in South-Central Los Angeles after he and his wife were awakened by alarming noises. The Hollidays sold the recording to Los Angeles TV station KTLA, which aired ninety seconds of it on its 10 pm local news programme on 4 March 1991, not much more than twenty-four hours after the assault had occurred. KTLA made the footage available to CNN, which subsequently distributed it to other networks, nationally and internationally, in the days that followed, turning the assault into a global media event. The televised tape sparked widespread public outrage, especially in the United States, prompting Los Angeles mayor, Tom Bradley, to establish an independent commission to investigate police brutality and racism in the LAPD. The commission's report, critical of the LAPD, was released on 9 July 1991, eight months before the video was deployed in *California v. Powell, Koon, Wind and Briseno* (1992). During the trial proceedings, however, the video was made to perform for the defence. Jury members were made to watch the videotape more than thirty times at different speeds, frame by frame, in freeze-frames, forwards and backwards and in slow motion with voice-over narration. Individual frames showed specific actions and reactions in isolation, and selected moments of the tape were shown repeatedly. Hours and hours of court time spent on a few minutes of video resulted in a marked contrast between the duration of the original footage and the amount of time spent viewing it. These techniques were part of how defence counsel convinced the jury to acquit the four officers of charges of assault and excessive force. Later, in April 1993, however, in a Federal civil rights trial, officers Koon and Powell were found guilty of civil rights violations while officers Wind and Briseno were acquitted.

For many film and media scholars, the defence lawyers' success in convincing the jury to acquit the LAPD officers served to underline the importance of thinking about how technically reproducible images embody profound ambiguities, tensions and contradictions. A focus of the scholarship during this time when discussions of the 'King case' were prominent in theoretical debates around the technical image and its cultural status and meanings was the idea that visual evidence is fugitive, in that it can have multiple and provisional meanings. The interpretations of the video produced in the courtroom by the defence illustrated for many what Petro (1995: x) describes as 'the evidential force and the powerful indeterminacy of the image and its reception'. Petro (1995: x) takes up Barthes's ([1981] 2000: 93) conceptualization of the photograph as 'certain but fugitive testimony' to articulate the tension at the centre of academic debate about the referential capacities of the image. Petro (1995: xiv) reasons that 'as the fate of the Rodney King video powerfully demonstrates, photographic testimony is always (and at once) overloaded yet insubstantial – open to multiple interpretation and debate'. Song (2005: 86) likewise maintains that the acquittal of the officers showed that the distance between sign and referent could be 'irrefutably and perilously wide'. Schwartz (2009: 9–10) argues, however, that discussions among film and media scholars about the uses of the King video in court typically lack an understanding of how such referentiality is conceptualized in the US legal system. As I outlined at the outset of this book, in film theory the image as indexical trace has been associated with the inscription of a moment in time and with the unstaged, unrehearsed, pro-filmic event. Schwarz points out:

> In court, the cinema of indexicality is not the same as in film theory. In cinema, such indexicality is an implicit result of the medium itself and works to give the spectator an impression of reality. In court, film's indexicality is a result of the combination of a particular image and the testimony authenticating it, making the process of creating a particular image explicit. Evidentiary film's indexicality functions to purvey the facts of an event to the jury.

In court, indexical traces, as remnants of a material connection with a referent at a time in the past, must be contextualized and interpreted, their meanings deciphered and verified.

As treatment of the King video by the defence illustrated so powerfully for many film and media scholars, courtrooms can be characterized as sites of contest over the past, where events are subject to conflicting interpretations, reconstructions and processes of resignification as prosecution and defence teams battle over the most likely and convincing version of what has happened. This has contributed to making courtrooms potent institutional settings for the deployment of reenactment. I propose that the treatment of the King video by the defence demonstrates that replay technologies can enable us to 'replay' film and media events in ways that re-*enact* those events. Control over the temporalities of technical repetition has become so commonplace that this must impact on our understanding of the reenactment as a practice and a representational form that always entails the act of repetition. I am not suggesting that the retiming of moving images by means of replay technologies always and inevitably results in reenactment. Rather, I argue that, in some instances, retiming can make an original film or video perform again in a way that constitutes a form of reenactment.

Across this book, I have examined a variety of reenactments that are commonly recognized as such as well as others that do not fall into familiar ideas or forms of the reenactment but that can be thought of as reenactments in the ways that they repeat, perform and interrogate events. In so doing, I have aimed to build a conceptualization of the reenactment that can position more recognized and less familiar forms for the reenactment in relationship with one another. My focus in this final chapter of the book on debates among legal and forensic scholars and practitioners about the treatment of computer-generated reenactments in the courtroom as well as debates among film and media scholars about the 'King case' brings together my ruminations about the emergence of digitally produced reenactments begun in Chapter 3 with ideas about the relationship between retiming and reenactment initiated in Chapter 4. And the concerns explored in this chapter also resonate with reflections about the relationships between reenactment and mediatized events discussed in Chapters 1 and 2. Fundamental to my argument in this book is the belief that the reenactment cannot be understood outside of its mediation and I have identified some of the ways that the transformations that the reenactment has undergone as a representational form are tied to changes in digital and photochemical media. Computer-generated reenactments are understood to be part of a continuum of media use in litigation and reflect the increasing prominence of a range of media in legal trials, which has prompted some litigators and legal scholars to suggest that, as Schofield (2016: 3) puts it, 'Court environments, which have been one of the last bastions of the oral tradition, are slowly being transformed into cinematic display environments'. Even so, as I will show, there remains an inextricable relationship between testimony and reenactment in the courtroom, evident in the regulation of computer-generated reenactments and in the treatment of the Rodney King video.

Computer animations as demonstrative evidence

It is important to distinguish between the two main forms of computer-generated reenactment that have become admissible in US courts: scientific computer simulations and computer animations, both of which are more common in civil rather than criminal trials. Computer simulations involve specific, limited data being entered in a computer program to reconstruct an event based on the rules of that program (usually those associated with scientific principles such as the laws of physics or mathematics) and their admissibility has evolved from the standards for admitting expert scientific testimony and theories (see Chatterjee 1995). Computer simulations can be admitted as substantive evidence to help prove an issue in a case. Substantive evidence requires a high threshold for acceptance: it can only be presented to establish the truth or falsity of an alleged matter of fact in a case. Computer animations, which are my focus in this chapter, can only be admitted as demonstrative evidence, which means they are used to illustrate or clarify a version of the events being explained by an eyewitness or expert. Much discussion about a growing body of standards and guidelines that are developing in the United States around the regulation of computer animations focuses on what can be admitted as demonstrative evidence. US courts have the most extensive precedents, with computer-generated reenactments first admitted during the 1980s, and have consequently been a source of guidance for the management of similar reenactments in other jurisdictions, such as Australia and the UK (see Schofield 2009). The emerging guidelines and judgements associated with their admission continue to be re-evaluated. To be admissible, first, an animation must be authenticated as accurate by an authenticating witness and its relevance to the arguments about the facts at issue in the case must be established. Computer animations are admitted as demonstrative evidence when they are considered to a visual aid, akin to charts, maps, models, experiments and diagrams, and are commonly admissible when they help the trier of fact – the judge or jury who carries the responsibility of determining the issues of fact in a case – to more quickly and easily understand, visualize and remember details of complex and unfamiliar issues, processes or events being explained by an eyewitness or an expert (Savage 1991; Chatterjee 1995; Schofield 2016). Indeed, Schofield (2009) describes computer animations as 'unparalleled in their capabilities for presenting complex evidence'. Computer animations are employed in the courtroom to improve communication with the trier of fact. The focus is on the presentation of information to an audience. They are designed to perform for a judge and jury rather than investigate. They are considered especially useful for holding and maintaining juror's attention and condensing what would otherwise be lengthy testimony.

As with other forms of demonstrative evidence, the criteria for admissibility require a judge to weigh the probative value of a computer animation against its prejudicial effect. In the United States, this is associated with Rule 403 of the Federal Rules of Evidence (rules adopted by US Congress in 1975 and subsequently enacted in many states across the country), which outlines the following factors which may render evidence inadmissible: 'unfair prejudice, confusion of the issues, or misleading the jury, or by considerations of undue delay, waste of time or needless presentation of cumulative evidence'. Imwinkelried (cited in Hennes 1994: 2163) argues that 'the juror ideally should ascribe to an item of evidence only the probative value that the item deserves' but if 'the jury is likely to misestimate and overvalue the probative worth of the item' that would constitute an inferential error. A primary concern in the legal community is that the probative value of a computer animation will be outweighed by its potential to unfairly prejudice jurors. The rules of evidence have typically been applied strictly to computer animations because of their perceived persuasiveness (Webster and Bourn 2016). Computer animations will be so memorable, evocative and authoritative, and convey such an 'aura of reliability' (Chatterjee 1995), it is commonly argued, that they may 'dwarf other more probative, yet less vivid, testimony and evidence' (Hennes 1994: 2167) and therefore 'win the hearts and minds' of the jury who will give the evidence undue weight and influence.

This consternation about the impact of computer-generated reenactments on legal decision makers typically reflects and builds on some of the dominant perceptions about media spectatorship broadly associated with the admission of films and videos into evidence. Discussions about the use of computer animations in the legal community tend to circulate around the issue of how to conceptualize juries' familiarities with, and relationships to, film, television, video and digital media more generally, given the increasing pervasiveness and influence of media on our everyday lives and ways of understanding ourselves and our worlds. The notion that we live in a post-literate society dominated by broadcast, online and mobile media informs a commonly held idea that jurors are more likely to pay attention, absorb, remember and be persuaded by information presented by audiovisual means rather than written or spoken word. Hennes (1994: 2125, 2179) argues, for example, that 'television and videotape, because of their prevalence and acceptance as a form of receiving relevant information, enhance the effects that sight has upon mental recognition and retention'. Hennes (1994: 2181) goes as far as to suggest that 'jurors may not be able to prevent the cognitive overvaluing that occurs when viewing a videotaped reenactment'. Schofield (2016: 20) articulates another common idea: 'Moving images tend to mesmerize, and they can relax an individual's critical nature. This means that viewers are inclined towards a "seeing is believing" attitude, as they do with television.' When it comes to thinking about digital technologies, the concerns can ramp up even more. Webster and Bourn (2016: 441) argue, for example, that 'in a society enthralled by cutting-edge technology, the danger that juries will give undue weight to computer-generated evidence over less-glamorous forms of evidence is very real'. Hoenig (2012) likewise proposes: 'Advances in computer-generated graphics now portray imagery so sophisticated, so authoritative, so evocative that the pictorial details can dwarf the testimonial foundation that justifies its admissibility.' These kinds of arguments mimic the ontological and epistemological concerns about film expressed in US courts as far back as the 1920s and 1930s (see Schwartz 2009: 14–15). Schwartz (2009: 26–7), for example, discusses John Henry Wigmore's concerns in *Treatise on the Anglo-American System of Evidence*, published in 1923, that the persuasiveness of motion pictures left the bias involved in the construction of filmic reconstructions invisible. There are some challenges to this dominant view. Fiedler (2003: 310), for example, argues that given jurors are familiar with the idea that visual images displayed in a movie or television program have been manipulated, they are unlikely to believe it at face value.

Legal scholars' accounts of mediation and spectatorship have drawn primarily from frameworks associated with psychology and social science research methods to help them tease out the complexity of these concepts. The idea that, as Schofield (2016: 3) argues, computer animations are 'inherently persuasive' or that, as Hennes (1994: 2142) claims, they make a 'forceful mental impression' builds on a body of research that suggests that the presentation of evidence to jurors using a variety of visual aids, including photographs and videotapes, is more persuasive than verbal descriptions. This leads to the conclusion that, as Dunn, Salovey and Feigenson (2006: 229–30) explain, 'trial lawyers profit from jurors' reliance on visual media when arguing cases – the more a trial presentation incorporates familiar media forms, the more persuasive it is likely to be'. Several studies (Kassin and Dunn 1997; Bennett, Leibman and Fetter 1999; Dunn, Salovey and Feigenson 2006) that have surveyed jurors and attempted to assess some of the assumptions about the persuasiveness of computer animations have produced mixed results. Kassin and Dunn found animations to be more persuasive, for example, while Bennett, Leibman and Fetter did not. For Dunn, Salovey and Feigenson (2006: 242), their results suggest that if an animation 'depicts an unfamiliar scenario' then it may be more likely to 'persuade jurors to render a verdict in favour of the side presenting the display'. On the other hand, they point out that their results also suggest that computer animation was less persuasive if a juror was already more familiar with the type of event, such as a car crash, and could more easily visualize it. They conclude that the impact of a computer animation on a jury can vary depending on the type of trial.

The idea that computer animations may be more persuasive when representing events that are less familiar to audiences reflects an ongoing concern in the legal community that the integration of these investigative processes within an animation means that jurors are being presented with a finished product and served the information 'on a plate', ready-made, potentially encouraging them to take the information at 'face value', rather than treat the reenactment as illustrating a hypothesis that has been developed based on a range of information and processes (Savage 1991; Selbak 1994). As representations of testimony about how a sequence of events took place, computer animations produced for the courtroom retain an engagement with the investigative capacities of the reenactment, drawing on data and evidence compiled from a range of sources. In *People v. Duenas* (2012), for example, the testimony of a biomechanics expert working for the prosecution was accompanied by a four-minute computer animation showing how a shooting occurred, developed using details drawn from police and coroner reports, crime scene measurements and photographic records (Hoenig 2012). The presentation of the reenactments in the courtroom, however, does not give emphasis to what King (2012) calls the 'epistemological melodrama' that characterizes the production of reenactments in television programs such as *Secrets of Lost Empires* (Nova, 2000) and *Leonardo's Dream Machines* (ITN Factual, 2003). These series bring together experts from different 'communities of practice' to reconstruct ancient technologies such as the Roman Baths or collaborate on the construction of models of Da Vinci's drawings. King (2011: 132) conceives of this kind of reality television programming, in which the different agendas, skills and expertise of participants are on show, as working with the idea of 'reenactment as an experimental knowledge practice', where discontinuities, conflicts and collaborations are acknowledged. The police procedural television series *CSI* and *Bones*, discussed in Chapter 3, also regularly dramatize this kind of epistemological melodrama. In the courtroom, however, these processes occur prior to the commencement of the trial and are not necessarily part of the courtroom presentation.

While acceptance of videotaped evidence has become routine, Hennes (1994: 2125) argues that consternation about accuracy, repeatability and dramatization means that 'as the content of the videotaped evidence moves closer to dramatizing the issues in dispute ... judicial scrutiny and instances of exclusion increase', especially for criminal trials. Hennes (1994: 2142) points to the exclusion of a computer animation in *Lopez v. State* (1983), where the Texas Court of Appeals ruled that 'any staged re-enacted criminal acts or defensive issues involving human beings are impossible to duplicate in every minute detail and are therefore inherently dangerous', as initially influential on subsequent decisions. However, as Savage (1991: 443), among others, points out, precisely because it is likely to be practically impossible, exact duplication is not required. Events are made up of many contingencies that can never be repeated exactly. Instead, litigators must be able to show that the conditions associated with a reenactment are 'substantially similar' to the conditions associated with the actual events and that they illustrate appropriately the testimony of the witness. In this respect, *New York v. McHugh* (1984) is widely considered an influential early admission of a computer animations into a US courtroom. It was a road accident reconstruction used to illustrate the contention that weather conditions had caused an accident. In such an example, time of day, road and traffic conditions, traveling speed, skill level of the drivers and the angle of impact need to be substantially similar (see Selbak 1994: 346–7). Rulings in two highly publicized criminal cases, *New Jersey v. Spath* (1990) and *People v. Mitchell* (1991), also initiated what Hennes (1994: 2128) describes as a 'significant shift in judicial philosophy' regarding the admissibility of crime scene reenactments. In *New Jersey v. Spath*, the reenactment showing the trajectory of a bullet was permitted but not ultimately used. In *People v. Mitchell* (1991), the prosecution was permitted to submit a modified computer animation that illustrated the trajectory of bullets as well as the victim's and defendant's movements based on forensic evidence and the prosecution's theory about what had occurred.

So, the primary concerns about the admissibility of computer-generated reenactments in US courtrooms relate to their accuracy and persuasiveness. Much of the discussion about the regulation of computer animations and the mitigation of these concerns focuses on how they will be presented. Several strategies have been advised and employed. Concerns about how legal decision makers respond to the persuasiveness of computer animations have been addressed through a common requirement that jurors be given cautionary or limiting instructions before viewing a computer animation. Such instructions are recommended or mandated to remind juries that the animations are not documentation of the events, or an exact recreation of the events, but rather a representation that aids in understanding one potential version of those events provided in testimony: a version that supports either the prosecution or the defence's interpretation of the evidence. In the courtroom, as in other contexts explored in this book, the referential status of a reenactment must be declared and clearly signalled to its audience. This explanation of the referential status of these reenactments is connected to their status as demonstrative evidence, designed to serve an illustrative function: to show, explain and educate their audience. The guidelines that regulate the presentation of computer animations in court to help the trier of fact recognize and treat computer animations as reenactments and demonstrative evidence serve to emphasize one of the ideas that dominated film and media scholars accounts of the use of King video in court: that the past is contested and events are always open to multiple interpretations. There are differing responses within the legal community about the significance of this framework for the presentation of computer animations to the trier of fact. Hoenig (2012) points out, for example, that the California Supreme Court in *People v. Duenas* (2012) upheld that once computer animations meet appropriate standards for accuracy and fairness, courts should not obstruct the admission of computer animations if jurors are properly instructed. But Webster and Bourn (2016), who provide a survey of the cautionary requirements in the case law across US circuits and states, argue that the fact that such cautionary instructions have become so widespread remains an indication of the capacity of computer animations to persuade juries.

Another of the dominant strategies for mitigating persuasiveness and communicating the referential status of a computer animation is to place limitations on the degrees of realism associated with a representation. This has become another means to signal to a jury that the animation is a representation of the version of the events put forward in the testimony and not an exact recreation of the events. In *People v. Mitchell* (1991), for example, the prosecution was required to replace a human-like figure representing the victim with a geometric shape to underscore to the jury that the animation represented a theory rather than a proven fact (see Selbak 1994: 359). The referential relationship that the reenactment sets up between itself and a pre-existing event has typically been associated with the iconic sign in Peirce's taxonomy, characterized in terms of resemblance. For computer animations, the requirement that they are 'substantially similar' to the events they represent means they must replicate conditions associated with an event. But, as the example in *People v. Mitchell* (1991) illustrates, the notion of resemblance does not necessarily extend to visual likeness, in part because of concerns about persuasiveness. The idea that persuasiveness can be mitigated through the regulation of aesthetics is reflected in *Commonwealth v. Serge* (2006), where the Pennsylvania Supreme Court ruled that an animation showing bullet trajectories and the positions of the victim and defendant was 'not unfairly prejudicial because it did not include inflammatory elements, such as sounds, facial expressions, lifelike movements, transitions, or evidence of injury such as blood' (Smart 2007: 393). Schofield (2016: 21) even proposes that practitioners who create computer animations for litigation should study filmmaking techniques designed to provoke emotion and identification to help them eliminate these techniques from the animations they produce. This approach to aesthetics is also the legacy of ongoing efforts to manage the incorporation of film and video evidence into legal proceedings. Schwartz (2009: 10, 68–70) points out that evidentiary films and videos are expected to function as 'nonsubjective seeing' and as such 'any affect they contain must be screened out as prejudicial'. Even in more straightforward uses of video in courts, such as videotaped depositions, decisions associated with shot choice, camera angles, sequences of shots and editing techniques have become carefully regulated.

In the case of computer animations, however, the issue of point of view becomes more complicated since it is possible for experts to interact with and shift viewpoints within an animation as they explain their account (see Selbak 1994: 362–3). Fiedler (2003: 314–15) points out that computer animations presented in court can 'violate reality' in terms of the points of view they can provide: flying through a scene, giving a view from under an object, removing visual obstructions or using a split screen. Computer animations build an experience of the data and relevant evidence using programs that utilize 3D modelling to generate points of view for the trier of fact that can only be represented digitally. Schofield (2009) even points out that the collection, analysis and interpretation of forensic evidence has been also impacted significantly by digital technologies, with digital collection technologies enabling the data to be imported easily into computer modelling. While the animations may retain their referential relationship to the events they represent – by drawing on measurements of crime scenes, for example, collating data and identifying contingencies associated with an event – their rendering involves generating digital images from numerical digital models by means of computer software.

Clearly, computer animations can be used to visualize and explain information about a sequence of events that would not be visible to the naked eye. However, the ability to reconstruct events that could not be seen by an eyewitness does not, of course, always need digital rendering. We only have to think of Errol Morris's infamous use of close-up, slow-motion reenactments in the documentary film *The Thin Blue Line* (1988) of police officer Teresa Turko, tossing her milkshake to the ground. As Morris (2008) explains, these reenactments reconstruct perspectives on the crime that would not have been available even if Morris and his crew had been on the scene with a camera at the time that they were occurring:

> It wasn't a *cinema verité* documentary that got Randall Dale Adams out of prison. It was a film that re-enacted important details of the crime. It was an *investigation* – part of which was done with the camera. … [A] 35-millimeter film crew and many, many cameras – cameras taking multiple angles, high angles from overhead, low angles at tire-level looking under the car, even angles *inside* the suspect vehicle. [original emphasis]

The crew worked to reconstruct specific actions from points of view that only the cinematography and editing processes make available, giving audiences a view of the events of the crime that they would not otherwise be able to see other than through this cinematic reconstruction.

These reenactments in *The Thin Blue Line*, like those that are admissible in court, are constructed based on police drawing of the crime scene, which showed the location where the milkshake had landed; police interviews with Turko; Morris's own interviews with Dale Holt, the principle internal affairs investigator; and the internal affairs report. Morris focuses on the spilt milkshake as an instance of relational evidence, investigating its location in relation to the other objects within the crime scene to establish the direction and path in which it was thrown as well as to establish the timing and sequence of Turko's actions. Reenacting the trajectory of the milkshake based on discrepancies in the accounts of what happened, Morris makes the case that, contrary to her initial testimony, Turko did not get out of the patrol car when Wood got out. Morris concludes that, against procedure, she only exited – tossing her milkshake as she did so – as her partner was shot five times by the driver of the suspected vehicle. Morris (2008) favoured these kinds of reenactments because, as he describes, 'they redirect our attention and allow us to see things that would be otherwise invisible'. Computer animations can go even further by providing digital representations of small- or large-scale processes such as DNA replication or weather patterns (see Schofield 2016). They can also take the form of exemplars that show, for example, how a body part functions or how it can be damaged. They give greater emphasis to, and potentially expand, the range of events being examined and contested during a trial by giving event-status to activities of a scale that is best represented digitally. In this respect, computer animations not only draw on the history of the incorporation of evidential film and video in court but are also associated with digital ontologies that are becoming increasingly dominant in contemporary screen culture. In Rodowick's view (2007: 104), in the 'emerging ontology of the digital', the point of reference for the representation of events 'will be to mental events – not physical reality moulded to the imaginary, but the free reign of the imaginary in the creation of images *ex nihilo* that can simulate effects of the physical world (gravity, friction, causation) while also overcoming them'. The production and reception of these reenactments are being shaped by, and shaping, expanding cross-institutional understandings of digital imagery.

Significantly, many of the strategies for presenting computer animations in court also resonate with the treatment of the King video by the defence in *California v. Powell, Koon, Wind and Briseno*, their acceptance in US courtrooms overlapping with the era of the King case and the debates that surrounded it. These include showing a reenactment at different speeds, using slow motion, freezing at specific points and making use of narration, presented concurrently or successively, from experts and eyewitnesses. The crossover of these strategies lends weight to the idea that the treatment of the video by the defence made the video function as a form of reenactment, as I will discuss in more detail shortly. Conversely, it also suggests that the incorporation of computer animations into the courts draws on existing strategies associated with the presentation of evidential films and videos. Indeed, Schwartz (2009: 9) argues, for example, that the tactics employed by the defence in *California v. Powell, Koon, Wind and Briseno* were themselves the legacy of strategies for contesting and presenting moving images that had been evolving in US courtrooms since the 1970s.

King video as fugitive testimony

One of the characteristics that connects these computer animations with the retiming of the King video is that both utilize reenactment to make certain events visible, palpable and understood by their audiences in new ways. As has likewise been regularly articulated within the legal community, Morris (2008) understands his use of reenactment as a means of 'presenting the crime' in order that 'it could be understood' by audiences. The reenactments become, he says, a way of 'reducing the crime to essential questions' that serve to 'focus our attention on some specific detail or object that helps us look beyond the surface of images to something hidden, something deeper – something that better captures what really happened'. The approach to the King video by the defence likewise focuses attention on specific details of the events.

A central aspect in the LAPD defence strategy was the rescreening of Holliday's video footage in slow motion, without audio, while the officers themselves and expert witnesses performed voiceover narrations interpreting every single action and reaction contained in the footage. In a 'frame-by-frame' analysis of the videotape, Sergeant Charles Duke, an instructor at the Los Angeles Police Academy and an expert witness for the defence, maintained that nothing more than reasonable force was used against King and that every one of the fifty-six blows from the officers' batons was fully justified (see Linder 2001). Michael Stone, Officer Powell's defence lawyer, described this strategy as the defence team getting 'the jurors to look at the case not from the eye of the camera, but from the eye of the officers' (quoted in Taylor Gibbs 1996: 49). The police officers gave detailed accounts of their motives as the slow-motion footage rolled. The interviews with the defendants led to the slowed-down video footage painting a picture of four police officers concerned for their own safety in the face of a dangerous, provocative, out-of-control suspect. For example, Officer Powell, prompted by his lawyer, described his mental state, as he inflicted savage blows on King, as 'completely in fear for my life, scared to death' (quoted in Nichols 1994: 28). Officer Briseno, as he watched himself on the video, testified that his heavy stomping on King's shoulders was an effort to get the suspect to ground so that his fellow officers could cease clubbing him with their batons. He did not follow police procedure and simply hold King down with his knee, he said, because he feared getting accidentally struck by a baton (see Linder 2001). Duke's and the officer's evidence, combined with the retiming of the video of the attack on King, effectively rechoreographed a vicious and unwarranted assault as an action in line with appropriate police procedure.

The retiming of the video with accompanying commentary effectively presented the jury with a reenactment in which that which had not previously been visible was now made so: King as aggressor and the LAPD officers in fear. The dispute in the courtroom did not centre on whether King had been beaten fifty-six times with a metal baton, kicked seven times and struck with two blasts of 100,000 volts from a TASER electrical stun gun, all of which the videotape helped to establish. (Despite hours of court time devoted to it, scrutiny of the tape failed to determine whether King had been struck on the head by any of the baton blows, an act which would have automatically convicted the police officers of excessive force.) The issue was about whether the physical force used was appropriate or excessive for the situation from the point of view of a 'reasonable' police officer. The retiming of the video was crucial in undoing its previous associations with assault. The defence could convince the controversially hand-picked jurors to accept this interpretation of the events caught on video by making the video itself perform as evidence of officers following police procedure. Further, the prosecution's decision not to put King on the stand during the trial meant that his beaten body was represented during the trial solely by the videotape. His body had also previously been known primarily in its circulation in the video on television news programmes. The assault on King left him bruised and battered. 'I felt beat up and like a crushed can', he told a grand jury in March 1991 (quoted in Linder 2001). But the retiming of the assault on King's videotaped body, and of his actions and reactions, ultimately resulted in the disappearance of King's actual beaten body from the trial.

After the Hollidays sold the recording of the assault on King to Los Angeles TV station KTLA, they ended up filing a copyright infringement against several television stations over its use. But on 11 June 1993, US District Court judge Irving Hill ruled that the tape was of such significant national interest that in this instance the right of the public to view the footage outweighed any property rights Holliday might hold. The footage, he said, was 'as important, or more important, than My Lai', referring to the incident in which video news reports of the My Lai massacre in Vietnam were crucial in turning public opinion against the American intervention into the Vietnam War (Holland 1993). To the mind of Holliday's attorney, James Jordan, the videotape was 'the most viewed and, I daresay, the most important videotape of the twentieth century' (quoted in Tomasulo 1996: 75). Of course, the significance of amateur video footage as evidence of crimes and other events of interest to news media has only increased since then with the widespread adoption of mobile phones and the easy upload of such footage to social media and news websites. At the time of writing, phone footage of George Floyd's death on 25 May 2020 has sparked ongoing protests and riots across the United States and globally. Minneapolis police officer Derek Chauvin has been charged with second-degree murder and second-degree manslaughter for kneeling on Floyd's neck for nearly nine minutes. And this is just one example of footage of brutality circulating online as individuals, communities and organizations continue to mobilize to try to address this violence and the issues with which it is entangled.

As I observed in the Introduction, Schwarz (2004: 101) contends that the impact of cinema, radio and television (and now increasingly online streaming) on our societies requires that we think about historical time as occupying different velocities, scales and speeds. For White (1995: 23), the use of the King video in the courtroom is an example of how 'electronic media can manipulate recorded images so as literally to "explode" events before the eyes of viewers'. The defence demonstrated how the ability to play around with time's directionality through contemporary replay technologies can problematize the parameters of a film or media event. Fiske (1996: 918) puts it very aptly when he argues that since 'any event can be put into discourse in different ways … the critical relationship is between the different discursive constructions of that event, rather than between a representation of an event and the event itself'. When the King video was employed in the 1992 court case, one of the major tasks of the LAPD officers' defence team was to cast doubt on the status of the video as a 'primal scene' for police brutality (Song 2005: 69) and to dislodge the meanings contained in the video as it had circulated on television, directing its meaning away from this dominant interpretation. Tomasulo (1996: 76) argues that for the defence to succeed 'the King video had to be converted specifically into a *narrative* text' to ensure that the events in the footage became intelligible to the jury within a specific interpretive framework. Hence his essay's title: 'I'll see it when I believe it'. Nichols (1994: 22) likewise explains that the performative and rhetorical strategies employed by the defence lawyers 'systematically set out to construct an interpretive frame of which the videotape itself would serve as confirmation'. The jury's decision to acquit the police officers was not, Nichols contends, 'a question of ultimate truth, but of how a specific outcome occurs in a particular interpretive arena, through specific strategies and rhetorical moves'. In the aftermath of the widespread circulation of the King video and the first verdict acquitting the police officers, Fiske and Glynn (1995: 505) argued that

> the image saturation of late capitalist society … has volatilized any notion of a stable and singular reality principle. In these conditions, truth loses its finality and objectivity, multiplies and becomes a process of constant resimulation and contestation.

The reworking of the temporal structure of the King video produced reenactments that certified the video's status as fugitive testimony for film and media scholars by anchoring the video in an interpretive framework that contradicted the 'meaning' of the video that was circulating in the public domain. The new meanings ascribed to the events associated with the assault on King serve to highlight the idea that reenactments are not authorized by their external referents but rather by the performative rhetorical frames that produce an event after the fact.

Conclusion

By means of retiming, the assault on King and his reactions to it have been made to perform differently through a reworking of the temporal structure of the original moving image form. In the preceding chapters, I argued that performance plays a crucial role in the way in which the reenactment authenticates itself as historically accurate and is thus central to the ways in which a reenactment announces itself *as* a reenactment. The shifting parameters *of* performance – in terms of both what is recognized as performance and new locations of and for performance – impact on understandings of the reenactment. Performance is no longer only what happens in front of the camera. We now have digital performances in which there are no 'real' actors and performances produced through the manipulation of existing moving imagery. As Rodowick (2007: 16) proposes, 'One can say that the sampling and reworking of a digital image is a new performance of it.' This kind of performance is not reliant upon what happens in front of the camera but rather on what happens in and through the reworking of audiovisual material. Tomasulo (1996: 70–1) argues, 'Our concepts of historical referentiality (what happened), epistemology (how it happened), and historical memory (how we interpret it and what it means to us) are now determined primarily by media imagery.' Access to the past is increasingly defined by technologies that facilitate control and manipulation of moving images. The combination of a retimed video in the King case, the courtroom performances by the officers and the testimony of the defence's expert witnesses made the recorded events perform in new ways, giving each image new meaning and undoing the logic of the actions and reactions represented on the tape when it ran in 'real time' on television.

Computer animations designed for the courtroom have also been explicitly understood by scholars, litigators and judges as involving performance. As with the King video, these are performances driven by testimony. Moving images are made to perform through narration, manipulation of the temporality of the events being represented and opportunities for perspective taking with audiences being invited to explore events and actions from different points of view. Debate about the regulation of how computer animations perform in the courtroom has focused on thinking about how they will be received by their audiences, namely the trier of fact. In the King case, it was eyewitness footage, which was understood as having an indexical relationship to events in question, that was made to perform for the defendants and expert witnesses in an effort to convince the trier of fact to accept a particular perspective on how those events took place. Computer animations, in contrast, are digitally rendered to replicate and illustrate certain conditions associated with a series of events in an effort to convince the trier of fact to accept the particular perspective explained an expert witness. In the King case, the performances of the video involved forms of retiming and reiteration that were facilitated by replay technologies. The performances associated with computer animations in the courtroom draw on digital technologies that, as Rodowick (2007: 104) describes, 'can simulate effects of the physical world (gravity, friction, causation) while also overcoming them'. As such, there are no 'real' actors in either kind of performances. Instead it is the witnesses who perform in the courtroom and who can make moving images perform too.

Conclusion

Across this book I have examined various transformations that the reenactment has undergone through its relations with and incorporation into different forms of technical media. Grouping together an array of film, television and video examples in this book has helped me to embrace the reenactment's uneven and indiscriminate manifestations. By examining some of the shifting forms and functions of the reenactment and by drawing on specific concepts and debates in film theory, my aim has not been to produce a singular definition of the reenactment but rather to track some of its forms and manifestations and to do so as a way of tracing the increasing inseparability between 'media times' and 'historical times' (Schwarz 2004). I have drawn on key areas of film theory that have been particularly useful for thinking this through. These include debates about the circulatibility of the technically reproducible image, the shifting status of the indexical sign, the workings of cinematic temporality and the movement of film and cinema across media platforms. I have explored how the shifting parameters of technical reproducibility, indexicality, performance and events, and the nature of their interrelationships, also signal the shifting parameters of reenactment as a form of historical representation.

I have characterized the two conflicting agendas in the reenactment in terms of the reenactment being caught between the attempt to emphasize faithful repetition, which secures its authority as a form of historical representation, and the attempt to emphasize its theatrical, performative nature, which enables it to declare itself a reenactment. The negotiation between repetition and theatricality in the reenactment has been continually reworked. This negotiation has developed in relation to changes in the functions, status and referential relationships of the film and television genres in which the reenactment has appeared as well as wider transformations in the production and distribution of screen-based media. In this book, I have shown not only that the tension between these conflicting agendas makes the reenactment a dynamic and highly self-reflexive representational form but also that it makes the reenactment an exemplary accomplice in the pursuit of the relationships between temporality, theatricality and referentiality in contemporary historical representation.

Necessarily predicated on staging a past event, the reenactment shows up the ways in which shifts in the status of theatricality in film and television are connected to ideas of reference. My examinations of the reenactment's self-reflexive, presentational mode of address have frequently been tied to investigations of the reenactment's relationship to spectatorship. In the Introduction, I aligned the reenactment's theatricality with Gunning's (1990) efforts to draw attention to the exhibitionism that characterized the first decade of cinema and its persistence underground long after, arguing that the self-conscious exhibitionism of the reenactment shifted status with the emergence and solidification of the conventions and referential distinctions of narrative cinema. In Chapter 1, I explored some of the approaches to self-reflexivity associated with in-person reenactment, a strategy that enables subjects to stage and perform events associated with their own lives. Chapter 2 showed how film reenactments work to foreground investment in the theatrical dimensions of the pro-filmic field and I argued that they did so to ensure that spectators recognize them as the performance of a past event. I argued in Chapter 3 that this self-reflexive, presentational mode of address that has characterized the reenactment remains crucial to the recognition of a reenactment *as* a reenactment in the digital era even as the terrain of the pro-filmic field becomes increasingly diluted in contemporary image production. I showed that it is still possible to conceptualize theatricality in the reenactment without recourse to the theatrical dimensions of the pro-filmic field.

In Chapters 2 and 3, the relationship between theatricality and reference is explored in relation to the indexical sign. By analysing the ways in which reenactments regularly imitate or place indexical traces in the mise en scène, especially sets, props, costumes and performances, I showed how the concept of the indexical trace has played an important authenticating role in the film and television reenactment. In an increasingly digital media environment, however, rather than indexical traces being made to perform an authenticating function for the reenactment, I argued that we have entered a moment in which investment in the theatricality of the reenactment can authorize the trace. I pursued this argument through Peirce's work on the index. I examined the relationship between the two primary subcategories of Peirce's indexical sign and highlighted his enthusiasm for deictic indices – defined by demonstrative and performative acts that direct and focus attention. Focussing on the relationship between deictic indexicality and the reenactment, I argued that the traditional oppositions between reenactment and trace, index and theatricality must be rethought.

Discussions of indexicality were not the only outcome, however, of the investigations I undertook in Chapter 2. I also established that in a media environment characterized by rapid and easy movement of technically reproducible images across media platforms, reenactments frequently certify themselves as authentic through the reenactment of film and media events already circulating in the public domain. It was in fact in Chapter 1 that I first asked whether an event can be separated from its mediation. Here I proposed that reenactments are anchored less by the historical event on which they are based than by the performative, rhetorical frames they establish to depict the event. Continuing this idea into Chapter 5, I made the case that control over the technical timing of film and media events can enable us to replay these events in ways that can reenact them, making that which is familiar perform differently. Chapters 3 and 5 also explored how emerging ontologies of the digital are making it possible to produce reenactments that could not be seen with the naked eye or even captured by a camera, making visible and palpable new points of view on events so small in scale that they may have previously had little event status at all.

Clearly, it is not simply the idea of the event, but also performance in the reenactment, that has been shaped by the emergence of digital image production and the increasing circulation and distribution of technically reproducible images across media platforms. I have explored, for example, how the circulation of film and media events shapes performance in the reenactment and how a performance can become an event or turn the past into an event. In Chapter 2, I focussed on how actors' performances in contemporary biopics are measured in relation to the audiovisual documentation of events in the lives they perform. In Chapter 4, I considered how the actors' performances in the remake of *Psycho* (dir. Gus Van Sant, 1998) were shaped by the playing of the original *Psycho* (dir. Alfred Hitchcock, 1969) on DVD on the set of the remake and discussed how in *What Farocki Taught* (Jill Godmilow, 1998) the original performances were periodically superimposed over those of the remake as a double exposure. In Chapters 4 and 5, I focussed on the question of how the forms of retiming available through contemporary replay technologies can engage the tension between performance and repetition that is central to the reenactment as a representational form. A central focus of the book has been on the relationship between performance and demonstration. I have explored this relationship in detail across Chapters 1, 3 and 5. In all three chapters, I discuss examples of performances that are produced in an effort to show, explain and testify to audiences certain specific ideas and arguments about how a series of events took place. The different manifestations across these chapters range from documentary subjects performing events in which they had previously participated to crime reconstructions and courtroom presentations.

Doane (2002: 160) maintains that in the early years of the cinema 'the requirement of external spectatorial knowledge was not atypical, but rather, constituted something of a norm. The spectator was often expected to have knowledge of another text (for example, newspaper accounts of a current event)'. This expectation, crucial to early film reenactments, has continued to be important for the reenactment throughout the twentieth century and into the twenty-first. In Chapter 1, I explored some of the debates about how in-person reenactment can be understood as a means to 'talk back' to institutional ideologies and media representations that have shaped popular perceptions circulating around the actions of individuals and communities. In Chapter 2 I looked at the functions of external spectatorial knowledge in three biopics where documentaries about the same subjects are also in circulation. In Chapter 5, the example of the Rodney King video illustrated how a media text circulating in one arena could be made to hold different meanings when re-presented in another. In Chapter 4, I explored how shot-for-shot remakes engage in dialogue with originals that already exist in technically reproducible form. Further, I showed how the production notes for Van Sant's *Psycho* cross-reference the filmmaking technologies of Hitchcock's original film to frame the remake as the reenactment of key aspects of the production process, turning the original production of *Psycho* into an event. In Chapters 3 and 5 I considered some of the processes and principles involved in the production and regulation of reenactments for the purposes of crime scene investigation and litigation. I reflected on how the tensions between the investigative and demonstrative dimensions of reenactment play out in terms of audiences' ability to access and recognize the variety of texts and sources that inform a reenactment's production.

While the reenactment has become an increasingly pervasive form of historical representation in screen-based media, reenactments continue to be closely tied to the institutional, historical, social and cultural circumstances of their making. As such, the questions of what a reenactment is and of what 'to reenact' entails continue to be important and valuable questions to raise. But they are questions that to date have rarely been posed in the disciplinary field of film and media studies. How and why these questions have not been adequately attended to in film and media studies before is, in part, because they are complex questions to answer. In film, as I have shown, the reenactment operated briefly as genre during the first decade of the cinema, then it became more associated with a form of historical representation that was found across media in different genres and across different cultural forms. The digital era has brought about further transformations to the reenactment, primarily because the digital image's challenges to understandings of photographic reference have impacted on ideas of historical representation. But as I have demonstrated, asking these questions in an effort to uncover and interrogate diverse and evolving manifestations of the reenactment can actually help us account for these changing expressions of reference in technically reproducible media. Addressing these questions can provoke new insights into the relations between media times and historical times and the increasingly mediated nature of our event culture. Reenactments continue to be entangled with evolving conceptualizations of the ontological and epistemological dimensions of the moving image. This is so across the range of institutions and genres that shape how they manifest and how they are authenticated. Given the reenactment's prevalence as form of historical representation in screen-based media, we need to continue to ask these questions as we grapple with the multifarious implications of ongoing transformations in our media environments.

References

Agnew, V. (2004), 'Introduction: What Is Reenactment?' *Criticism*, 46 (3): 327–39.
Agnew, V. (2007), 'History's Affective Turn: Historical Reenactment and Its Work in the Present', *Rethinking History*, 11 (3): 299–312.
Allen, M. (2007a), 'Introduction: This Much We Know...', in M. Allen (ed.), *Reading CSI: Crime TV under the Microscope*, 3–14, London: I.B. Tauris.
Allen, M. (2007b), 'So Many Different Ways to Tell It: Multi-Platform Storytelling in *CSI*', in M. Allen (ed.), *Reading* CSI: *Crime TV under the Microscope*, 57–72, London: I.B. Tauris
Anderson C., and J. Lupo (2003), 'Hollywood Lives: The State of the Biopic at the Turn of the Century', in S. Neale (ed.), *Genre and Contemporary Hollywood*, 91–104, London: British Film Institute.
Arntfield, M. (2011), 'TVPD: The Generational Diegetics of the Police Procedural on American Television', *Candian Review of American Studies*, 41 (1): 75–95.
Baker, G. (2004), 'An Interview with Pierre Huyghe', *October*, 110: 80–106.
Bangma, A. (2006), 'Preface Two – Contested Terrains', in A. Bangma, S. Rushton and F. Wurst (eds), *Experience, Memory, Reenactment*, Rotterdam: Piet Zwart Institute.
Barthes, R. ([1972] 1992), *S/Z*, trans. Richard Miller, Oxford: Blackwell.
Barthes, R. ([1981] 2000), *Camera Lucida: Reflections on Photography*, trans. R. Howard, London: Vintage, Random House.
Bazin, A. (1960), 'The Ontology of the Photographic Image', *Film Quarterly*, 13 (4): 4–9.
Bazin, A. ([1967] 1971), *What Is Cinema?* trans. H. Gray, Berkeley: University of California Press.
Bazin, A. (2001), 'Science Film: Accidental Beauty (1947)', in A. Masaki Bellows, M. McDougall and B. Berg (eds), *Science Is Fiction: The Films of Jean Painleve*, 144–7, Cambridge, MA: MIT Press.
Bellour, R. (1987), 'The Pensive Spectator', *Wide Angle*, 9 (1): 6–10.
Benjamin, W. (1968), *Illuminations*, ed. H. Arendt, trans. H. Zohn, New York: Schocken Books.
Bennett, R., J. Leibman and R. Fetter (1999), 'Seeing Is Believing; or Is It? An Empirical Study of Computer Simulations as Evidence', *Wake Forest Law Review*, 34: 257–94.
Bibikova, I. (1990), 'The Design of Revolutionary Celebrations', in V. Tolstoy, I. Bibikova and C. Cooke (eds), *Street Art of the Revolution: Festivals and Celebration in Russian, 1918-33*, trans. F. Longman, F. O'Dell and V. Vnukov, London: Thames and Hudson.
Bingham, D. (1999), '"I Do Want to Live!": Female Voices, Male Discourse, and Hollywood Biopics Author(s)', *Cinema Journal*, 38 (3): 3–26.

Bingham, D. (2010a), *Whose Lives Are They Anyway? The Biopic as Contemporary Film Genre*, New Brunswick: Rutgers University Press.

Bingham, D. (2010b), 'Living Stories: Performance in the Contemporary Biopic', in C. Cornea (ed.), *Genre and Performance: Film and Television*, 76–95, Manchester: Manchester University Press.

Bingham, D. (2013), 'The Lives and Times of the Biopic', in R. Rosenstone and C. Parvulescu (eds), *A Companion to the Historical Film*, 233–54, Chichester: Wiley-Blackwell.

Black, D. L. (2009), 'Hollywood Comes to San Francisco', *Milk* [Film], Dir. Gus Van Sant. United States: Universal.

Blackson, R. (2007), 'Once More … with Feeling: Reenactment in Contemporary Art and Culture', *Art Journal*, 66 (1): 28–40.

Blackwelder, R. (2003), 'Respect from Theron Out', *SPLICEDwire*. Available online: http://splicedwire.com/03features/ctheron.html (accessed 3 November 2020).

Boorstin, D. ([1961] 1992), *The Image: A Guide to Pseudo-Events in America*. New York: Vintage.

Bordwell, D. (1993), *The Cinema of Eisenstein*, Cambridge, MA: Harvard University Press.

Bourriaud, N. (2002), *Postproduction*. New York: Lukas & Stenberg.

Boyle, D. (2009), 'Trauma, Memory, Documentary: Re-enactment in Two Films by Rithy Panh (Cambodia) and Garin Nugroho (Indonesia)', in B. Sarkar and J. Walker (eds), *Documentary Testimonies: Global Archives of Suffering*, 155–72, New York: Routledge.

Boyle, D. (2016), 'On a Morality of Filing: A Conversation between Rithy Panh & Deirdre Boyle', *CineAction*, 97: 39–44.

Bruzzi, S. (2006), *New Documentary*, London: Routledge.

Bruzzi, S. (2015), 'Re-enacting Trauma in Film and Television: Restaging History, Revisiting Pain', in C. Wassmann (ed.), *Therapy and Emotions in Film and Television*, 89–98, New York: Palgrave Macmillan.

Bruzzi, S. (2016), 'Acting Out and Working Through: Documentary Re-enactment', ZDOK Do It Again, Zurich, 19 May. Available online: https://blog.zhdk.ch/zdok/files/2017/07/referat_bruzzi_2016.pdf (accessed 3 November 2020).

Bruzzi, S. (2020), *Approximation: Documentary, History and the Staging of Reality*, New York: Routledge.

Buck-Morss, S. (2000), *Dreamworld and Catastrophe: The Passing of Mass Utopia in East and West*, Cambridge, MA: MIT Press.

Byers, M., and V. M. Johnson, eds. (2009), *The CSI Effect: Television Crime and Governance*. Lanham, MD: Lexington Books.

Camhi, L. (2004), 'The Banal Faces of Khmer Rouge Evil', *New York Times*, 16 May.

Cannon, D. (2004), 'The *CSI* Shot: Making It Real', *CSI: Crime Scene Investigation* [TV programme] DVD commentary, United States: Momentum Pictures.

Cavagna, C. (2004), 'Interviews: Charlize Theron'. Available online: http://www.aboutfilm.com/features/monster/interviews.htm (accessed 28 July 2020).

Cavell, S. (1982), 'The Fact of Television', *Daedalus*, 111 (4): 75–96.

Chatterjee, I. (1995), 'Admitting Computer Animations: More Caution and New Approach Are Needed', *Defence Counsel Journal* 62 (1): 36–46.

Cheshire, G. (1998), '*Psycho* – "Psycho" Analysis: Van Sant's Remake Slavish but Sluggish', *Variety*, 6 December. Available online: https://variety.com/1998/film/reviews/psycho-psycho-analysis-van-sant-s-remake-slavish-but-sluggish-1200456298/ (accessed 3 November 2020).

Chisum, J. (2002), 'An Introduction to Crime Reconstruction', in B. Turvey (ed.), *Criminal Profiling: An Introduction to Behavior Evidence Analysis*. London: Elsevier Academic Press.

Chisum J., and B. E. Turvey (2000), 'Evidence Dynamics: Locard's Exchange Principle and Crime Reconstruction', *Journal of Behavioral Profiling*, 1 (1): 1–10.

Clover, C. (1987), 'Her Body, Himself: Gender in the Slasher Film', *Representations*, 20: 187–228.

Cole, S. (2015), 'A Surfeit of Science: The "CSI effect" and the Media Appropriation of the Public Understanding of Science', *Public Understanding of Science*, 24 (2): 130–46.

Collingwood, R. G. ([1956] 1994), *The Idea of History*, Oxford: Oxford University Press.

Comolli, J.-L. (1978), 'Historical Fiction: A Body too Much', *Screen*, 19 (2): 41–53.

Conklin, Gardner, et al. (2002), *Encyclopaedia of Forensic Investigation*, Westport, CT: Oryx Press.

Cook, A. (2004), 'The Use and Abuse of Historical Reenactment: Thoughts on Recent Trends in Public History', *Criticism*, 46 (3): 487–96.

Corner, J. (1996), *The Art of the Record: A Critical Introduction to Documentary*, Manchester: Manchester University Press

Custen, G. (1992), *Bio/Pics: How Hollywood Constructed Public History*, New Brunswick: Rutgers University Press.

Custen, G. (2000), 'The Mechanical Life in the Age of Human Reproduction: American Biopics, 1916–1980', *Biography*, 23 (1): 127–59.

Dannatt, A. (2001), 'Where Fact and Fiction Meet', *Art Newspaper*, 2 January.

Dayan, D., and E. Katz (1992), *Media Events: The Live Broadcasting of History*, Cambridge: Harvard University Press.

De Groot, J. (2016), *Consuming History: Historians and Heritage in Contemporary Popular Culture*, London: Routledge.

Deller, J. (2002), *The English Civil War Part II: Personal Accounts of the 1984–85 Miners' Strike*, London: Artangel.

Dening, G. (1994), *Mr Bligh's Bad Language: Passion, Power and Theatre on the Bounty*, Cambridge: Cambridge University Press.

Dijck, J. van (2001), 'Bodies without Borders: The Endoscopic Gaze', *International Journal of Cultural Studies*, 4 (2): 220–36.

Doane, M. A. (2002), *The Emergence of Cinematic Time: Modernity, Contingency and the Archive*, Cambridge, MA: Harvard University Press.

Doane, M. A. (2007a) 'Indexicality: Trace and Sign: Introduction', *differences*, 18 (1): 1–6.

Doane, M. A. (2007b) 'The Indexical and the Concept of Medium Specificity', *differences*, 18 (1): 128–52.

Doane, M. A. (2007c) 'Review: *Death 24x a Second: Stillness and the Moving Image*', *Screen*, 48 (1): 113–8.

Dobson N. (2009), 'Generic Difference and Innovation in *CSI: Crime Scene Investigation*', in M. Byers and V. M. Johnson (eds), *The CSI Effect: Television, Crime and Governance*, 75–89, Lanham, MD: Lexington.

Druxman, M. (1975), *Make It Again, Sam: A Survey of Movie Remakes*, South Brunswick, NJ: A. S. Barnes.

Dunn, M., P. Salovey and N. Feigenson (2006), 'The Jury Persuaded (and Not): Computer Animation in the Courtroom', *Law & Policy* 28 (2): 228–48.

Dyer, R. (1986), *Heavenly Bodies: Film Stars and Society*, London: BFI.

Ebert, R. (1998), 'Review: *Psycho*', *RobertEbert.com*. Available online: https://www.rogerebert.com/reviews/psycho-1998 (accessed 3 November 2020).

Eberwein R. (1998), 'Remakes and Cultural Studies', in A. Horton and S. McDougal (eds), *Play It Again, Sam: Retakes on Remakes*, 15–33, Berkeley: University of California Press.

Elder, C. (2009), 'Colonialism and Reenactment Televison: Imagining Belonging in Outback House', in V. Agnew and J. Lamb (eds), *Settler and Creole Reenactment*, 193–207, London: Palgrave MacMillan.

Ellis, J. (1998), 'Cinema and Television: Laios and Oedipus', in T. Elsaesser (ed.), *Cinema Futures: Cain, Abel or Cable?*, 127–35, Amsterdam: Amsterdam University Press.

Elsaesser, T. (2002), 'Introduction: Harun Farocki', *Senses of Cinema*, 21. Available online: http://sensesofcinema.com/2002/harun-farocki/farocki_intro/ (accessed 3 November 2020).

Elsaesser, T. (2005), 'Harun Farocki: Filmmaker, Artist, Media Theorist', *Afterall* 11: 54–63.

Elsaesser, T. (2007), 'Discipline through Diegesis: The Rube Film between "Attractions" and "Narrative Integration"', in W. Strauven (ed.), *Cinema of Attractions Reloaded*, 205–23, Amsterdam: Amsterdam University Press.

Epstein, R. (2004), 'Director's Commentary', *The Times of Harvey Milk*, [Film] Dir. Robert Epstein, United States: Telling Pictures.

Erickson, R. (2009), 'The Real Movie: Reenactment, Spectacle, and Recovery in Pierre Huyghe's *The Third Memory*', *Framework*, 50 (1–2): 107–25.
Farocki, H. (2016), '"Keep the Horizon Open": An Interview with Harun Farocki', *Senses of Cinema*, 79. Available online: http://sensesofcinema.com/2016/feature-articles/harun-farocki-interview/ (accessed 3 November 2020).
Feigenson N., and M. Dunn M (2003), 'New Visual Technologies in Court: Directions for Research', *Law and Human Behavoir*, 27: 109–26.
Fiedler, B. S. (2003), 'Are Your Eyes Deceiving You? The Evidential Crisis Regarding the Admissibility of Computer-Generated Evidence', *New York Law School Law Review*, 48 (1–2): 295–321.
Fiske, J. (1996), 'Admissible Postmodernity: Some Remarks on Rodney King, OJ Simpson and Contemporary Culture', *University of San Francisco Law Review*, 30: 4.
Fiske, J., and K. Glynn (1995), 'Trials of the Postmodern', *Cultural Studies*, 9 (3): 505–21.
Forrest J., and L. R. Koos (2002), 'Reviewing Remakes: An Introduction', in J. Forrest and L. R. Koos (eds), *Dead Ringers: The Remake in Theory and Practice*, Albany: State University of New York Press.
Fowler, P. (1992), *The Past in Contemporary Society: Then, Now*, London: Routledge.
Fox, M. (2014), 'Harun Farocki, Filmmaker of Modern Life, Dies at 70', *New York Times*, 4 August. Available online: https://www.nytimes.com/2014/08/04/arts/harun-farocki-filmmaker-of-modern-life-dies-at-70.html (accessed 3 November 2020).
Fox Searchlight (1999), *Boys Don't Cry* [Press Kit] Dir. Kimberley Peirce, United States: Fox Searchlight Pictures.
Franko, M. (2018), 'Introduction: The Power of Recall in a Post-Ephemeral Era', in M. Franko (ed.), *The Oxford Handbook of Dance and Reenactment*, 1–16, Oxford: Oxford University Press.
Frow, J. (1999), 'Review of Horton and McDougal', in A. Horton and S. McDougal (eds), *Play It Again, Sam: Retakes on Remakes*', *Screening the Past*, 7. Available online: http://tlweb.latrobe.edu.au/humanities/screeningthepast/shorts/reviews/rev0799/jfbr7a.htm (accessed 3 November 2020).
Fuhs, K. (2012), 'Re-imagining the Nonfiction Criminal Narrative: Documentary Reenactment as Political Agency', *Concentric: Literary and Cultural Studies*, 38 (1): 51–78.
Gapps, S. (2003), 'Authenticity Matters: Historical Re-enactment and Australian Attitudes to the Past', *Australian Cultural History*, 23: 105–16.
Gaudreault, A. (2007), 'From "Primitive Cinema" to "Kine-Attractology"', in W. Strauven (ed.), *The Cinema of Attractions Reloaded*, 85–44, Amsterdam: Amsterdam University Press.
Gever, M. (2005), 'The Spectacle of Crime Digitised: *CSI: Crime Scene Investigation* and Social Anatomy', *European Journal of Cultural Studies*, 8 (4): 445–63.

Giles, H. (2016), 'Recreating the Battle of Orgreave – the 2001 Reenactment'. Available online: https://www.battleoforgreave.com/recreating-the-battle-of-orgreave (accessed 28 July 2020).

Godmilow, J., and A.-L. Shapiro (1997), 'How Real Is the Reality in Documentary Film', *History and Theory*, 36 (4): 80–101.

Green, D., and J. Lowry (2003), 'From Presence to the Performative: Rethinking Photographic Indexicality', in D. Green (ed.), *Where Is the Photograph?*, 47–60, Brighton: Photoworks/Photoforum.

Greenberg, H. R. (1991), 'Raiders of the Lost Text: Remaking as Contested Homage in *Always*', *Journal of Popular Film and Television*, 18 (4): 164–72.

Griffiths, A. (2003), '"Shivers Down Your Spine": Panoramas and the Origins of the Cinematic Reenactment', *Screen*, 41 (1): 1–36.

Griffiths, A. (2008), *Shivers Down Your Spine: Cinema, Museums, and the Immersive View*, New York: Columbia University Press.

Gunning, T. (1990), 'The Cinema of Attractions: Early Film, Its Spectator and the Avant-Garde', in T. Elsaesser and A. Barker (eds), *Early Cinema: Space, Frame Narrative*, 56–62, London: BFI.

Gunning, T. (1991), *D. W. Griffith and the Origins of American Narrative Film*, Urbana: University of Illinois Press.

Gunning, T. (1994), 'An Aesthetic of Astonishment: Early Film and the (In)Credulous Spectator', in L. Williams (ed.), *Viewing Positions: Ways of Seeing Film*, 114–33, New Brunswick: Rutgers University Press.

Gunning, T. (1995), 'Tracing the Individual Body: Photography, Detectives, and Early Cinema', in L. Charney and V. Schwarz (eds), *Cinema and the Invention of Modern Life*, 15–45, Berkeley: University of California Press.

Gunning, T. (1999), 'Tom Gunning on *What Farocki Taught*', University of Notre Dame, 4 August. Available at: https://www3.nd.edu/~jgodmilo/gunning.html (accessed 3 November 2020).

Gunning, T. (2007), 'Moving away from the Index: Cinema and the Impression of Reality', *differences*, 18 (1): 29–52.

Hansen, M. (1991), *Babel and Babylon: Spectatorship in American Silent Film*, Cambridge, MA: Harvard University Press.

Healy, C. (2009), 'Impossible Historical Reenactments: Invisible Aboriginies on TV', in V. Agnew and J. Lamb (eds), *Settler and Creole Reenactment*, 171–92, London: Palgrave MacMillan.

Hennes, D. B. (1994), 'Manufacturing Evidence for Trial: The Prejudicial Implications of Videotaped Crime Scene Reenactments', *University of Pennsylvania Law Review*, 142 (6): 2125–81.

Hewison, R. (1987), *The Heritage Industry: Britain in a Climate of Decline*, London: Methuen.

Hoenig, M. (September 2012), 'Admissibility of Computer-Generated Animations and Simulations', *New York Law Journal*, 10. Available online: https://www.herzfeld-rubin.com/blog/admissibility-of-computer-generated-animations-and-simulations/ (accessed 28 January 2021).

Hoffer T., and R. Nelson (1999), 'Docudrama on American Television', in A. Rosenthal (ed.), *Why Docudrama? Fact-Fiction on Film and TV*, 64–77, Cabondale: Southern Illinois University Press.

Holland, G. (1993), 'Media Had Right to King Video Tape, Judge Rules', *Copley News Service*, 11 June.

Horeck, T. (2004), *Public Rape: Representing Violation in Fiction and Film*, London: Routledge.

Horeck, T. (2007), 'From Documentary to Drama: Capturing Aileen Wuornos', *Screen*, 48 (2): 141–59.

Horton, A., and S. McDougal (1998), 'Introduction', in A. Horton and S. McDougal (eds), *Play It Again, Sam: Retakes on Remakes*, 1–11, Berkeley: University of California Press.

Hoyne, A. (2009), 'Doing It Again: Re-enactment in Contemporary British Art (1996–2007)', PhD diss., University of Melbourne.

Jeffries, S. (2008), 'Master Manipulator', *Guardian*, 31 March. Available online: http://www.theguardian.com/film/2008/mar/31/Austria (accessed 3 November 2020).

Jenkins, P. (2003), 'Interview with Patty Jenkins and BT' and 'The Making of *Monster* Featurette', *Monster* [Film] Dir. Patty Jenkins, United States: Dej Productions.

Jermyn, D. (2007), 'Body Matters: Realism, Spectacle and the Corpse in *CSI*', in M. Allen (ed.), *Reading* CSI: *Crime TV under the Microscope*, 79–89, London: I.B. Tauris.

Kahana, J. (2008), 'Reenactment', *Columbia University Press Blog*, 6 August. Available online: https://www.cupblog.org/2008/08/06/345/ (accessed 3 November 2020).

Kahana, J. (2009), 'Introduction: What Now? Presenting Reenactment', *Framework: The Journal of Cinema and Media*, 50 (1–2): 46–60.

Kapsis, R. (1992), *Hitchcock: The Making of a Reputation*. Chicago: Chicago University Press.

Kassin, S., and M. Dunn (1997), 'Computer-Animated Displays and the Jury: Facilitative and Prejudicial Effects', *Law and Human Behavior*, 21: 269–81.

King, K. (2004), 'Historiography as Reenactment: Metaphors and Literalisations of TV Documentaries', *Criticism*, 46 (3): 459–75.

King, K. (2012), *Networked Reenactments: Stories Transdisciplinary Knowledges Tell*, Durham, NC: Duke University Press.

Krohn, B. (2000), *Hitchcock at Work*, London: Phaidon.

Lamb, J. (2008), 'Historical Re-enactment, Extremity, and Passion', *Eighteenth Century*, 49 (3): 239–50.

Larcher, I. (2005), 'Documentary Criticised for Reenacted Scenes', *New York Times*, 29 March. Available online: http://www.nytimes.com/2005/03/29/movies/29docu.html?_r=1&scp=14&sq=Mighty+Times%3A+The+Children%92s+March&st=nyt (accessed 3 November 2020).

Latour, B. (1991), *We Have Never Been Modern*, trans. C. Porter, Cambridge, MA: Harvard University Press.

Lederman, M. (2007), 'The Power of the Trailer Park', *The Globe and Mail*, 27 October. Available online: http://www.theglobeandmail.com/arts/the-power-of-the-trailer-park/article20403968/ (accessed 3 November 2020).

Leitch, T. (2002), 'Twice-Told Tales: Disavowal and the Rhetoric of the Remake', in J. Forrest and L. R. Koos (eds), *Dead Ringers: The Remake in Theory and Practice*, 37–62, Albany: State University of New York Press.

Leitch, T. (2006), 'How to Steal from Hitchcock', in D. Boyd and R. Barton Palmer (eds), *After Hitchcock: Influence, Imitation, and Intertextuality*, 251–70, Austin: University of Texas Press.

Levy, D. (1982), 'Re-constituted Newsreels, Re-enactments and the American Narrative Film', in R. Holman (ed.), *Cinema 1900/1906: An Analytical Study*, 243–58, Brussels: Fédération Internationale des Archives du Film.

Limbacher, J. (1979), *Haven't I Seen You Somewhere Before? Remakes, Sequels and Series in Motion Pictures and Television, 1896–1978*, Ann Arbor, MI: Pierian.

Linder, D. (2001), 'The Trials of Los Angeles Police Officers in Connection with the Beating of Rodney King'. Available online: http://law2.umkc.edu/faculty/projects/ftrials/lapd/lapdaccount.html (accessed 3 November 2020).

Lipkin, S. N. (2002), *Real Emotional Logic: Film and Television Docudrama as Persuasive Practice*, Carbondale: Southern Illinois University Press.

Lipkin, S. N. (2011), *Docudrama Performs the Past: Arenas of Argument in Films Based on True Stories*, Newcastle upon Tyne: Cambridge Scholars.

Locard, E. (2002), in G. Conklin et al. (eds), *Encyclopaedia of Forensic Investigation*, Westport, CT: Oryx Press.

Loock, K. (2017), 'Remaking Funny Games: Michael Haneke's Cross-Cultural Experiment', in I. R. Smith and C. Verevis (eds), *Transnational Film Remakes*, 177–94, Edinburgh: Edinburgh University Press.

Lowenthal, D. (1985), *The Past Is a Foreign Country*, Cambridge: Cambridge University Press.

Lury, K. (2005), *Interpreting Television*, London: Hodder Education.

Lury, K. (2007), 'So Many Different Ways to Tell It: Multi-Platform Storytelling in *CSI*', in M. Allen (ed.), *Reading CSI: Crime TV under the Microscope*, 57–72, London: I.B. Tauris.

Lutticken, S. (2005). *Life, Once More: Forms of Reenactment in Contemporary Art*. Rotterdam: Witte de With.

Margulies, I. (2003), 'Exemplary Bodies: Reenactment in *Love in the City*, *Sons* and *Close Up*', in I. Margulies (ed.), *Rites of Realism: Essays on Corporeal Cinema*, Durham, NC: Duke University Press.

Margulies I. (2019), *In Person: Reenactment in Postwar and Contemporary Cinema*, Oxford: Oxford University Press.

Marquis, E. (2013), 'Conceptualizing Documentary Performance', *Studies in Documentary Film* 7 (1): 45–60.

Martyn, P. (2011), '"I Know What It's Like to Be the Outsider": Hilary Swank on Her Journey from Trailer Park to Tinseltown', *The Daily Mail*, 7 January.

Massera, J.-C. (2000), 'The Lesson of Stains', in B. Holmes (trans.), *Pierre Huyghe: The Third Memory*, Paris: Editions du Centre Pompidou.

McCalman, I. (2004), 'The Little Ship of Horrors: Reenacting Extreme History', *Criticism*, 46 (3): 477–86.

McCalman, I., and P. Pickering (2010), 'From Realism to the Affective Turn: An Agenda', in I. McCalman and P. Pickering (eds), *Historical Reenactment: From Realism to the Affective Turn*, 1–17, London: Palgrave Macmillan.

McDonough, T. (2004), 'No Ghost', *October*, 110: 107–30.

McDougal, S. (1998), 'The Director Who Knew too Much: Hitchcock Remakes Himself', in A. Horton and S. McDougal (eds), *Play It Again, Sam: Retakes on Remakes*, 52–69, Berkeley: University of California Press.

Mendelsohn, C. (2004), 'The Writers Room', *CSI: Crime Scene Investigation* [TV programme] DVD commentary, United States: Momentum Pictures.

Metz, C. (1974), *Film Language: A Semiotics of the Cinema*, trans. M. Taylor, New York: Oxford University Press.

Morris, E. (2008), 'Play It Again, Sam (Re-enactments, Part One)', *New York Times*, 3 April. Available online: http://opinionator.blogs.nytimes.com/2008/04/03/play-it-again-sam-re-enactments-part-one/ (accessed 3 November 2020).

Mulvey, L. (2004), 'Passing Time: Reflections on Cinema from a New Technological Age', *Screen*, 45 (2): 142–55.

Mulvey, L. (2006), *Death 24x a Second: Stillness and the Moving Image*, London: Reaktion Books.

Musser, C. (1991), *Before the Nickelodeon: Edwin S. Porter and the Edison Manufacturing Company*, Berkeley: University of California Press.

Musser, C. (1994), *The Emergence of Cinema: The American Screen to 1907*, Berkeley: University of California Press.

Musser, C. (2007), 'Rethinking Early Cinema: Cinema of Attractions and Narrativity', in W. Strauven (ed.), *The Cinema of Attractions Reloaded*, 389–416, Amsterdam: Amsterdam University Press.

Naremore, J. (1973), *Filmguide to Psycho*. Bloomington: Indiana University Press.

Naremore, J. (2002), 'Remaking *Psycho*', in S. Gottlieb and C. Brookhouse (eds), *Framing Hitchcock: Selected Essays from the Hitchcock Annual*, 387–95, Detroit: Wayne State University Press.

Nichols, B. (1991), *Representing Reality: Issues and Concepts in Documentary*, Bloomington: Indiana University Press.

Nichols, B. (1994), *Blurred Boundaries: Questions of Meaning in Contemporary Culture*, Bloomington: Indiana University Press.

Nichols, B. (2008), 'Documentary Reenactment and the Fantasmatic Subject', *Critical Inquiry*, 35 (1): 72–89.

Nichols, B. (2013), 'Irony, Cruelty, Evil (and a Wink) in *The Act of Killing*', *Film Quarterly* 67: 2, 25–9.

Nowell-Smith, G. (1990), 'On History and the Cinema', *Screen*, 31 (2): 160–71.

Opam, K. (2017), 'Obsessed Fans are Using Shot-for-Shot Blockbuster Remakes as Their Personal Film School', *The Verge*, 20 July. Available online: https://www.theverge.com/2017/7/20/16006112/revenge-of-the-sith-shot-for-shot-fan-films-raiders-tim-hoekstra-eric-zala (accessed 3 November 2020).

Oppenheimer, J. (2012), 'Perpetrators' Testimony and the Restoration of Humanity: S21, Rithy Panh', in J. ten Brink and J. Oppenheimer (eds), *Killer Images: Documentary Film, Memory and the Performance of Violence*, 243–55, New York: Wallflower Press.

Paget, D. (1998), *No Other Way to Tell It: Dramadoc/Docudrama on Television*, Manchester: Manchester University Press.

Paget, D. (2002), 'Acting a Part: Performing Docudrama', *Media International Australia*, 104 (1): 30–41.

Palmer, D. (2001), '"I Know What Is It's Like to Be an Outsider": Hilary Swank on Her Journey from Trailer Park to Tinseltown', *Daily Mail*, 7 January. Available online: http://www.dailymail.co.uk/home/you/article-1341187/Hilary-Swank-journey-trailer-park-Tinseltown-I-know-like-outsider.html (accessed 28 January 2021).

Panh, R., and C. Bataille (2014), *The Elimination: A Survivor of the Khmer Rouge Confronts Hist Past and the Commandant of the Killing Fields*, trans. John Cullen, New York: Other Press.

Panse, S. (2007), '"The Bullet Confirms the Story Told by the Potato": Materials without Motives in *CSI: Crime Scene Investigation*', in M. Allen (ed.), *Reading* CSI: *Crime TV under the Microscope*, 153–66, London: I.B. Tauris.

Passafuime, R. (2008), 'Sean Penn Interview for *Milk*', *The Cinema Source*, 24 November. Available online: http://www.thecinemasource.com/?interview=sean-penn-interview-for-milk (accessed 28 July 2020).

Patton, P. (2010), *Deleuzian Concepts: Philosophy, Colonization, Politics*, Stanford, CA: Stanford University Press.

Peirce, C. S. (1932), *Collected Papers of Charles Sanders Peirce*, ed. C. Hartshorne and P. Weiss, 8 vols, Cambridge, MA: Harvard University Press.

Peirce, C. S. (1955), *Philosophical Writings of Peirce*, ed. J. Buchler, New York: Dover.

Peirce, C. S. (1991), *Peirce on Signs: Writings on Semiotics by Charles Sanders Peirce*, ed. J. Hoopes, Chapel Hill: University of North Carolina.

Peirce, C. S. (1992), *The Essential Peirce: Selected Philosophical Writings*, ed. N. Houser and C. Kloesel, 2 vols, Bloomington: Indiana University Press.

Peirce, K. (1999), 'Featurette', *Boys Don't Cry* [Film] DVD commentary, United States: Twentieth Century Fox.

Petro, P. (1995), 'Introduction: History Happens', in P. Petro (ed.), *Fugitive Images: From Photography to Video*, vii–xiv, Bloomington: Indiana University Press.

Pickering, P. (2010), ' "No Witnesses. No Leads. No Problems": The Reenactment of Crime and Rebellion', in I. McCalman and P. Pickering (eds), *Historical Reenactment: From Realism to the Affective Turn*, 109–32, New York: Palgrave Macmillan.

Pidduck, J. (2001), 'Risk and Queer Spectatorship', *Screen*, 42 (1): 97–103.

Pierson, M. (2009), 'Avant-Garde Re-enactment: *World Mirror Cinema*, *Decasia* and *The Heart of the World*', *Cinema Journal* 49 (1): 1–19.

Protopopoff, D., and M. Serceau (1989), 'Faux remakes et vraies adaptations', in D. Protopopoff and M. Serceau (eds), *Le Remake et l'adaptation*, Paris: CinemaAction.

Ranciere, J. (2009), *The Emancipated Spectator*, New York: Verso.

Rebello, S. (1991), *Alfred Hitchcock and the Making of* Psycho, New York: Harper Perennial.

Renov, M. (2004), *The Subject of Documentary*, Minneapolis: University of Minnesota Press.

Robinson, D. (2015), 'Harun Farocki: Serious Games', *Artlink*, 1 March. Available online: https://www.artlink.com.au/articles/4303/harun-farocki-serious-games/ (accessed 28 January 2021).

Rodowick, D. N. (2007), *The Virtual Life of Film*, Cambridge, MA: Harvard University Press.

Rosen, P. (2001), *Change Mummified: Cinema, Historicity, Theory*, Minneapolis: University of Minnesota Press.

Rosenthal, A. (1999), 'Introduction', in A. Rosenthal (ed.), *Why Docudrama? Fact-Fiction on Film and TV*, Carbondale: Southern Illinois University Press.

Rushton, S. (2006), 'Preface One – Tweedledum and Tweedeledee Resolved to Have a Battle', in A. Bangma, S. Rushton and F. Wust (eds), *Experience, Memory, Re-enactment*, Rotterdam: Piet Zwart Institute.

Santas, C. (2000), 'The Remake of *Psycho* (Gus Van Sant, 1998): Creativity or Cinematic Blasphemy?' *Senses of Cinema*, 10. Available online: http://sensesofcinema.com/2000/feature-articles/psycho-2/ (accessed 3 November 2020).

Santos Aquino, R. (2012), 'Necessary Fictions: From Cinema Verite to Cine, ma Verite', *CINEJ Cinema Journal*, 1 (2): 51–61.

Savage, E. (1991), 'Videotaped Reenactments in Civil Trials: Protecting Probative Evidence from the Trial Judge's Unbridled Discrtion', *John Marshall Law Review*, 24 (2): 433–62.

Schaeffer, B. (2000), 'Cutting the Flow: Thinking *Psycho*', *Senses of Cinema*, 6. Available online: http://sensesofcinema.com/2000/conference-for-the-love-of-fear/psycho/ (accessed 3 November 2020).

Schneider, R. (2011), *Performing Remains: Art and War in Times of Theatrical Reenactment*, New York: Routledge.

Schofield, D. (2009), 'Animating Evidence: Computer Game Technology in the Courtroom', *Journal of Information Law & Technology*, (1): 1–21.

Schofield, D. (2016), 'The Use of Computer Generated Imagery in Legal Proceedings', *Digital Evidence and Electronic Signature Law Review*, 13: 3–25.

Schwartz, L.-G. (2009), *Mechanical Witness: A History of Motion Picture Evidence in U.S. Courts*, Oxford: Oxford University Press.

Schwarz, A. (2007), ' "Not This Year!" Reenacting Contested Pasts Aboard *The Ship*', *Rethinking History* 11 (3): 427–46.

Schwarz, B. (2003), ' "Already the Past": Memory and Historical Time', in S. Radstone and K. Hodgkin (eds), *Regimes of Memory*, 135–51, New York: Routledge.

Schwarz, B. (2004), 'Media Times/Historical Times', *Screen*, 45 (2): 93–105.

Searle, A. (2002), 'Monsters Inc.', *The Guardian*, 5 November.

Selbak, J. (1994), 'Digital Litigation: The Prejudicial Effects of Computer-Generated Animation in the Courtroom', *Berkeley Technology Law Journal*, 9 (2): 338–67.

The Shorter Oxford English Dictionary (2002), Oxford: Oxford University Press.

Slyce, J. (2003), 'Jeremy Deller: Fables of the Reconstruction', *Flash Art International* 36: 74–7.

Smart, C. (2007), 'The Computer Must Be Right: Computer Generated Animations, Unfair Prejudice and Commonwealth v. Serge', *Temple Journal of Science Technology and Environmental Law*, 26 (2): 387–404.

Sobchack, V. (1990), ' "Surge and Splendor": A Phenomenology of the Hollywood Historical Epic', *Representations*, 29: 24–49.

Song, M. H. (2005), *Strange Future: Pessimism and the 1992 Los Angeles Riots*, Durham, NC: Duke University Press.

Staiger, J. (1996), 'Cinematic Shots: The Narration of Violence', in V. Sobchack (ed.), *The Persistence of History*, 39–54, New York: Routledge.

Stevens, D. (2005), 'Them Dry Bones: Fox's New Foresnics Drama is *CSI* with Older Corpses', *Slate*, 13 September. Available online: http://www.slate.com/articles/news_and_politics/surfergirl/2005/09/them_dry_bones.html (accessed 3 November 2020).

Stokel-Walker, C. (2018), 'Shrek Is Love, Shrek Is Life. Shrek Is Retold by a Group of 200 Committed Amateurs in the Weirdest Film You'll See This Year', *Wired*, 30 November. Available online: https://www.wired.co.uk/article/shrek-retold-crazy-fan-remake (accessed 3 November 2020).

Swank, H. (2000), Interview on *The Movie Show* [TV programme], SBS, 8 March. Available online: https://www.sbs.com.au/movies/video/11682371946/Interview-with-Kimberly-Peirce-and-Hilary-Swank (accessed 3 November 2020).

Tait, S. (2006), 'Autopic Vision and the Necrophilic Imaginary in *CSI*', *International Journal of Cultural Studies*, 9 (1): 45–61.

Taylor, R. (2002), *October*, London: BFI.

Taylor Gibbs, J. (1996), *Race and Justice: Rodney King and O. J. Simpson in a House Divided*, San Francisco, CA: Jossey-Bass.

Tobias, S. (1999), 'Kimberly Peirce', *A.V. Club*, 27 October. Available online: http://www.avclub.com/articles/kimberly-peirce,13626/ (accessed 3 November 2020).

Tomasulo, F. (1996), ' "I'll See It When I Believe It": Rodney King and the Prison-House of Video', in V. Sobchack (ed.), *The Persistence of History*, 69–88, New York: Routledge.

Tomic, M. (2013), 'Fidelity to Failure: Re-enactment and Identification in the Work of Mike Kelly and Paul McCarthy', *Oxford Art Journal* 33 (3): 437–56.

Turnbull, S. (2007), 'The Hook and the Look: *CSI* and the Aesthetics of the Television Crime Series', in M. Allen (ed.), *Reading* CSI: *Crime TV under the Microscope*, 15–32, London: I.B. Tauris.

Universal Pictures (1998), 'Press Kit', *Psycho*, dir. Gus Van Sant, Universal Pictures and Imagine Entertainment.

Verevis, C. (2006a), *Film Remakes*, Edinburgh: Edinburgh University Press.

Verevis, C. (2006b), 'For Ever Hitchcock: *Psycho* and Its Remakes', in D. Boyd and R. Barton Palmer (eds), *After Hitchcock: Influence, Imitation, and Intertextuality*, 15–29, Austin: University of Texas Press.

Verowoert, J. (2005), 'Production Pattern Associations on the Work of Harun Farocki', *Afterall* 11: 65–78.

Vidal B. (2014), 'Introduction: The Biopic in its Critical Contexts', B. Vidal and T. Brown (eds), *The Biopic in Contemporary Film Culture*, 1–32, New York: Routledge.

von Geldern, J. (1993), *Bolshevik Festivals, 1917–1920*, Berkeley: University of California Press.

Walker, J. (2012), 'Moving Testimonies: "Unhomed Geography" and the Holocaust Documentary of Return,' in J. Lothe, S. Rubin Suleiman and J. Phelan (eds), *After Testimony: The Ethics and Aesthetics of Holocaust Narrative for the Future*, 269–88, Columbus: Ohio State University Press.

Weber, S. (1996), *Mass Mediauras: Form, Technics, Media*, ed. A. Cholodenko, Stanford, CA: Stanford University Press.

Webster, B., and T. Bourne (2016), 'The Use of Computer-Generated Animations and Simulations at Trial', *Defense Counsel Journal* 83 (4): 439–59.

Weissmann, E., and K. Boyle (2007), 'Evidence of Things Unseen: The Pornographic Aesthetic and the Search for Truth in CSI', in M. Allen (ed.), *Reading CSI: Crime TV under the Microscope*, 90–102, London: I.B. Tauris.

White, H. (1995), 'The Modernist Event', in P. Petro (ed.), *Fugitive Images: From Photography to Video*, 17–38, Bloomington: Indiana University Press.

Winston, B. (1999), ' "Honest, Straightforward Re-enactment": The Staging of Reality', in K. Baker (ed.), *Joris Ivens and the Documentary Context*, 160–70, Amsterdam: Amsterdam University Press.

Winston, B. (2013), 'Introduction: The Documentary Film', in B. Winston (ed.), *The Documentary Film Book*, 1–32, London: BFI.

Wollen, P. ([1969] 1998), *Signs and Meaning in the Cinema*, London: BFI.

Film and television

1900 House (1999–2000), [TV programme] UK: Wall to Wall Television/Channel 4.

The Act of Killing (2012), [Film] Dir. Joshua Oppenheimer, Denmark: Final Cut for Real DK.

Aileen: Life & Death of a Serial Killer (2003), [Film] Dir. Nick Broomfield, UK: Lafayette Films.

Aileen Wuornos: The Selling of a Serial Killer (1992), [Film] Dir. Nick Broomfield, UK: Lafayette Films.

Alfred Hitchcock Presents (1955–62), [TV programme] United States: Shamley Productions/Universal TV.

Ali: Fear Eats the Soul (1974), [Film] Dir. R. W. Fassbinder, West Germany: Tango Film.

All My Babies: A Midwife's Own Story (1953), [Film] Dir. George Stoney, United States.

Ambulance at the Accident (1897), [Film] Dir. William Heise, United States: Edison.

Ambulance Call (1897), [Film] United States: Edison.

America's Most Wanted (1988–2012), [TV programme] United States: Fox.

Basic Training (1971), [Film] Dir. Frederick Wiseman, United States: Basic Training Company.

The Battle of Chile (1975–9), [Film] Dir. Patricio Guzman, Chile.

The Battle of Orgreave (2001), [Film] Dir. Mike Figgis, UK: Channel 4.

The Birth of a Nation (1915), [Film] Dir. D. W. Griffith, United States: David W. Griffith Corp.

Bones (2005–17), [TV programme] United States: Fox.

Bophana: A Cambodian Tragedy (1996), [Film] Dir. Rithy Panh, Cambodia/France: Catherine Dussart Productions.

Boys Don't Cry (1999), [Film] Dir. Kimberly Peirce, United States: Fox Searchlight/ Killer Films.
The Brandon Teena Story (1998), [Film] Dir. Susan Muska and Gréta Olafsdóttir, United States: Bless Bless Productions.
Cape Fear (1961), [Film] Dir. J. Lee Thomson, United States: Melville-Talbot Productions/Universal Pictures.
Cape Fear (1991), [Film] Dir. Martin Scorsese, United States: Amblin Entertainment/ Universal Pictures.
Chile, Obstinate Memory (1997), [Film] Dir. Patricio Guzman, Chile/France/Canada: La Sept-Arte; Les Films d'Ici, National Film Board of Canada.
CNET Central (1996–9), [TV programme] United States: CBS.
Coal Face (1935), [Film] Dir. Alberto Cavalcanti, UK: GPO Film Unit.
The Colony (2005), [TV programme] Australia: SBS Independent.
The Conversation (1974), [Film] Dir. Francis Ford Coppola, United States: Paramount Pictures.
Conviction (2010), [Film] Dir. Tony Goldwyn, United States: Pantheon.
CSI: Crime Scene Investigation (2000–15), [TV programme] United States: Jerry Bruckheimer Television.
CSI: Miami (2002–12), [TV programme] United States: Jerry Bruckheimer Television.
CSI: NY (2004–13), [TV programme] United States: Jerry Bruckheimer Television.
Diagnosis Murder (1992–2001), [TV programme] United States: Viacom Productions.
Dial M for Murder (1954), [Film] Dir. Alfred Hitchcock, United States: Warner Bros.
Dog Day Afternoon (1975), [Film] Dir. Sidney Lumet, United States: Artists Entertainment Complex/Warner Bros.
Dragnet (1951–9), [TV programme] United States: Mark VII Ltd.
E! News (1991–), [TV programme] United States: E! Network.
Execution by Hanging (1905), [Film] United States: Mutoscope/Biograph.
Far from Poland (1984), [Film] Dir. Jill Godmilow, United States.
Frontier House (2002), [TV programme] UK: Wall to Wall Television/Channel 4.
Gaslight (1939), [Film] Dir. Thorold Dickinson, UK: British National Films.
Gaslight (1994), [Film] Dir. George Cukor, United States: MGM.
The Godfather (1972), [Film] Dir. Francis Ford Coppola, United States: Alfran Productions/Paramount Pictures.
Granton Trawler (1934), [Film] Dir. John Grierson, UK: GPO Film Unit.
The Great Train Robbery (1903), [Film] Dir. Edwin Porter, United States: Edison.
High School (1968), [Film] Dir. Frederick Wiseman, United States: Osti Productions.
Hill Street Blues (1981–7) [TV programme] United States: NBC/MTM Enterprises.
Histoire(s) du cinéma (1998), [Film] Dir. Jean-Luc Godard, France: Gaumont.
Homicide: Life on the Street (1993–9), [TV programme] United States: NBC.

Hospital (1970), [Film] Dir. Frederick Wiseman, United States: National Education Television.
In the Name of the Father (1993), [Film] Dir. Jim Sheridan, UK/Ireland: Universal Pictures.
Inextinguishable Fire (1969) [Film] Dir. Harun Farocki, Germany.
The Jeanne Parr Show (1978), [TV programme] United States: CBS.
JFK (1991), [Film] Dir. Oliver Stone, United States: Warner Bros.
Juvenile Court (1973), [Film] Dir. Frederick Wiseman, United States: Zipporah Films.
Law and Order (1969), [Film] Dir. Frederick Wiseman, United States: National Education Television.
Law & Order (1990–), [TV programme] United States: NBC.
Leonardo's Dream Machines (2003), [TV programme] UK: ITN Factual.
Man on Wire (2008), [Film] Dir. James Marsh, UK/United States: Discovery Films.
The Man Who Knew Too Much, (1934), [Film] Dir. Alfred Hitchcock, UK: Gaumont British Picture Corporation.
The Man Who Knew Too Much (1956), [Film] Dir. Alfred Hitchcock, United States: Paramount Pictures.
Mayday (2003–) [TV programme] UK: Cineflix.
Miami Vice (1984–90) [TV programme] United States: Michael Mann Productions/Universal TV.
Mighty Times: The Children's March (2004), [Film] Dir. Bobby Houston and Robert Hudson, United States: HBO.
Milk (2008), [Film] Dir. Gus Van Sant, United States: Focus Features.
Million Dollar Baby (2004), [Film] Dir. Clint Eastwood, United States: Warner Bros.
Monster (2003), [Film] Dir. Patty Jenkins, United States: Media 8 Entertainment.
Nanook of the North (1922), [Film] Dir. Robert Flaherty, United States: Les Freres Revillon/Pathe Exchange.
Night Mail (1936), [Film] Dir. Harry Watt and Basil Wright, UK: GPO Film Unit.
North by Northwest (1959), [Film] Dir. Alfred Hitchcock, United States: MGM.
October (1927), [Film] Dir. Sergei Eisenstein, USSR: Sovkino.
A Perfect Murder (1998), [Film] Dir. Andrew Davis, United States: Warner Bros.
Police Story (1973–7), [TV programme] United States: Columbia Pictures Television.
Prime Suspect (1993–2003), [TV programme] UK: Granada Television.
The Prisoner of Zenda (1913), [Film] Dir. Edwin Porter, United States: Famous Players Film Company.
Psycho (1960), [Film] Dir. Alfred Hitchcock, United States: Shamley Productions.
Psycho (1998), [Film] Dir. Gus Van Sant, United States: Universal Pictures.
Psycho II (1983), [Film] Dir. Richard Franklin, United States: Universal Pictures.
Psycho III (1986), [Film] Dir. Anthony Perkins, United States: Universal Pictures.
Psycho IV: The Beginning (1990), [Film] Dir. Mick Garris, United States: Universal TV.

Quincy, ME (1976–83), [TV programme] United States: Glen A. Larson Productions/ Universal TV.
Rear Window (1994), [Film] Dir. Alfred Hitchcock, United States: Paramount Pictures.
S-21: The Khmer Rouge Killing Machine (2003), [Film] Dir. Rithy Panh, Cambodia/ France.
Schindler's List (1993), [Film] Dir. Steven Spielberg, United States: Universal Pictures.
Seconds from Disaster (2004–18), [TV programme] United States/UK: National Geographic.
Secrets of Lost Empires (2000), [TV programme] United States: Nova.
The Ship (2002), [TV programme] UK: BBC.
Shoah (1985), [Film] Dir. Claude Lanzmann, France: New Yorker Films.
Shrek (2001), [Film] Dir. Andrew Adamson and Vicky Jenson, United States: DreamWorks.
Shrek Retold (2018), [Film] Dir. Grant Duffrin.
Stalin (1993), [TV programme] United States: HBO.
Star Wars Episode III: Revenge of the Sith (2005), [Film] Dir. George Lucas, United States: Lucas Film.
Tenderloin Tragedy (1907), [Film] United States: Biograph.
The Thin Blue Line (1988), [Film] Dir. Errol Morris, United States: Miramax.
The Times of Harvey Milk (1984), [Film] Dir. Rob Epstein, United States: Black Sand Productions.
Titicut Follies (1967), [Film] Dir. Frederick Wiseman, United States: Zipporah Films.
The Trench (2002), [TV programme] UK: BBC.
Vertigo (1958), [Film] Dir. Alfred Hitchcock, United States: Paramount Pictures.
Welfare (1975), [Film] Dir. Frederick Wiseman, United States: Zipporah Films.
What Farocki Taught (1998), [Film] Dir. Jill Godmilow, United States.

Artworks, exhibitions and performances

Ahistoric Occasion: Artists Making History, curated by Nato Thompson (Massachusetts Museum of Contemporary Art, 27 May–22 April 2006).
Akropolis in *Poor Theatre* (Elizabeth LeCompte, Wooster Group, Performing Garage, NYC, 2004).
The Battle of Orgreave (2001, Jeremy Deller).
Deep Play (2008, Harun Farocki).
Eat Fear/Angst Essen (2008, Ming Wong).
Experience, Memory, Re-enactment, curated by Anke Bangma and Florian Wüst (Piet Zwart Institute, TENT Centre for Visual Arts, Rotterdam, February–May 2004).
Fresh Acconci (1995, Paul McCarthy and Mike Kelly).

History Will Repeat Itself: Strategies of Re-enactment in Contemporary (Media) Art and Performance, curated by Inke Arns (Hartware MedienKunst Verein, Pheonixhalle, 8 June 2007).

Life, Once More: Forms of Reenactment in Contemporary Art, curated by Sven Lutticken (With de Witte Centre for Contemporary Art, Rotterdam, 27 January–27 March 2005).

The Milgram Reenactment (2002, Rod Dickinson).

Once More ... With Feeling (Reg Vardy Gallery, Sunderland, 2 November–16 December 2005).

Playback_Simulated Realities, curated by Sabine Himmelsbach (Edith-Ruß-Haus für Mediakunst, Oldenburg, 3 September–11 November 2006).

Re-enact (Casco, Mediamatic, Amsterdam, 12 December 2004).

Remake (1994, Pierre Huyghe).

Serious Games (2009–10, Harun Farocki).

Service of the Goods (2013, Jean-Paul Kelly).

Seven Easy Pieces (2005, Marina Abramovic).

A Short History of Performance, Parts I–IV (Whitechapel Art Gallery, 2002–6).

Shulie (1997, Elisabeth Subrin).

The Storming of the Winter Palace, dir. Nikolai Evreinov, Winter Palace Square, Petrograd, 7 November 1920.

The Third Memory (2000, Pierre Huyghe).

Videograms of a Revolution (1999, Harun Farocki).

Workers Leaving the Factory in Eleven Decades (2006, Harun Farocki).

Case law

Commonwealth v. Serge [2006] 896 A.2d (Penn. Super. Ct).

Lopez v. State [1983] 651 S.W.2d 413 (Tex. Ct. App. 1983).

New Jersey v. Spath [1990] No. SGJ263908 (N.J. Super. Ct. Crim. Div. filed 5 Dec. 1990).

New York v. McHugh [1984] 476 N.Y.S.2d 721.

People v. Duenas [2012] Cal. LEXIS 7251; 55 Cal. 4th 1; 2012 WL 3155944 (Cal. Sup. Ct. 6 August 2012).

People v. Mitchell [1991] No. 12462 (Cal. Super. Ct. Marin County indictment filed 17 September 1991).

People v. Powell et al. [1992] (Los Angeles Superior Court 5 March 1992).

Powell v. Superior Court, 232 Cal. App. 3d 785, 283 Cal. Rptr. 777 (1991).

United States v. Koon [1993] 833 F. Superir 769 (C.D. Cal. 4 Aug. 1993).

Index

1900 House 3, 87

Academy Awards 31, 64–5, 71–6
actualities 12–14
Act of Killing, The (Oppenheimer, 2012) 42
Agnew, Vanessa 2–4
Aileen: Life & Death of a Serial Killer (Broomfield, 2003) 64, 67
Aileen Wuornos: The Selling of a Serial Killer (Broomfield, 1992) 64–5
Alfred Hitchcock Presents 140
American Civil War 8, 50
Ambulance at the Accident (1897) 11
Ambulance Call (1897) 11–12
anachronism 137, 142
Angelator 27, 97, 99–100, 103, 110, 113–14
appropriation 60–1, 130–1, 142–3
autoremake 120 (*see also* remake)

Barthes, Roland 22, 95, 147
Battle of Orgreave, The (Figgis, 2001) 26, 33–4, 47–54
Bazin, Andre 22, 100, 102
biopic 24–6, 57–86, 117, 125, 167–8
Bingham, Dennis 60–1, 63, 70–2
Birth of a Nation, The (Griffith, 1915) 15–16, 18
Bones (2005–17) 27, 87–114, 153
Boys Don't Cry (Peirce, 1999) 26, 59–64, 66, 72–6, 79–80, 84, 86
Brandon Teena Story, The (Muska and Olafsdottir, 1998) 60–2, 64, 66, 72–4, 80
Bruzzi, Stella 37, 40, 42, 51, 92, 117, 141

California v. Powell, Koon, Wind and Briseno (1992) 28, 146–7, 158–60
celebrity 61, 68, 86

centenary of cinema 25, 139
cinema of attractions 14–16, 114–15
cinematic metaphor 102, 104, 106
cinéma vérité 30–1
close-up 53, 72–3, 99–100, 106–10, 157
Collingwood, R. G. 2, 87
computer animations 100, 145, 149–59, 164
computer simulations 100–1, 104–5, 110, 113–14, 149
Conviction 75
credit sequence 66, 85, 93
crime reconstruction
    courtroom 148, 154, 168
    police procedural television 87, 89–91, 93, 97, 100, 168
CSI: Crime Scene Investigation (2000–15) 27, 88–93, 95–114
CSI-shot 27, 99, 106, 110
Custen, George 58, 60–1, 63, 65, 86

deictic index 23, 105–11, 114–15, 167
delayed cinema 136, 139
demonstrative evidence 145, 149–50, 155, 167, 169
detective fiction 87–9, 91, 103, 114
digital image 20, 25, 101–2, 104, 115, 157–8, 163, 167, 169
direct cinema 30
Doane, Mary Ann 12–14, 18, 21–3, 57, 64, 90, 106, 109, 168
docudrama 18–20, 24
documentary 6, 12, 25–6, 29, 56, 63–72, 76–85, 131–5, 157–8
Dog Day Afternoon (Lumet, 1975) 34, 41, 44–7
double exposure 128, 132–4, 168
Dragnet (1951–9) 89, 103
dramatization 3–4, 6, 16, 26, 77, 85, 154
DVD 122, 124–5, 127, 168

Ebert, Roger 67, 70, 123
Eisenstein, Sergei 8–10
Elsaesser, Thomas 15, 115, 131, 142
embodied impersonation 71–2
endoscopic camera 104, 112
English Civil War Society 48–9
event
    audio 76–7, 80–2
    bodily 25, 35, 37–8, 55, 99–100, 114
    contested 34–5, 40–1, 46–7, 50–1, 53, 155, 158
    crime under investigation 89–93, 95–8, 111–13, 147–50, 155–6
    current, topical or newsworthy 11–13, 19–20, 161
    documented 16, 26, 35, 59, 63–4, 70, 76–8, 163, 168
    historical 9–10, 16–18, 34–5, 50–1
    mediatized 25–6, 45–8, 52–8, 148–9, 161–3
    media 25, 28, 34, 47–8, 52–3, 62–3, 81, 85–6, 146, 148, 162–3, 167
    narrative 27, 91–3, 95–6
    pro-filmic 22, 29–30, 32, 58, 147–8
    reconstruction 97–100, 110–13, 149–59
    staged 9, 12–13, 30–9, 42–5, 49–56
    television 43–4, 52–3, 77–8, 80–2, 146–7, 163
    unstageable 27, 99–101, 114
evidence
    computer-generated 151, 153, 155, 156–7
    demonstrative, 149–50, 155, 156, 160–1
    Federal Rules of Evidence 150–1
    motion picture 147, 151–2, 154, 161
    physical or trace 88, 90–1, 93, 96–100, 107, 113–14
    relational 158
    substantive 149

fame 61–2, 86
Far from Poland (Godmilow, 1984) 134–5
Farocki, Harun 27–8, 118–19, 127–36, 141–3
forensic
    anthropology 89, 93
    evidence 100, 154, 157
    investigation 27, 87–92, 95–100, 112–13, 145
    technology 27, 93, 96, 98, 100, 102
freeze-frame 67, 127, 146
fugitive testimony 145, 147, 159, 162

genre (*see also* actualities, biopic, detective, docudrama, documentary, police procedural, remake) 1–2, 4, 6, 10, 11, 13–15, 24, 91, 99, 141, 165, 169–70
Godfather, The (Coppola, 1972) 45
Godmilow, Jill (*see also* individual works) 27, 118–19, 127–36, 141, 168
Griffith, D. W. 16–18
Gunning, Tom 14–16, 23, 88, 102, 114, 135, 166

heritage 2, 7, 48–9
Hill Street Blues (1981–7) 88–9, 103
historical film 58, 64–6, 68, 70–1, 77
Hitchcock, Alfred (*see also* individual works) 27–8, 118, 120–2, 125–30, 137–42, 168–9
Holliday, George 28, 146, 159, 161
Hollywood 27, 60, 64–5, 75–6, 106, 129–30, 139–40
Holmes, Sherlock 87–8

iconic sign 22, 156
indexical sign 21–3, 27, 57, 95, 102, 105–11, 115, 147–8, 164–7 (*see also* indexical trace and deictic index)
indexical trace 22–3, 27, 57, 61, 85, 90–2, 95, 97, 101–2, 105–11, 115, 147–8, 166–7
Inextinguishable Fire (Farocki, 1969) 27–8, 118, 127–36
in-person reenactment 25–6, 29, 33, 44, 47, 50, 53, 55–6, 166, 168

Kahana, Jonathan 25, 29–33
Khmer Rouge 25, 33–4, 40–1
King, Katie 3, 48, 90, 153
King, Rodney 28, 146–9, 155, 158–64, 168

living history 2–3, 7, 26, 34, 50, 52–3
Locard, Edmund 90
Lopez v State (1983) 154
Lutticken, Sven 7–8, 10, 48, 54

Man Who Knew Too Much, The
　　(Hitchcock, 1934 and 1956) 120–1
Margulies, Ivone 25, 29, 31, 33, 38, 42,
　　44, 54–5
mass spectacle 9–10
memory
　bodily 37, 51, 55
　collective 55, 61, 123
　historical 50–1, 163
　living 45, 47, 50–1
　mediated 7, 45, 47
　performing 19, 39
　popular 62
Miami Vice 88–9
Mighty Times: The Children's March
　　(Houston and Hudson, 2004) 31
Milk (Van Sant, 2008) 26, 59–66, 68–72,
　　75–6, 80–5
Million Dollar Baby (Eastwood, 2004) 75
minority appropriation 60–1
Monster (Jenkins, 2003) 26, 59–69, 71,
　　74–9, 84, 86
Morris, Errol 157–9
Mulvey, Laura 21, 123–5, 127, 139–40
Musser, Charles, 11, 13, 16

Nanook of the North (Flaherty, 1922) 29,
　　38
New Jersey v. Spath (1990) 154
New York v McHugh (1984) 154
newsreel 8, 12–13
Nichols, Bill 25, 29–30-2, 38–9, 44, 135,
　　160, 162
Night Mail 38
Nowell-Smith, Geoffrey 8, 12–13, 18

October (Eisenstein, 1927) 8–10

Panh, Rithy 25, 33–41
Peirce, Charles Sanders 21–3, 57, 90,
　　95, 102, 105–7, 156, 167 (*see also*
　　indexical sign)

Peirce, Kimberly (*see also* individual
　　works) 26, 59, 62, 66
People v Duenas (2012) 153, 155
People v. Mitchell (1991) 154, 156
performance art 7–8
photochemical image 22, 57, 102, 104, 149
Pickering, Paul 2–3, 87
police procedural television 27, 87–8,
　　90–2, 96, 98, 153
Powell v. Superior Court (1991)
prejudicial 150–1, 156
primal scene 79, 162
probative value 150–1
Psycho (Hitchcock, 1960) 27–8, 118–21,
　　124–8, 136–42, 168–9
Psycho (Van Sant, 1998) 27–8, 118–22,
　　124–8, 136–42, 168–9

rape 60, 75, 78–80
reality television 3, 24, 87, 153
Rear Window (Hitchcock, 1954) 122,
　　130, 141
reenactment societies 26, 34, 48–52
remake (*see also* shot-for-shot remake and
　　autoremake) 27–8, 117–42, 168–9
researched detail 26, 57–61, 63, 65, 70, 72,
　　77, 79, 85, 90
retiming 28, 125–6, 148, 159–61, 163–4, 168
Rodowick, D. N. 20–1, 102–3, 123, 138,
　　158, 163–4,
Rosen, Philip 21–2, 58, 65, 77, 79, 102, 105

Schneider, Rebecca 8, 50, 55–6, 141–2
Schwarz, Bill 4–5, 161, 165
shot-for-shot remake 27, 117–18, 122–5,
　　127–31, 135–6, 141–2, 168
slasher movie 141
slow-motion 104, 157, 160
Spanish-American War 11–13
spectacle
　biopic 65, 79
　cinema of attractions 14, 24, 114
　CSI-shot 104, 106
　living history 1–2
　mass spectacle 9–10
　police procedural television 96–7
　public spectacle 86

spectatorship
    cinema 121, 123, 125
    courtroom 145, 151–2
    DVD 125, 127
    pensive spectator 127
    television news 142
stars 42, 44, 47, 70–1, 75–6, 86
Stefano, Joseph 121
Storming of the Winter Palace, The (1920) 8–10

technical reproducibility 4–6, 20–1, 33, 56, 117, 122, 127, 146, 165
testimony 22–3, 35–40, 79–80, 88, 132, 147–51, 153–5, 159, 162–4
Thin Blue Line, The (Morris, 1988) 157

Third Memory, The (Huyghe, 2000) 26, 33–4, 41–8, 51
Times of Harvey Milk, The (Epstein, 1984) 64–6, 68, 70–1, 80–5

Van Sant, Gus (*see also* individual works) 26–7, 59, 83, 118–30, 136–42, 168–9
Verevis, Constantine 117, 120, 123–4, 141
Vidal, Belen 58, 61, 63, 70
Vietnam War 129, 132, 135, 161

What Farocki Taught (Godmilow, 1998) 27–8, 118–19, 127–36, 141–3, 168
Winston, Brian 25, 29–30, 38
Wojtowicz, John 26, 41–7

www.ingramcontent.com/pod-product-compliance
Lightning Source LLC
Chambersburg PA
CBHW061830300426
44115CB00013B/2319